COGNITION AND WORK

Northwestern University
Studies in Phenomenology
and
Existential Philosophy

General Editor Anthony J. Steinbock

COGNITION AND WORK

A Study concerning the Value and Limits of the Pragmatic Motifs in the Cognition of the World

Max Scheler

Translated from the German by Zachary Davis

Northwestern University Press
Evanston, Illinois

Northwestern University Press
www.nupress.northwestern.edu

English translation copyright © 2021 by Northwestern University Press.
Published 2021. All rights reserved.

Originally published in German in 1926 under the title *Erkenntnis und Arbeit.*

Printed in the United States of America

10 9 8 7 6 5 4 3 2 1

Library of Congress Cataloging-in-Publication Data
Names: Scheler, Max, 1874–1928, author. | Davis, Zachary, 1972– translator.
Title: Cognition and work : a study concerning the value and limits of the pragmatic motifs in the cognition of the world / Max Scheler ; translated from the German by Zachary Davis.
Other titles: Erkenntnis und Arbeit. English | Northwestern University studies in phenomenology & existential philosophy.
Description: Evanston, Illinois : Northwestern University Press, 2021. | Series: Northwestern University studies in phenomenology and existential philosophy | Originally published in German in 1926 under the title Erkenntnis und Arbeit.
Identifiers: LCCN 2020057157 | ISBN 9780810142695 (paperback) | ISBN 9780810142701 (cloth) | ISBN 9780810142718 (ebook)
Subjects: LCSH: Knowledge, Theory of. | Pragmatism.
Classification: LCC BD163 .S24813 2021 | DDC 121—dc23
LC record available at https://lccn.loc.gov/2020057157

To Stella and Wyatt

Contents

Acknowledgments

I would not have been able to complete this translation without the tremendous support of many different people. Christian Sternad and Susi Gottlöber were instrumental in helping me with numerous struggles rendering Scheler's difficult German into English. Although he passed away before the completion of this project, I would like to thank Manfred S. Frings for his encouragement of the project and his work as editor of the German volume. Karin Frings has also provided great support for the project. She welcomed me into her home so that I could consult Manfred's translations, finished and unfinished; supported my stay in Albuquerque, New Mexico, so that I could consult the Scheler archives at the University of New Mexico; and helped compile and ready the materials for the Manfred S. Frings archives at Southern Illinois University (SIU) at Carbondale. With a generous grant from the library at SIU, I was also able to consult the Frings archives for further assistance on translation.

Over the many years it took to complete this project, I have pestered my colleagues at both the Max Scheler Gesellschaft and the Max Scheler Society of North America for assistance. Among these colleagues, I would like to specifically recognize Michael Gabel, Eugene Kelly, Wolfhart Henckmann, Mathias Schlossberger, Guido Cuisnato, Olivier Agard, Joachim Fischer, and Günter Fröhlich. This work would also not have been possible without the continued financial support of St. John's University and the encouragement of my colleagues in the Department of Philosophy there. I would also like to share my indebtedness to the editorial staff at Northwestern University Press, particularly Anne Gendler, for their continued patience and diligence in seeing the project to its end.

Most importantly, I would like to thank those closest to me for their unwavering support. My wife, Lanessa, has offered the most enthusiastic support for the project and has been my most trusted ear in rendering passages into English. I would like to dedicate this project to the two persons I love most in the world, my two children, Stella and Wyatt. Without their love and understanding, I would not have been able to complete this arduous translation.

Translator's Introduction

The following text is the English translation of Max Scheler's *Erkenntnis und Arbeit* (*Cognition and Work*), which appeared in 1926, just two years before his death, and was published jointly with two other works in a volume titled *Die Wissensformen und die Gesellschaft* (*The Forms of Knowledge and Society*).[1] As Scheler notes in his foreword to the first edition of that book, the two major works contained in it, *Probleme einer Soziologie des Wissens* (*Problems of a Sociology of Knowledge*) and *Cognition and Work*, serve as an "entrance" into his metaphysical cognition and thinking.[2] Scheler passed away before completing his promised work on metaphysics. A collection of unpublished manuscripts and notes are all that remain of it, many of them now published in volume XI of Scheler's collected works (the *Gesammelte Werke*). The two main works in the 1926 volume, *Cognition and Work* and *Problems of a Sociology of Knowledge*, function, according to Scheler, as a complement to one another,[3] but they very much stand alone as independent texts.[4] The third text in the 1926 volume was a much shorter essay, *Universität und Volkshochschule* (*University and Adult Education Program*), which was first published in 1921.

Of the three works, *Cognition and Work* was the oldest in its development. In his foreword to the 1926 volume, Scheler writes that the publication of *Cognition and Work* makes good on a long-standing promise.[5] As early as part 1 of *Formalism in Ethics and Non-Formal Ethics of Values*, which was published in 1913, Scheler mentions his forthcoming work *Work and Cognition*, which is to address the problem of perception.[6] It is not clear what led to the delay in the completion of that work. Certainly, the outbreak of World War I must have been a significant factor in diverting his attention. Scheler wrote extensively not only during the war, where he defended German aggression, but also afterward, when he sought to find a means to rebuild Germany. Although Scheler hints in *Formalism in Ethics* at the forthcoming work on perception which would eventually become *Cognition and Work*, the latter work introduces novel concepts and approaches to perception that are not found in his earlier work. Though *Cognition and Work* may have been conceived quite early, it is very much a work from Scheler's later phase of research and thought.

There are considerable overlaps among all three works in the 1926 volume, particularly with regard to the first two. Scheler's later work on philosophical anthropology helps to shed light on the central problem treated in all three works in the volume. All three works are an attempt to describe the relation between spirit (*Geist*) and life (urge, drive, or impulse: *Drang*), which Scheler would later describe as two independent and irreducible movements not only of the human being, but of the cosmos itself. Spirit and life are certainly not new themes in Scheler's work. These later works, however, mark a significant change in his approach to understanding not only how spirit and life are unique movements, but also how these two independent movements relate to one another. As his later metaphysics demonstrates, Scheler is willing to move in a much more speculative direction than he had in his earlier phenomenological works. *Cognition and Work*, as well as *Problems of a Sociology of Knowledge*, are the transition pieces into this more speculative turn.

Cognition and Work is not speculative in nature, but the work does test the traditional boundaries of phenomenology and the types of phenomena possible to investigate. The work is composed of three main investigations: a critique of philosophical pragmatism, a phenomenological account of perception, and a phenomenological account of reality. There is a certain temporal structure to the work. Scheler's critique of pragmatism in the first part makes good on a long-standing promise to publish a work on pragmatism, a project he had begun almost twenty years earlier. The middle section on perception marks his first and only attempt to develop a phenomenology of perception, and with it he engages deeply with contemporary scientists and psychologists on current research in perceptual experience and meaning. The final section is the shortest of the three and serves mainly as an introduction to the problem of reality, an investigation that Scheler takes up in greater earnest in later works. Hence, the work brings together the past, present, and future horizons of Scheler's interests.

At first glance, these three different investigations in *Cognition and Work* may appear unrelated and the text in its entirety to be just a collection of writings, rather than a unified whole. To some extent this first impression is justified, and it is not difficult to imagine these three parts of the text being published as separate essays. However, the structure, and thus the unity, of the text stems from a question Scheler raises at the very beginning of the work: What is the meaning of the human being? In a later work, *The Human Place in the Cosmos*, Scheler writes that no question has been more central to his reflections from the very first stirrings of his philosophical consciousness.[7] The opening pages of *Cognition and Work* pose this question in terms of a historical shift in the modern period regarding the meaning of the human being. No longer is the human being understood as *homo rationalis,* but rather as a mere *homo faber* or toolmaker. Those readers who are familiar with Scheler's earlier work will understand that he raises this question in the context of his deep-seated suspicions of the modern worldview. As most poignantly articulated in his early work *Ressentiment,* Scheler maintains that the modern human being is in crisis, a crisis stemming from a reversal in the order of values.[8] In the so-called modern era, the value of utility has risen in prominence and is privileged over the value of life. As a result of this reversal, modernity has ushered in the rise of liberal individualism, late capitalism, and the mechanistic view of nature. As I make clear below, Scheler's central task in *Cognition and Work* is to show the gross shortcomings of the modern mechanistic view of nature and offer a new, "dynamic" description of nature and the type of existence that living beings have in it.

At the outset of *Cognition and Work,* Scheler places this modern reversal of values in the context of the problem of cognition (*Erkenntnis*) and knowledge (*Wissen*). A theory of cognition (*Erkenntnistheorie*) has been a long-standing concern for Scheler, as well as a source of frustration. His frustration lies in part in the fact that he has yet to provide a full theory of cognition, given that he recognizes that all of his work up to this point has assumed such a theory. An additional source of frustration is that most contemporary accounts of cognition have only accounted for one type of cognition, namely, the type assumed by the positive sciences. *Cognition and Work* was not intended to provide a theory of cognition, but rather to serve as the launching pad for a forthcoming treatment that Scheler was unable to complete before his death. Though he cites a number of authors and their respective definitions of cognition, Scheler does not offer one of his own. In fact, he remains purposely unclear as to a proper definition of cognition. The reason for this ambiguity is to highlight the many different kinds of cognition relative to particular types of investigations; for example, the types of cognition taking place in art, metaphysics, the natural sciences, and the natural worldview. In lieu of a definition of cognition, Scheler does describe the different measures of cognition, measures such as true and false, adequate and inadequate. In a much earlier work, *Phenomenology and a Theory of Cognition,* Scheler does provide a suggestion as to what he means by cognition: "The absolute measure of any 'cognition' is and remains the *self-givenness* of the fact." By "self-givenness" Scheler means a coincidence (*Deckung*) "between what is meant and that which is given in the experiencing of it."[9] A theory of cognition is thus not a theory of truth, though truth can certainly be a type of cognition. Rather, it is an account of what is evident. Scheler's account of perception in *Cognition and Work* shows that there is a type of cognizing which is taking place prior to any conscious awareness of it, a cognizing that humans share with other living beings. For Scheler, there is a level of cognition that is pre-linguistic and nonconceptual.

In contrast to the absence of a definition of cognition, Scheler does provide one for knowledge. Knowledge, Scheler maintains, is an ontological relation, a relation wherein a being participates in the being-thus (*Sosein*) of another being.[10] A bit later in the text, Scheler calls this relation of participation "love."[11] *Cognition and Work* marks the first time Scheler defines knowledge as both an ontological relation and as a relation of love. Scheler had addressed the relation of love to cognition in an earlier essay, "Love and Cognition" ("Liebe und Erkenntnis").[12] In this work, the relation was one of foundation. Scheler argued that the primary act for any knowing or cognizing the world is the act of love. The later work, *Cognition and Work*, serves as Scheler's attempt to clarify and deepen the relation between love and cognition. Knowledge in the most universal sense is the goal of all cognition.[13] Understood ontologically, knowledge is a becoming, a becoming other.[14] If cognition is the coincidence of the meant and the given, then the goal of cognition is for the meant to become what is given.

Scheler is not at all clear how we are to understand this ontological process of becoming other. Complicating matters is his use of the term "being-thus" (*Sosein*). Throughout *Cognition and Work* Scheler contrasts being-thus with existence (*Dasein*). This may lead one to assume that Scheler is working from the traditional distinction between essence and existence. Yet, Scheler will also use the German word *Wesen*, which in certain contexts means essence. The being-thus of an object and the essence of an object are related. It is from the being-thus of an object that the essential characteristics and qualities of an object can be intuited. The being-thus of an object is its particular objectiveness, the objective sense of a given object pertaining specifically to that object. An object may share essential qualities with other objects, but it has its own being-thus.

While there are many questions that remain unanswered in regard to Scheler's notion of knowledge, his intent is to introduce a notion of knowledge that rejects the neo-Kantian notion of it, a notion that dominated much of epistemology at this time. The neo-Kantians, according to Scheler, held that all knowing is an act of construction. A division thus exists between the way in which the world is and the way the world is known. Scheler seeks to dismantle such a division, a division that assumes a deep mistrust in the relation between the world and humans. According to him, the world is not a chaotic system to which the mind brings order. Knowing is a loving and trusting participation in the way in which the world is.

From this general definition of knowledge as an ontological relation, Scheler describes three different types of knowledge: redemptive knowledge (*Erlösungswissen*), erudition (*Bildungswissen*), and mastery knowledge (*Herrschaftswissen*). These three types of knowledge are wholly distinct and irreducible to one another, with each having its own unique origination and subject matter. Redemptive knowledge springs from the feeling of awe and concerns the highest ground of being-thus and existence, and seeks to know where we are heading. Erudition springs from the feeling of wonder and concerns both the "unfolding of the person" and what the world is. Metaphysics is a particular kind of erudition. Mastery knowledge springs from fear and seeks to gain some practical knowledge of the world in order to then control it. Positive science is one kind of mastery knowledge. Although these three types of knowledge are distinct from one another, there is a ranking among them. While genetically, in the life of a person, mastery or practical knowledge is the first type of knowledge to be acquired, it serves only as the first step toward the highest goal of knowledge. Erudition does not grow out of mastery knowledge, but it is the next step in the grand becoming of knowledge. Similarly, redemptive knowledge follows erudition and is the deepest type of knowledge. Although for Scheler the awareness and cognition of the world begin in our practical relation to it, the origins of erudition and redemptive knowledge are there from the start and account for how human beings are able to move from the practical to the metaphysical and religious forms of knowledge. As Scheler writes, "all knowledge is ultimately from the divine and for the divine."[15]

Most of *Cognition and Work* is dedicated to a clarification—and critique—of mastery or practical knowledge. In addition to the value reversal assumed in the positive sciences, there is also a reduction of the three kinds of knowledge to a single type, namely mastery knowledge. This is also Scheler's main criticism of pragmatism as well. However, rather than attempt to show the failures of the positive sciences and pragmatism to recognize both redemptive knowledge and erudition, Scheler seeks to show how they have failed to fully understand the nature of mastery knowledge. This is why he begins the main text of *Cognition and Work* with an analysis of pragmatism.

Scheler's critique of pragmatism in *Cognition and Work* is one of the earliest and most sustained treatments of pragmatism in Germany. For this reason, *Cognition and Work* is often cited as the work most responsible for the reception of pragmatism in Germany, a reception that Hans Joas has characterized as one marred by a misunderstanding.[16] For instance, Max Horkheimer cites *Cognition and Work* in his book critiquing pragmatism, *Eclipse of Reason*. It is not my interest here to either defend or contest the extent to which Scheler misunderstood pragmatism. He appears to have read relatively little of the American pragmatists. In *Cognition and Work,* he cites only Charles Peirce's essay "How to Make Our Ideas Clear" and William James's *Pragmatism: A New Name for Some Old Ways of Thinking.* He only mentions John Dewey once and only with regard to the development of the "school of work." Whether Scheler understood or misunderstood pragmatism may remain an open question, but it is clear that he had a very limited reading of the American pragmatists.[17]

The earliest reception of American pragmatism in Germany took place many years before the publication of *Cognition and Work.* Many in Germany had become aware of the emergence of pragmatism in the United States much earlier, and the reception of pragmatism in Germany can be traced back to Wilhelm Jerusalem's German translation of James's *Pragmatism,* a translation published in 1908.[18] That same year was the III. Internationalen Kongress für Philosophie in Heidelberg, where a contentious discussion of pragmatism figured prominently in the conference.[19] Scheler did not attend the Kongress. However, Moritz Geiger, a fellow member of the Munich phenomenological circle, did. Although we don't know the extent to which pragmatism was a topic in the circle's meetings in Munich, there does seem to have been much interest in pragmatism at this time. Scheler held a seminar on pragmatism in Munich during the 1909–1910 winter semester. His earliest manuscripts on pragmatism also stem from this period as well. In addition to Scheler, Adolf Reinach, another member of the Munich circle, included pragmatism in his lectures on cognition during the 1909–1910 winter semester. Reinach also published a lengthy obituary upon James's death in 1910.[20] Many of the criticisms leveled against pragmatism at the Kongress and by Reinach are consistent with Scheler's critique of pragmatism in *Cognition and Work.* For instance, James's account of truth and meaning in terms of their consequences or "cash value" came under great scrutiny by many attendees of the Kongress, as well as by Reinach and Scheler.[21]

Scheler's interest in pragmatism is much broader and more expansive than these early critiques. He begins his analysis by first situating pragmatism within the history of philosophy, or more specifically the history of modern philosophy. Scheler claims, for instance, that Hobbes was essentially the "grandfather" of pragmatism.[22] By situating pragmatism within a particular history of modern thought, a thought that embraces nominalism, Scheler aims to show that it harbors reductive tendencies similar to that tradition. This reduction concerns the meaning of knowledge and its different types. According to Scheler, pragmatism fails to understand that it is possible to suspend our practical relation to the world and comprehend the world as it is in essence—and even possibly gain insight into the *Weltgrund*, the ground of all being. Suffering from a type of blindness to the possibility of both erudition and redemptive knowledge, pragmatism reduces all forms of knowledge to a single type, namely mastery knowledge. Thus Scheler sees in pragmatism the same danger posed by the positive sciences: the rendering of all metaphysical and religious knowledge as merely meaningless and ungrounded speculation.

If Scheler was interested in pragmatism merely for the threat it posed to our understanding of knowledge and thus our understanding of the meaning of the human being, there would be no reason for such a long engagement with the movement of pragmatism, nor any reason to devote an entire work to its significance. While pragmatism may have its "errors," Scheler does argue that there is a "relative correctness" to pragmatism. In pragmatism, Scheler finds an important ally to overcome the mechanistic view of nature found not only in the positive sciences, but also in much of modern philosophy. As is the case for Scheler, pragmatism rejects any form of disinterested scientific inquiry, as if one were to do science for the sake of science itself. All scientific inquiry, according to pragmatism, assumes the interest of the scientist, and assumes a practical project or aim. In this regard, there is no objective science and no universal truth. At the level of practical or mastery knowledge, there is only truth relative to the specific project or aim of the scientific inquiry. Pragmatism thus does not make the mistake of the positive sciences and claim that its knowledge of truth is the only meaningful one. Rather, pragmatism recognizes that claims of truth at the practical level are "existentially relative." By contrast, the positive scientist fails to grasp that she is already caught up in a practical relation to the world and that the mechanistic view of nature presupposes a distinctive aim with regard to nature; namely, the desire to control and dominate nature according to its fixed mechanistic laws. The virtue of pragmatism is that it acknowledges its own relativity, and its inability to comprehend nature outside of any practical orientation. Hence, pragmatism is aware that its knowledge of nature is not value-neutral or practically neutral. For Scheler, pragmatism has much to offer by way of our understanding of mastery knowledge and our practical relation to the world. Its shortcomings lie in its blindness to the other forms of knowledge that are not practical in nature and which assume a very different idea of truth and evidence.

In clarifying the relative virtues of pragmatism, Scheler makes sense of the apparently abrupt transition from his critique of pragmatism to a philosophy of perception in *Cognition and Work*. Not only does he aim to articulate a different account of perception from those given within the framework of a mechanistic view of nature, but he also tries to show how central a role attention plays at the most primary levels of perceptual experience. As Scheler writes, "Without some degree and some direction of *drive attention*, without *value* grasping, and furthermore without the beginning of a *motor* process, *a perception*, no matter how simple it may be, *can in no way take* place."[23] Pragmatism helps to demonstrate that the practical level of experience is already value-latent and that the perceiver is practically invested in the perceived world.

As was also the case for Edmund Husserl in his work *Analyses concerning Active and Passive Synthesis*, Scheler's phenomenological account of perception was a direct response to Kant's *Critique of Pure Reason*, and in particular his attempt to develop a transcendental aesthetic. Both Husserl and later Maurice Merleau-Ponty, in his *Phenomenology of Perception*, provide a much more exhaustive account of perception at the so-called passive or pre-personal level of existence than Scheler does in his relatively brief account. Nonetheless, Scheler's account should be considered just as original as both Husserl's and Merleau-Ponty's phenomenology of perception, though it has not garnered the same amount of attention.

There are a number of aspects that contribute to the uniqueness of Scheler's approach to a phenomenology of perception. I wish only to highlight two of them. The first concerns the means by which he engages with his contemporaries on the problem of perception. Pragmatism, in many respects, had first filtered into Germany via the sciences and not philosophy. Many of the leading German psychologists and physicists at the time had already incorporated aspects of pragmatism as a means to develop a different approach than the one offered by the positive sciences and the mechanistic view of nature. In *Cognition and Work*, Scheler works directly from many of these thinkers, men such as Ernst Mach, Hans Driesch, Wolfgang Köhler, and Hugo Münsterberg, when developing his own account of perception and the manner in which a living being interacts and makes sense of its environment. The purpose of this engagement was to place the sciences into a type of conversation with phenomenological investigations. In particular, Scheler was trying to develop a dynamic theory of material and movement that understood beings and things in the environment as centers and fields of force.[24] While, on the one hand, Scheler was working to provide a phenomenological ground for the sciences and the account of perception, he was, on the other hand, working on his metaphysics and specifically the movement of life. For this reason, he was interested not only in human perceptual experience but also in the manner by which all living beings relate to the world perceptually. In this respect, a dialogue with the sciences was a means to learn from biologists, physicists, and psychologists about the natural world and the psychic life of living creatures.

The second aspect that distinguishes Scheler's phenomenology of perception from his fellow phenomenologists is his account of the life-drives and their fundamental role in perceptual experience. In the work that accompanied *Cognition and Work,* namely *Problems of a Sociology of Knowledge,* Scheler introduces a distinction between the real and ideal factors of history.[25] This is one of the first indications by him of his later distinction between spirit and drives (or life).[26] The real factors of history are rooted in the drive structure of the human being and are the material conditions for the realization of culture. The ideal factors are rooted in spirit and are endeavors such as art, philosophy, and economics.[27] The relation between these two factors is one wherein the ideal factors guide and direct the real factors, opening the "sluice gates" for particular spiritualized expressions of the real factors to become manifest.[28] Scheler's central concern in *Cognition and Work* is the activity of the drives in perceptual experience. In seeking to show the limitations of the mechanistic view of nature, he demonstrates that the body is not simply reacting passively to sensations, sensations which would then be interpreted or formed by concepts. The drives are already directing the living being in its environment in accord with their basic vital urge to achieve an optimal life course.[29] The mechanistic view of nature takes the drives for granted and fails to realize that all perception is drive-motor conditioned.

Scheler had already established in *Formalism in Ethics and Non-Formal Ethics of Values* that the primary relation the human being has to the world is a relation to value. Things in the world are given as of value prior to them being given as objects or known as such. Scheler's analysis of perception in *Cognition and Work* provides an opportunity for him to deepen the analysis in respect to the life drives. The phenomenological account of perception is taking place at the biological level of experience, and in this regard Scheler is not restricting his analysis of perception to only human beings. His account is meant for the perceptual experience of all living beings. To be clear, Scheler is not describing what perceptual experience is like for other living beings. Not only does the drive structure vary greatly among living beings, but human beings are also spiritual beings, which allows for a much different type of perceptual experience. Nevertheless, Scheler is giving an account of the structure of perception at the biological or vital level of existence, and thus of the structure of perception for all living beings.

For Scheler, mere living beings do not have a world, but live in an environment or milieu. Only persons have a world. The relation a living being has to the environment is ecstatic, and is mediated by the life drives. For a living being, the environment is never an object of reflection, nor are the objects in it. Objects in the environment are not given as intentional objects, but as environmental things (*Umweltdinge*). For instance, the tree is not given as a tree, but as a thing of vital interest, as something to provide shelter or food, or perhaps to provide fuel for a fire. Environmental things do not have sense in the strict sense, and living beings certainly do not have concepts of these environmental things. However, environmental things have a vital significance. Hence, the environment is not a chaotic bundle of stimuli to which the living being blindly reacts. The environment is always given in relief, with those objects of vital interest coming to the foreground and those of non-interest receding into the background.

Later, in *The Human Place in the Cosmos,* Scheler will attribute practical intelligence to living beings, an intelligence that is relative to the complexity of the living being.[30] Perception is the means by which the living being develops greater practical intelligence, an intelligence that will allow the living being to thrive. The learning takes places through a process of trial and error. Practical intelligence is not the same as mastery knowledge. As I have described above, knowledge concerns the grasping of the essence and being-thus of an object. At the biological level, practical intelligence concerns the success and failure that a living being has in moving through its environment.

While the living being does not have concepts of environmental things, it does have images (*Bilder*) of them. The notion of images is first introduced in *Cognition and Work.* Scheler defines an image as an objective appearance that is transcendent of consciousness and is fully irreal.[31] Images are transcendent and irreal because they are a reflection, a type of mirroring, of the environmental object given, but this is an appearing of more than can be given in any single stimulus or multiple stimuli from the fields and centers of force at play in the environment. Images are, in this sense, more than what a being is aware of with regard to what is immediately given. These images, contrary to empiricists like Hume, are not the sum of sensations or impressions. For Scheler, there is no such thing as a "pure sensation."[32] Every sensation is an admixture of both stimulus and drive attention.[33] The image or objective appearance is prior to any sensation. Images arise by virtue of a relation between "dynamic factors," that is, the centers and fields of force, and the specific type of living being.[34] Relative to its particular drive structure, each type of living being has its particular selection or ordering of the things in its environment. These images get filled in, so to speak, by the stimulus upon the particular sense organs and become associated and disassociated from one another. From the outset, the content of perception consists of the image and the particular sensations. As a living being interacts with its environment, it learns through perception how best to navigate within that environment, and comes to have a more precise image of the things in it. Over the course of the life of the living being, the image of the environment develops and the living being comes to learn how to fit into its environment.

The preliminary nature of Scheler's phenomenology of perception gives rise to more questions than it answers. For instance, it is not at all clear why Scheler chooses to use the word "image" to describe the objective appearing of environmental things to the living being. Do images or pictures appear to living beings? Why make use of this representational model for perception? This question become even more problematic in Scheler's account of fantasy. With his account of perception, Scheler opens up many paths for phenomenological inquiry. What is clear from his account in *Cognition and Work* is that phenomenology must contend with the great complexity and various forms of structuring that are developed at the biological level of existence. Perception assumes this dynamic relation between the forces of the environment and the drives of the living being. Already at this level, living beings exhibit a tremendous intelligence.

In the final section of *Cognition and Work*, Scheler takes up the problem and experience of reality. That he undertakes such a project marks a decisive break from Husserl. For Husserl, the "real" or the reality of an object is bracketed. Phenomenology is to concern itself with the way in which an object is given, its sense—and not its being or existence. Heidegger makes a similar break from Husserl when he examines the meaning of being in *Being and Time.* This is not the place to lay out the differences in the phenomenological approaches to the problem of existence and the real taken by Husserl, Heidegger, and Scheler. It is sufficient only to point out that Scheler's approach in *Cognition and Work* is fundamentally different from both Husserl's and Heidegger's approaches.

For Scheler, a phenomenological account of reality begins with the question: How is the real given? It is an attempt to answer the most basic metaphysical question: How do we know that the world is indeed real? As a means to answer this question, Scheler returns once again to the life drives of the living being. The real is given in the experience of "resistance."[35] Following again the strict distinction between spirit and the life-drives, Scheler asserts that resistance is an experience that is only accessible to living beings. The being real of an object has nothing to do with the objective sense of an object in our intellectual acts.[36] Spirit, in other words, does not experience reality as such. Although the reality of the world and the sense (or meaning) of the world are of two distinct origins, there is in the human being, the finite person, an increasing synthesis of the real and the sense of the world.[37] The two distinctive movements of life and spirit are two distinct modes of access, but they are movements that work in solidarity with one another to make sense of the real world.

Resistance is, as Scheler admits, a very "vague and undifferentiated" experience. Like Dilthey, he rejects the idea that resistance is a sensation given to the senses. To make this point, Scheler makes use of the resistance felt at the end of a stick. If resistance was a sensation of the sense, the resistance would be felt in the hand holding the stick as it is pressed against the wall. Yet, one feels the resistance at the end of the stick, not in one's hand. Dilthey tried to account for this problem by suggesting that resistance was a sensation of the will. For Scheler, sensations do not resist. Rather it is the "thing itself," the thing understood as a force center, which resists. Resistance is an experience of the "active self."[38] The experience of resistance is to a certain extent paradoxical. It is, on the one hand, the most fundamental experience of any living being. However, on the other hand, spirit has no access to this experience and thus cannot know what it means. An account of the experience of reality asks the impossible. It requires that we describe the world that we "have" ecstatically prior to us knowing the world, prior to any consciousness of the world as such.[39]

At the end of *Cognition and Work*, we are in many ways brought back to the very origins of cognition itself. The suffering in the experience of resistance gives rise to reflection and thus to the birth of the ego.[40] Cognition begins with the stark reality that there is a world. There are, for Scheler, "laws of pre-givenness." For instance, the "outer world" is pre-given to the "inner world," and the "with-world" (the world with others) is pre-given to the individual ego.[41] Because consciousness presupposes the having of the world ecstatically, Scheler insists that phenomenology not only account for the experience of reality, but also for the manner in which humans as vital beings inhabit an environment and orient themselves among the other fields and centers of forces. The renewed metaphysical spirit that Scheler calls for at the conclusion of *Cognition and Work* was meant as a new challenge for phenomenology, a challenge to return to the most fundamental relation that humans have to the world.

Notes

1. This book in its entirety was later published as *Die Wissensformen und die Gesellschaft*, vol. VIII of Scheler's *Gesammelte Werke* (*Collected Works*), to which the bracketed page numbers in this edition refer.

2. Max Scheler, "Vorwort," in *Die Wissenformen und die Gesellschaft,* vol. VIII of *Gesammelte Werke,* ed. Maria Scheler (Bern: Francke Verlag, 1980), 11.

3. Scheler, "Vorwort," 9.

4. An earlier and shorter version of *Problems of a Sociology of Knowledge* did appear two years earlier in a collection of essays with the title "Attempts toward a Sociology of Knowledge."

5. Scheler, "Vorwort," 13.

6. Max Scheler, *Der Formalismus in der Ethik und die Materiale Wertethik: Neuer Versuch der Grundlegung eines Ethischen Personalismus,* vol. II of *Gesammelte Werke,* ed. Maria Scheler (Bern: Francke Verlag, 1966), 169; translated by Manfred S. Frings and Roger L. Funk as *Formalism in Ethics and Non-Formal Ethics of Values: A New Attempt toward the Foundation of an Ethical Personalism* (Evanston, Ill.: Northwestern University Press, 1973), 156.

7. Max Scheler, *Die Stellung des Menschen im Kosmos,* in *Späte Schriften.* vol. IX of *Gesammelte Werke,* ed. Manfred S. Frings (Bern: Francke Verlag, 1980), 9; translated by Manfred S. Frings as *The Human Place in the Cosmos* (Evanston, Ill.: Northwestern University Press, 2009), 3.

8. Max Scheler, *Das Ressentiment in Aufbau der Moralen,* in *Vom Umsturz der Werte: Abhandlungen und Aufsätze,* vol. III of *Gesammelte Werke,* ed. Maria Scheler and Manfred S. Frings (Bern: Francke Verlag, 1955), 33–148.

9. Max Scheler, *Phänomenologie und Erkenntnistheorie,* in *Schriften aus dem Nachlass I, Zur Ethik und Erkenntnislehre,* vol. X of *Gesammelte Werke,* ed. Maria Scheler (Bern: Francke Verlag, 1957), 398; my translation.

10. Max Scheler, *Erkenntnis und Arbeit,* in *Die Wissenformen und die Gesellschaft.* vol. XIII of *Gesammelte Werke,* ed. Maria Scheler (Bern: Francke Verlag, 1980), 203.

11. Scheler, *Erkenntnis und Arbeit,* 204.

12. The English translation of "Liebe und Erkenntnis" has translated *Erkenntnis* as "knowledge," which is understandable. It is not until Scheler's later work that the distinction between cognition and knowledge is maintained by him. See Max Scheler, "Liebe und Erkenntnis," in *Schriften zur Soziologie und Weltanschauungslehre,* vol. VI of *Gesammelte Werke,* ed. Maria Scheler (Bern: Francke Verlag, 1963), 77–99; translated as "Love and Knowledge" in Max Scheler, *On Feeling, Knowing, and Valuing: Selected Writings,* ed. Harold J. Bershady (Chicago: University of Chicago Press, 1992), 147–65.

13. Scheler, *Erkenntnis und Arbeit,* 203.

14. Scheler, *Erkenntnis und Arbeit,* 204.

15. Scheler, *Erkenntnis und Arbeit,* 211.

16. Hans Joas, *Pragmatism and Social Theory* (Chicago: University of Chicago Press, 1993), 94–121.

17. Scheler does cite other works such as *The Varieties of Religious Experience* by William James in other places, and he certainly read James's *Principles of Psychology.*

18. William James, *Der Pragmatismus: Ein neuer Name für alte Denkmethoden,* trans. Wilhelm Jerusalem (Leipzig: Klinkhardt, 1908).

19. For a fuller account of the early reception of pragmatism in Germany, see Zachary Davis, "The Possibility of Phenomenology: Scheler's Confrontation

with Pragmatism," in *Erkennen—Handeln—Bewähren: Phänomenologie und Pragmatismus,* vol. 2 of *Scheleriana,* ed. Michael Gabel and Matthias Müller (Nordhausen: Verlag Traugott Bautz, 2015), 118–33.

20. Adolf Reinach, "William James und der Pragmatismus," in Adolf Reinach, *Sämtliche Werke: Textkritische Ausgabe in 2 Bände,* ed. Karl Schuhmann and Barry Smith (Munich: Philosophia Verlag, 1989).

21. Gerschon Seliber provides an account of these criticisms during the Kongress in "Der Pragmatismus und seine Gegner auf dem III. Internationalen Kongress für Philosophie," in *Archiv für systematische Philosophie* 15, no. 3 (1909). In his obituary on James, Reinach also offers his critique of James's notion of truth (Reinach, "William James und der Pragmatismus").

22. Scheler, *Erkenntnis und Arbeit,* 222.

23. Scheler, *Erkenntnis und Arbeit,* 284.

24. Scheler, *Erkenntnis und Arbeit,* 289.

25. Max Scheler, *Probleme einer Soziologie des Wissens,* in *Die Wissenformen und die Gesellschaft,* vol. XIII of *Gesammelte Werke,* ed. Maria Scheler (Bern: Francke Verlag, 1980), 39; translated by Manfred S. Frings as *Problems of a Sociology of Knowledge* (Boston: Routledge and Kegan Paul, 1980), 53.

26. For a full account of Scheler's understanding of the real and ideal factors, and how the interplay between these factors is responsible for the growth and sense of a culture, see Kenneth Stikkers's "Introduction" in Max Scheler, *Problems of a Sociology of Knowledge,* trans. Manfred S. Frings (New York: Routledge and Kegan Paul, 1980), 1–32.

27. Scheler, *Probleme,* 19; Scheler, *Problems,* 35.

28. Scheler, *Probleme,* 40; Scheler, *Problems,* 54.

29. Scheler, *Erkenntnis und Arbeit,* 283.

30. Max Scheler, *Die Stellung des Menschen im Kosmos,* in *Späte Schriften.* vol. IX of *Gesammelte Werke,* ed. Manfred S. Frings (Bern: Francke Verlag, 1976), 27; translated by Manfred S. Frings as *The Human Place in the Cosmos* (Evanston, Ill.: Northwestern University Press, 2009), 21.

31. Scheler, *Erkenntnis und Arbeit,* 287.

32. Scheler, *Erkenntnis und Arbeit,* 323.

33. Scheler, *Erkenntnis und Arbeit,* 316.

34. Scheler, *Erkenntnis und Arbeit,* 295.

35. Scheler, *Erkenntnis und Arbeit,* 365.

36. Scheler, *Erkenntnis und Arbeit,* 363.

37. Scheler, *Erkenntnis und Arbeit,* 360.

38. Scheler, *Erkenntnis und Arbeit,* 365.

39. Scheler, *Erkenntnis und Arbeit,* 370.

40. Scheler, *Erkenntnis und Arbeit,* 370.

41. Scheler, *Erkenntnis und Arbeit,* 374–75.

Note on Translation

Every translation assumes some interpretation of the text, and a translator must always contend with the very difficult and ambiguous question of whether to remain true to the text or to its meaning. Scheler's writing presents its own unique challenges, in part because he makes use of his own meanings of particular words and when necessary creates new ones. I have done my best to remain consistent with the other English translations of Scheler's work. There are, however, many inconsistencies among the many different English translations.

In some cases, I have left the original German word in brackets next to my translation. This was either due to the inherent ambiguity of the word, often a neologism from Scheler, or because the same English word was used to translate two different German words. An example of this latter problem is Scheler's use of the words *Wahrnehmung* and *Perzeption*. While *Wahrnehmung* literally means "taking as true," the generally accepted English translation of this word is "perception." The same is the case for the less frequently used German word *Perzeption*. For my translation, I have translated both words as "perception."

Throughout the text there are deeply troubling remarks and characterizations by Scheler regarding both race and gender. While it is the case that Scheler is pulling from much of the language and research prevalent at the time in which he was writing, certain passages entail significant racial, gender, and Eurocentric biases. I have chosen to retain Scheler's word choices both for the sake of accuracy in the translation and as a means to hold Scheler accountable.

Finally, I have included at the end of the translation an appendix containing the "Additions" from the unpublished works that Maria Scheler included in her edition of *Die Wissenformen und die Gesellschaft*, volume VIII of Scheler's *Gesammelte Werke*. The four manuscripts, namely, (a) "The 'Spirit' of Pragmatism and the Philosophical Concept of the Human Being" (ca. 1912 and 1909), (b), "Pragmatism and More Recent Natural Science" (ca. 1912 and 1909), (c) "Simultaneous Grounding of the Theory of Perception and the Theory of Formal-Mechanistic Natural Science," and (d) "The Pragmatist, the Idealist—and the Wise," were written at different times, and it is not clear from the afterword why Maria Scheler chose to include these particular manuscripts. However, for the sake of consistency with Scheler's collected works, I have chosen to include them as well. The first two manuscripts, (a) and (b), stem from notes written in 1912, and part 2 of manuscript (a) is the oldest, written in 1909. The second two manuscripts, (c) and (d), were written much later, in 1926–27 and 1923 respectively.

COGNITION AND WORK

1

The Problem

The pathos that the modern human being attaches to the word "work" has had a tremendous influence on the *philosophical view of cognition* and on the meaning of the *human being*. Its intensity has become all the greater as the modern human being attempts to wrestle itself loose from the ancient and Christian spiritual traditions and seeks to create for itself a worldview and ethos from its own conditions of life and existence. This pathos finds its most precise expression in the *Communist Manifesto*: work is the "sole creator of all education and culture." The best evidence for the increased intensity of this pathos is the emergence of "pragmatic thinking" in epistemology as well as in metaphysics. Is the human being "*homo rationalis*" and not merely "*homo faber*"? This is the decisive question that we must dare to raise.

Even for those who pay no mind to such speculative questions, the fact that the productivity of modern positive science, its continual, unending progress, and the worldwide success of modern technology in mastering nature all rest upon the very tight *unification of science with the technical-mechanical form* of the production of goods, is taken for granted to such a degree that the systematic and intimate *relationship between work and cognition* existing in our civilization is never called into question. This bond between work and cognition not only grounds the *defining characteristics* of the modern Western form of experimental science, a form of science guided by mathematical theory and distinct from all other forms of science that the world had to offer, for example Chinese, Indian, Greek, and medieval Western forms of science; but it also to no less degree grounds the distinctiveness of modern rational consumer-capitalism and its economic system, which distinguishes it from all other forms of capitalistic and non-capitalistic economies that we have ever come across in history. However indubitable the emergence of this unity may be and however clearly and decisively this unity severs the modern Western world from the collective pre-world [*Vorwelt*] and with-world [*Mitwelt*], as well as from all forms of contemplative "science" or, better said, theories of wisdom (to which the Chinese, Indian, and Greek sciences belong), however the emergence of this unity between work and cognition severs the modern Western world from any form of an economy that is merely satisfying needs—that is, an economy in which the experiences human beings have in their work are *handed down* within their professions without being systematically sought and are then practically related to areas in which new needs are *awakened* (e.g., telegraph, telephone, the electrical industry, indeed almost all of modern communications technology)—the emergence of this unity remains incredibly ambiguous.

[194] For the purpose of having an outline of our problem, let us initially pose the distinctly *antithetical either-or question* to which the preceding developed relations have not done justice: Is the modern technique of work and production of goods only a *subsequent and practical use* of *knowledge* about nature, nature's order, and its lawful connections which is, as far as it is concerned, *purely theoretical*? ("Purely theoretical" is meant here as that which concerns both the operations of thought and intuition and their forms that go into the acquisition of knowledge, and also the subjective ends and motives of the researcher who seeks to obtain this knowledge.) *Or* is the conscious (or unconscious) drive and *will to have mastery* over nature the *primum movens*, and accordingly are the particular experimental and technical experiences that were produced through the actual effects of this will the primary and leading experiences allowing us then to conclude that the new science is only a *subsequent formulation* of these experiences had in the *dealing with* and forming of nature: a logification, unification, and systemization of the successful and unsuccessful reactions that nature grants us based upon our practical work-access? If this latter description is the case, then it would at least be necessary to set as a goal of the discussion of the question whether the *forms* of thought and intuition with which modern science approaches what is given of nature, whether the methods and the particular cognition goals of modern science would themselves have been constructed through the *pre- and alogical positing* of this "will to power and mastery over nature" as well as through the success and failure of its effects—constructed in the course of this practical-technical adaptation to nature.

If this question is answered in the affirmative, it does in no way imply that the *individual* researcher posited in his intention and motivation a different aim than the so-called "*pure*" cognition of the thing, or that he as inquirer must already have some sense of the possible practical worth of his research work. Since Liebig's brilliant critique of the Baconian method of induction, such a banal use of subject intention has been unanimously and resoundingly contradicted by serious natural researchers and mathematicians as to make it not worth reviewing here. Yet, a more far-reaching and indirect utilitarianism is capable, and not with recourse to the self-valuation of truth, of setting this banality along a different course, a course already indicated keenly by Liebig. Along this course, any cognition of natural laws, which is utilized technically in the most fruitful manner, is not sought and found for the sake of this utilization, but is gained exclusively *from the method's own logic in pure theoretical intention.*[1] [195] Liebig's own cognitions construct examples of this course on the basis of organic chemistry, examples that have proven to be so fruitful for agricultural and soil fertilization technology. When the physicist Weber and the mathematician Gauss originally laid a wire in Gottingen between the physics institute and the astronomical observatory in order to understand the exact sidereal time through electrical waves, they did not immediately think that they had discovered the founding principles of the telegraph, an instrument that would be practically and technically useful for the rest of humanity. "We do not study the starry heavens and its laws in order to discover new laws according to which we could construct new machines, but rather we always make new machines that will free more humans from the burden of physical labor so they can research the heavens as well," said Henri Poincaré with Gallic antithesis, the same Poincaré whose nominalist theory of mathematics and natural science bears its own pragmatic elements. However, even if the more sophisticated pragmatism is correct in rejecting this banality, our above question is still in no way resolved with this rejection. H. Spencer teaches in his ethics that the maximum happiness of humans would construct the objective criteria of "good" and "bad," that the maximum good is only obtainable if no one would take it as a subjective goal and motive. The greatest happiness is obtained rather when the laws of justice, both innate and directly revealed to the individual, are followed; rules, according to Spencer, which are expressions of the accumulated experiences of the human species regarding success and failure, pleasure and displeasure of action, which lead more effectively to the goal of the objective maximum of happiness than the individual experience and reflection regarding these consequences. The truth of Spencer's theory is not our concern here.[2] The feelings of happiness on a *deeper* level are definitely only obtainable when they are *not* sought deliberatively. Could this not also be analogous? Could not the greatest practical objective use of knowledge be guaranteed first not through the striving for this use, but rather through the striving for *knowledge as such* as self-worth? The question whether the forms of thought and intuition, and further whether the methods and goals of the modern and superseding individual manner of research in the above sense are or are not determined *through the "will" to master nature,* is thus a question of a wholly different order. This question can never be grasped through the "psychology of the researcher."

Our intention is not to provide an exhaustive answer to the question posed here, for this could only be the task of a far more expansive work. We [196] can only provide some fundamental theoretical considerations that reveal new paths toward a solution to this question, which has up to this point been poorly formulated. The argument ultimately supporting these considerations is found in the publication of the research the author has dedicated for many years to the fundamental problems of epistemology.

In order to proceed in a systematic fashion, the *problem of work and cognition* would have to be investigated in a fivefold manner within the modern worldview. These five ways are:

1. *Historical and sociological.* This means, it would have to be shown in a fundamental synopsis of the history of science and philosophy and of the history of the technical forms of work, how the *cooperation of technology and science* took place in *detail,* what had command, how, on the one hand, the collective character of the sciences formed according to new technical aims and tasks, and, how, on the other hand, science had an effect on technology.[3] Pierre Duhem's research dedicated to the history of mechanics, thermodynamics, and the theory of energy, as well as Ernst Mach's works, touch upon many of these questions. Their research has made clear that the all-encompassing technical tasks have provided the impetus behind the various aspects of mathematics and natural science, and thus that the rigorous logifying and systemization of the discovered results was generally the *subsequent result.* It has also made clear that the *experiment* in particular as a pure means of research has slowly and originally grown out of the increasing leveling of the specific purposes that are both in part technical and in part playful interventions in nature. The isolation of the causes of the parts from an entire complex of the causes of the whole, their quantitative gradation, the entire system of types of "experimental induction," a phrase coined by J. S. Mill, in no way grew out of a pure will of cognition, but rather were *the result of technical interventions* that not only make an observation possible, but also bring forth what was wanted. The experiment is genetically, so to speak, only a *limit case* of a technical intervention. It is a technical intervention in which the specific aim originally desired is forgotten, and the specific aims level themselves to the general and comprehensive aims in order to obtain laws that allow, through an intervention in a part of nature, one not only to reach a predetermined aim, but also the epitome of *any possible* aim—when new needs arise. In the case when there is neither the desire nor the ability to realize or make the experiment possible in reality, the experiment becomes ultimately a "thought experiment"; that is, there is no desire to know how the object came to be in itself, but how [197] the object can be imagined so that the object *could* be made, if there were the material and force to do so, from the already existing parts and unam-

biguous signs for it. Newton undertook such a thought experiment when he imagines the Moon to be like a stone, whose parabolic trajectory, if thrown forcefully enough from a mountain peak, would ultimately go in circular motion around the Earth. Using the laws of free fall, established earlier by Galileo, to calculate the Moon's falling motion to the minutest of time lapses, Newton discovers which movement in conjunction with a tangential force strong enough to distance it from the Earth results in a circular motion.[4] In the deism of the seventeenth and eighteenth centuries, God himself becomes then merely an infinite "world engineer," who manufactured the world machine in such an exquisite manner that this machine can run optimally and harmoniously without divine world-direction, miracle, and revelation in any respect. Without a doubt, the new idea of power expressed simultaneously in Calvin's theology, Bodin's theory of sovereignty, and Hobbes's and Machiavelli's politics, an idea scientifically inspiring the period of the new inventions and discoveries, also selects anew the objects of cognition and determines anew its goals (i.e., the mechanistic explanation of nature). Francis Bacon wants only "to see in order to foresee," and "to foresee" and nothing more (for example, he had no interest in knowing the movements of the heavens' fixed stars), because this encourages human "power" over nature. G. B. Vico declares in the eighteenth century that we can only know something insofar as we would be capable of producing the object for ourselves.

What the theory of cognition is able to show convincingly is that the *pure* will to cognize, that logic, mathematics, and intuition would *never* lead us (as I. Kant and many researchers up to H. Driesch have believed) to a material or formal mechanistic explanation of the appearances of the nature of the soul (association psychology), or an explanation for the matter of dead nature, let alone of vital and spiritual reality. *History* reveal-ingly confirms this point. Indeed, the closer we are to the origin of the modern view of nature and the world, the better and more clearly we are able to make this point. This is only more emphatically confirmed, the closer we get to the origins of the modern view of nature and the world, or more precisely, the more closely we investigate the origins of the (*by no means constitutive*) *forms of thinking and intuition*. It is from the dynamic function of these forms that this worldview arose. The forms of thought and principles of the understanding, as Kant had compiled them in the *Critique of Pure Reason*, are only *one* possible kind of thinking of reason, and in no way are they reason itself. Certainly it is a kind of thinking that functionalized itself in and through experiences to become the highest value of knowledge, and the type of thinking of the new "will to power over nature" corresponding to this value was severed from all other "possible" [198] types of experience as the *only* possible experience. Because an *interest* direction and *value* bearing (and their preference rules) *precede* in general all possible perception[5] and intuition of the world, as well as all thinking as the grasping of meaning and facts [*Sachverhalt*], the so-called "mechanism" becomes the anticipatory schema in which the new bourgeois society captures the picture of the thing. Nothing is more certain than this: insofar as not only we human beings, but also "any living being" *can guide* nature and soul toward some particular goal through spontaneous movement, so must their appearance and being be rooted in the "movement" of transportable primary things (masses, electrons, etc.). Insofar as the world is not a mechanism, the world is certainly not guidable and controllable. It was neither the "pure understanding" nor the "pure spirit" that sketched out at the beginning of modernity the immense program of an all-encompassing mechanistic explanation of nature and the soul, a program outlined long before it was carried through in physics, chemistry, biology, psychology, sociology, etc. Rather, it was the new will to *power and work* of *a newly ascending society* aimed at *nature* that began gradually to suppress, on the one hand, the valuing estimation dominant during feudalism and feudal society, a mastery of human beings over *human beings* and the *organic world*, an estimation bound with the crude and broad enjoyment of the world; and began to suppress, on the other hand, the contemplative cognitive will of the priestly and monastic society which sought to grasp the *essence and form* of the world in order to mirror this spiritually. Any "kind of thinking," any of the structured, anticipatory schemas in which forms of worldviews and forms of science present the being-thus [*Sosein*] of the world, have *have originated through "functionalization,"* through the functionalization of a particular *detail* of *essential* intuitions and insights—a process I have described elsewhere.[6] A relativism and historicism, in O. Spengler's sense, in no way follow from this. If on some level existentially relative to its objects the world does not have *ontically* a formal, mechanistic side, then no subjective decisive judgment [*Machtwort*], no will to power could decipher such a side from world experience. Only the prevailing and specific choices of forms of thought are sociologically and historically determined, *not the forms* as such. Any of these schemas is further directed by an *ethos* form, through a living system of value-privileging [*Vor- und Nachsetzen*], a system of pre-loving. Moreover, any of these value systems persists through a dominant and *exemplary* social class. Nothing can better exemplify these laws than the social-historical origin of the modern worldview.

2. The problem of work and cognition is secondly an epistemological problem. This has already been shown by pragmatic philosophy from James to Nietzsche, from Bergson to Vaihinger. I will return to this problem in detail later. [199]

3. Our problem is also a *developmental physiological and psychological* problem, understood in several senses. For instance, there is the course of development of living beings, of the psychic accomplishment capacities of different kinds of animals in relation to each other and in relation to humans, of the maturation process from child to adult, and also of the development of knowledge of the historical human being. The question as to whether and to what extent conditional associations exist between the *drive* and *motor* behavior of the organism *and* the construction of its *view of the environment* (and similarly between work and its forms regulated by humans, and the forms of knowledge), and associations leading to the education *of the* organs and functions (physiological and psychical) that are necessary for the expansion of the worldview in the multiple respects, for example, of sensible and memory-related activity, is posed differently in respect to the diverse courses of development.

4. The problem of work and cognition can and must be thoroughly treated by the blossoming special field of physiology, *work physiology*, and it must be encouraged to do so in a multitude of directions of study. This science has studied in detail the interplay of the sensorial and the various motor processes of acts of work. These processes range from purposive consciousness and the workings of the cortex to the various simple as well as complex motor reflexes, which simultaneously delineates a chronogenetic series in the development of their constitutive areas of the nervous system and their special functions in the development of the brain stem (Monakow) up to the chemical energy sources in the muscle fiber. The same holds true for the *psychology* of work processes, and thank Kraepelin for the most elementary advances he made, especially the appearances of practice and fatigue of the different centers in question. Based on this initial advance, further investigations were undertaken concerning the psychopathic deficiency symptoms (character blindness, psychic blindness, psychic deafness, etc.) of sensory and memory, as well as those intellectual capacities linked to the deficiency of motor and involuntary drive factors in respect to the total system of efficiency. Bergson based his work *Matière et mémoire* on such kinds of symptoms as agnosia, apraxia, alexia, and aphasia, etc., In this work he primarily sought to provide a philosophical grounding for the theory of pragmatism using a particular interpretation of these symptoms.

5. Finally, in a more applied sense, our problem must assiduously concern itself with *pedagogy*. The idea of the so called "school of work" (Dewey, Kerschensteiner), in contrast to the so-called "school of erudition [*Bildung*]," has clearly grown out of the following question: whether one ought to first give a verbal definition in order to convey [200] to the

student the notion of specific weight, or whether one should first demonstrate to the student the type of process by which the specific weight of the body can be determined and then let the student practice it.

In the following exposition, I examine the problem of cognition and work from only the second and third points of view. I have already given a thorough account of the first and macroscopic point of view in my *Problems of a Sociology of Knowledge*. The investigation here of the same questions should, from the epistemological and developmental psychological point of view, complement and ground more deeply what was found in this earlier work.

The *pragmatic thesis*, in any of its various expressions and forms, subscribes to the "proposition" that all knowledge is genetically only the result of a kind of *inner action* and a preparation for a reshaping of the world. It is, moreover, for this reason that knowledge, based upon *any kind* of theoretical act such as intuition, perception, remembering, or thinking, must serve the action teleologically and value-theoretically. In what follows, the theory of *perception* is given more attention than the highly sophisticated constructions of the pragmatic theory of thinking (of concept formation, of judgment, of concluding, of the so-called axioms, of the meaning of natural principles and laws, of deduction and induction) for two reasons. First, I do so because the principles and fundamental errors of the pragmatic theory of thinking have, in my opinion, been impressively refuted by E. Husserl's *Logical Investigations*. Admittedly, this is still a refutation without precise determinations of the limits to which pragmatic motives and values actually come into play in scientific *thinking*. Secondly, I do so because I will give a comprehensive examination of the different forms of thinking that "pure logic" accepts in philosophy and science and their main areas (the logic of philosophy and the logic of science) in the still-unpublished first volume of my metaphysics, and I do not wish to repeat myself here.

2

The Essence and Meaning of Knowledge and Cognition

The Kinds of Knowledge

Only recently has it begun to dawn on philosophy that what has been called "epistemology" has mostly recognized only *one* kind of cognition, namely the kind of cognition in the *positive sciences*, and in the positive sciences only [201] certain arbitrarily privileged disciplines, whether it is the mathematical natural sciences or history. An "epistemology" of the "natural worldview," of "biology," an epistemology of the understanding of the objective sense-content of spiritual creations (of objective spirit) and subjective spiritual acts, an epistemology of objectifying psychology, of the observation of self and other, an epistemology of philosophy itself (or what E. Lask calls the "logic of philosophy"), and an epistemology of metaphysics; these are all still only in the beginning stages of development. What "knowledge" means in religion, art, mythology, and language, and how this knowledge is to be classified in the system of all knowledge, are questions that are only now beginning to be asked, after the long dreary period when philosophy had degraded itself to be the handmaiden of this or that specialized science. The clearest evidence for this sudden change is that Ernst Cassirer, the most important representative and proponent of the Marburg school,[1] the school in which "scientism" has taken its crudest form, has broken decisively from this contraction in epistemology.[2] From that school's general standpoint that the forms of thinking impose their functional laws on the objective world, Cassirer wants to know how the question "How is mathematical natural science possible?" can be broadened to cover all meaning and cultural constructs, such as language, myth, and religion. If all *ontological* measures are abandoned, it has yet to be shown how there would be some *semblance* [*Abstufung*] of right and wrong, true and false, or some kind of rank ordering between different systems or forms of thinking which establish themselves as different, and moreover how this approach can avoid the historical and sociological *relativism* of all worldviews and world interpretations.

Indeed, the *unity of the idea of knowledge* should not be forgotten in the new specification of the kinds and forms of knowledge and cognition. Nevertheless, it should no longer be possible for a book to be published—which may in fact be quite good for its specialized use—under the title "general epistemology."[3] Such a book may certainly treat the scientific theory of theoretical physics thoroughly, but then it also assumes thereby to have exhausted *every* force of human cognition. However, present-day schools determine the essence of "cognition" in fundamentally different ways, with determinations such as [202] "to develop judgments that lead to useful actions" (pragmatism), "the production of objects" (H. Cohen), "to portray the objectively existing forms of things" (Aristotle and Thomism), "intuitive identification in the becoming" (Bergson), "grasping how the relations in representations that are not like the things, but entirely dissimilar, relate the relations of the things" (Lotze et al.), "describing the intuitive facts with the least number of concepts and rules" (economism), "material forms of intuition" (Rickert), "to regain in part the relatively familiar in the relatively unfamiliar and to arrange it clearly with a minimum of signs" (M. Schlick), "to create instrumental fictions" (H. Vaihinger), and "to establish under one another an 'evident' comprehensive unity between meaning intuitions and all sensible and non-sensible intuitive contents with determinate meanings" (Husserl), to name only a few basic conceptions in present German philosophy. The basis for these hard-to-believe epistemological divergences regarding the basic concept of "cognition" lies not only in the *factual* issues involved, but also in the entirely *different kinds of knowledge* and *aims* of cognition that are thought about in each case.

The same holds true for theories regarding the standards of knowledge and cognition. There are far more standards than are customarily accepted—there are certainly some which are *independent* of one another—and moreover, the standard of "*true*" and "*false*" (the standard befitting only judgments as sense-pictures), which is commonly seen as the only standard, is actually only one standard among others. Thus, a consequence of recognizing only the standard of "true" and "false" is that other standards are overlooked. These overlooked standards include, for example, the standards of *intuitive* cognition; standards of "adequate" and "inadequate" with regard to the "fullness" of an object's features given in the intuited content; the difference between deception, disappointment, and intuited insight; the specific *epistemological* differences between a priori knowledge and a posteriori knowledge (i.e., between intuitive and rational knowledge); the fundamental and *distinct gradations* of the *existentially relative* nature of cognizable objects such as a spiritual subject in general, a finite spiritual being, a vital being in general, the human species in general, etc.; and the standards that serve as *signs* for the determination and presentation of cognitive sense content (clarity of the indication and economy of signs and their operative rules). Furthermore, there are differences in the use and meaning of the notion of "sense," as in the case of "having sense" [*Sinnhaft*] and being "free of sense" [*Sinnfreien*], or as in the parceling out of sense in the "meaningful" [*Sinnvolle*], the "nonsensical" [*Unsinnige*], and the "absurd" [*Widersinnige*]. Each of these notions of sense is valid in its own right and thus has a meaning independent of being "true" and "false," standards determining what *can* be true or false. In other words, a statement presupposes from the outset that a meaning would be positively granted to that statement, and that the statement would not be "free of sense" or "nonsense" or "absurd." These objective laws of sense correspond to the subjective laws of the *understanding* of sense and [203] "understandability."

The opposition of true–false is itself of three different kinds. It divides into the incontestably true and the oppositional true-false. All pure logical axioms themselves in their formal-ontic sense (and in contrast to their formulas) are incontestable, namely "true by insight." They define first that which is "formally true," or better expressed, what *can* be "correct" or rather "incorrect" (formally false). Thus, these axioms themselves are neither correct nor incorrect. Moreover, they are not "*materially true.*" This means that they do not correspond in their sense content with the intuitable existing state of affairs, with the "existence" of some positive meaningfulness, since the culturally edified manner of judgment, which questions whether an object is materially true or false (and the concepts contained in the judgment), must already be commensurate with the logical principles in order that they can only be true or false (in the material sense). One can only "see" or "not see" these principles, but one cannot "falsely see" them, which is a clearly absurd word concatenation. Hence, the rules of deduction, for example, cannot themselves function as higher propositions or as conclusions of deductions.[4]

For the teleological question, *to what end does knowledge serve*, and for the different but related question, what is the essential motivation to love and seek knowledge, there can be *no* answer that is the *same* for every kind of knowledge. This is the case if we think the kinds specifically according to the leading different standards that we use predominantly for knowledge.

The most general concept of knowledge, the aim of all cognition, has not been addressed by the definitions given above. Knowledge must be defined without using a particular kind of knowledge or something that already assumes in itself knowledge or "consciousness" (such as judgment, representation, deduction, etc.) in the definition. That is, the most general concept of knowledge must be defined by purely *ontological* concepts. It follows, then, that knowledge is a relation of being, and indeed a relation of being that presupposes the forms of being of the whole and part. It is the relation of *participation* of a being in the being-*thus* [*So*sein] of another being, a relation of participation wherein no change in this being-thus [*Soseinden*] is co-posited. The "known" becomes "part" of who "knows," but without in any respect budging from its position or being changed. This relationship of being is not a spatial, temporal, or causal relationship.

"*Mens*" or "*spirit*" is to us the X or the epitome of the act in the "knowing" being through which such participation is possible; it is that through which a thing, or better yet, the *being-thus* and only the being-thus of some being becomes an "*ens intentionale*," in contrast to the mere *existence* ("*ens reale*") that always and necessarily [204] remains *outside* and beyond that which is related to knowledge. The root of this X, the motivating moment for the execution of the acts which lead to some form of participation, can only be the *taking-part* transcending itself and its being. We call this, in the most formal sense, "*love*." Knowledge exists and only exists where the being-thus as strict identity is *both extra mente*, namely *in re, and also* and simultaneously *in mente* as "*ens intentionale*" or "object." The question of whether and how we come from our so-called "consciousness" to the things is still not a meaningful one for us yet. Consciousness or knowledge of knowledge (*con*-scientia) already *pre*supposes the having of *ecstatic* knowledge and can come to givenness through a *reflexive* act that directs itself originally to the knowledge-giving act. Without a tendency in the being that knows of moving from and out of itself to participate in a different being, no "knowledge" whatsoever is possible. I can see no other name for this tendency than "love," devotion. It is as if there is a dissolution of the limits of one's own being and being-thus through love. *The same* being-thus is grasped in both of the main classes of act that constitute our spirit, *intuition* and *thinking*, or rather image-having and meaning-having. It is also grasped (whether entirely or only in part) "*as the same*" in the strict sense of the word where the meant fully coincides with the intuited, or rather where all partial intuitions (mediated through the different modal functions of seeing, hearing, etc.) coincide with one another and further with memories and expectations, and where analogously the partial meanings that are fastened successively to the objective "meaning" of the thing bring about a complete meaning. In this experience of coincidence or this consequence of coincidental experiences (evidence), the thing makes clear its being-thus more and more adequately to spirit. All activities such as thinking, observing, and cognizing are only operations that lead to a "knowledge," but are not themselves knowledge.

If this "knowledge" is knowledge in the most general sense of the word, then it is clear that because knowledge is an ontological relation, its *goal,* that "for which" knowledge is and thus sought, cannot further be knowledge, but rather must in every case be a *becoming,* a *becoming other.* Nothing here is meant to reject the "what for" question of knowledge and to support "*la science pour la science,*" as is so often cited on behalf of those who stand in opposition to pragmatism. Epicurus already called it quite appropriately pure "vanity" to desire knowledge merely for the sake of wanting knowledge. The appeals to the scholar's vanity are no answer to a genuine philosophical question! As with everything that we love and seek, a *value* and a final ontic *sense* must befall knowledge. Knowledge for the sake of knowledge is as foolish as the "*l'art pour l'art*" of the aesthete. From the right "mind-set" (and nothing more), what is supported [205] in this answer is only that which is *negated* in philosophical pragmatism, namely the claim that all knowledge exists for the sake of utility—though there is indeed a knowledge that exists for the sake of practical *mastery* (not for the sake of utility or for the utility of mastery), or a better expression of this claim, whose selection of objects and object characteristics exists only for the sake of this mastery. Then a different, perhaps a higher-valued "what for" of the desire-to have-knowledge must be given, something like what C. von Sigwart meant in his *Logic* and later by J. G. Fichte, when he declared that knowledge is "part of the good" and our "moral ideal" to be that we "posit with free will," claims that stands in stark contrast to Plato, for whom the good is only οντως ον. Of course, it is generally admitted that this is only a phrase. For neither do we posit "freely" our moral ideal, nor does Sigwart tell us why we should immediately include knowledge in this ideal.

We have thus far only discovered that knowledge serves a *becoming.* The question now arises: *About what* is the becoming? *For whom* is the becoming? and *For what* is the becoming?

I believe there are three chief *goals of becoming* that knowledge can serve and does serve. First, there is service to the becoming and unfolding of the person who knows. This knowledge is "*cultural edification*" [*Bildungswissens*]. Second, there is service to the becoming of the world and (perhaps) the timeless becoming of the world's *utmost ground of being-thus and existence,* which come to their own "determination" of becoming in our human knowledge and in any possible knowledge regarding the world and world-ground or to that without which they cannot achieve their determination of becoming. This knowledge concerning the divine will is called "*redemptive knowledge.*" Third, there is the goal of practical domination and manipulation of the world for our human goals and purposes, and this embraces any knowledge on which pragmatism narrowly and even exclusively focuses. This is the knowledge of positive "science," "mastery knowledge," or "productive knowledge."

Does there exist an *objective rank order* among these three chief goals of becoming that knowledge serves? There is one, I think, that is very clear and immediately obvious. The trajectory of this rank order moves as follows. From "mastery knowledge" which serves the practical transformation of the *world* and the possible means through which we can transform the world, it moves on to "cultural edification" through which we broaden and unfold the being and being-thus of the *spiritual* person in us to a microcosm in which we seek to gain participation in the totality of the world, or at least according to its structural essential features, in the manner of our unique individuality. Then from "cultural edification" it moves further to "redemptive knowledge." That is, it moves to that knowledge in which our core person seeks to gain participation in the *highest being and ground of things* itself, or rather knowledge in which such participation is granted to the personal core through the highest ground itself; and also knowledge in which the highest ground of things, insofar as this ground "knows" itself and the world in us and through us [206], *itself* reaches its nontemporal goal of becoming, gains some kind of accord with itself, gains redemption from a "tension" and "primal oppositionality" lying within it. Thus nowhere is there a so-called "knowledge for the sake of knowledge," and there ought and "should" never be knowledge for the sake of knowledge. There has never and nowhere been such knowledge actually in this world.

When pragmatism assigns to the positive exact sciences primarily a practical mastery purpose, this is certainly *not wrong*. It is, however, vain foppishness to think of positive science as "good" or "noble" in giving freedom and power to human beings to direct and control the world. What is *false* in pragmatism is that, instead of regarding the technical positing of aims as one possibility for the possible objects of knowledge, it wants to render and thus primarily make comprehensible the *knowledge* of objects themselves, and ultimately the *idea* of knowledge in general, the idea of cognition and "truth," and further pure logic, etc., as "pragmatic." For whatever may be the selection principle for the objects of possible knowledge, *truth* must always be factual correspondence and further *knowledge* must always be participation in this selected being-thus.[5] Only for this reason can any knowledge, and even pragmatically rendered knowledge, be practically successful, because it is "true" participation, because the judgments are formally right and factually true. Yet, it is not only this one specific knowledge and "truth" that determines our actions to be *successful*. Pragmatism's so-called "new" concept of truth is utter nonsense.

A further prejudice of pragmatism is that it is entirely blind to the unique character and goal of becoming of both cultural edification and redemptive knowledge. Where it does appear to recognize the value rank order of knowledge goods, this value rank order is placed in the wholly *opposite* reverse order. In this order, in place of "cultural edification," that is, in place of the free self-unfolding of all the spiritual forces of the person and in place of the growth of spirit (subjectively and objectively) through the functionalization of essential knowledge in and through people, there is the mastery of nature and self. But in no way does the person and his or her growth exist for the sake of a maximum of mastery over nature. Although cultural edification has been very restrictively and narrowly developed, as it has in the ancient Chinese culture and in the heyday of the "humanistic" currents in the West, cultural edification will never be finished or become final. It *serves* any self-grasping of the original reality "in" the human being as one of its parts and functions, and serves any being-becoming of the macrocosmos in the being of the microcosmos of human consciousness, which has experienced in the history of metaphysics and religion the most diverse and unique interpretations.

[207] From these three knowledge ideals, the most recent history of the *West* and its independently developing cultural annex (America, etc.) has exclusively and systematically cultivated in ever-narrower ways the knowledge toward practical change in the world in the form of a division of labor, that is, the positive *specialized sciences.* In the course of history of the West, cultural edification as well as redemptive knowledge have increasingly receded into the background. Yet, only *half* of what could be of concern has been the focus of the knowledge of domination and control, namely, the part that serves to control and shape *external* nature (and inorganic nature in particular). This has pushed to the margins the *internal* life and soul technique, namely, the task of expanding as far as possible the power and dominion of the will and thereby of the spirit by means of the processes of the psychophysical organism—insofar as that organism is a temporal process ruled solely by vital laws. The *Asian* cultures have as great an advantage in the cultivation of *cultural edification* and *redemptive knowledge* and of technologically rendered knowledge directed at the psycho-vital world as Europe has in knowing how to master the external natural world.

Positivism and *pragmatism* are only the very narrow *philosophical formulations* of this real condition of the recent Western culture of knowledge. They both naively take the science of work to be the *only possible* form of knowledge in general. Pragmatism does have the significant advantage of *awareness* [*Bewusstheit*], contrary to the representatives of "*la science pour la science*" who pursue only de facto the work of science, i.e., a science that, entirely independent of the psychic desires of the researcher, is in general *objectively* senseless and purposeless when it does not serve the practical-technical transformation of the world. The pitfalls of this extreme narrowness on the part of positivism are far more hampering than they are for pragmatism because positivism's purely contemplative "theoretical" science already unjustifiably occupies the position in the human spirit for potential cultural edification and redemptive knowledge. For this reason, the *relative* rightness of pragmatic epistemology must continually be supported anew for the exact sciences rather than positivism.

It is not until this happens that the ideals of pure cultural edification and redemptive knowledge, their possible goals, their rudimentary spiritual dispositions, their means of thinking and intuition, their methods and techniques, can be so to speak discovered *once again* and arise out of the ruins of a civilization of purely work and the masses.

In order to recognize the unique character of cultural edification, it is necessary first to see that despite all of the necessary inner *cooperation of philosophy and science,* [208] the cognition goals and standards of these two kinds of knowledge are in *opposition.* According to Aristotle's accurate description, philosophy begins with the spiritual emotion of "wonder" that something of this constant being is *there.* Its movement of thought always aims ultimately at the question: How must have the ground and cause of the world totality been created so that "such and such a thing," such an essential *structure* of the world, is possible? Its object is, in the "*philosophia prima,*" the a priori essential structure of the world; and the question, a question renewed again and again, is: What is it that calls this or any thing of this being[6] into existence in general?

The science of production and work does not begin *its* "why" question with wonder. Rather it begins with the need—a need brought about by the surprise of the unusual, of the new, of events diverging from the "ordinary" course of the thing—to be able to "expect," predict, and ultimately either to create this "anomaly" at some other time, or to be able to *think* it by way of substituted signs as it would be created, as one would be able to "make" it. If the "anomaly," the surprising outcome, is annexed to the ideas regarding the ordinary course of the thing, and if the "laws of nature" are defined such that the event proves under certain given conditions to be the clear "consequence" of these lawful relations, then "science" is satisfied.

However, it is precisely here that the philosophical question originally arises. That question has absolutely *nothing* to do with the laws of the spatial-temporal coincidences of appearances and their numerically determined, measurable quantities, but on the contrary it concerns an inquiry into the persistent "*being*" and its causal effect-*origin,* into the sense and goal of what appears *there in general,* and this inquiry is entirely indifferent to spatial-temporal connections and quantities. Regarding these relational forms philosophy asks further, *What are they? What do they mean? What causes them?* This direction of the will to know must therefore learn with the same zeal, exactitude, and with the absolutely essential help of a peculiar spiritual *technique* to *refrain* from some mastery and controllability of all things and their becoming, just as the other will to knowledge has to prepare in advance and to *select* the processes of mastery, but has to *refrain* from any being of the thing.[7] That is, philosophy *begins originally* with the conscious bracketing of all possible desiring and practical spiritual dispositions and with the conscious bracketing of the "technical principles" by which the object of knowledge is chosen according to the order of possible mastery. Whether the inclusion of the technical choice principle and its bracketing [209] are to be practiced with clearly conscious and methodological intent depends strictly on whether a *general* cultivation and culture *of* knowledge is obtained, a knowledge which is possible for human beings to reach.

Because any possible practical disposition toward the world is vitally conditioned and any positive science aimed at mastery brackets the *specific* sensible and motor organizations of the earthly human being,[8] but in no way brackets "*the*" vital organization of the cognizing subject and its will to mastery in general, philosophy can be described as the attempt to gain a knowledge whose objects are *no longer existentially relative to life* and are not relative to *its* possible values. Consequently, science has to refrain from any possible questions regarding the essence of objects with which it deals, just as it refrains from the existential level of the thing's *absolute* reality. Its object is simultaneously the world of "*contingent being-so*" and of its mathematically formulable "laws," as well as the *vitally-existentially relative* world. Any question that cannot be settled through possible observation and measurement in conjunction with mathematical deduction is not a question for positive science. On the contrary, a question that can be settled in this manner, and which is further dependent upon an amount of inductive experience for the settlement, will never ever be a being question and therefore is not a fundamental question for philosophy.

Aside from the true-false standard which applies to any judgment-formulated knowledge and which is common to that knowledge, the standards (1) of the *a priori* (essence), and likewise the a priori for both truth and falsity, and (2) of the *absolute* reality of the objects of knowledge are for philosophy the decisive standards. The *first* standard is *most* decisive for the awakening of the personality's spiritual forces, i.e., for *cultural* edification, and the *second* standard is *most* decisive for *redemptive* knowledge as ultimate metaphysical knowledge. A person who is "educated" is not someone who knows or recognizes "many" coincidental being-thus of things, or someone who can predict and master the processes maximally according to rules. The educated person is thus not a "great scholar" or "researcher." Rather, the educated person is someone who has developed and functionalized a personal structure, an epitome which has united ideal and adaptable schemata into a style for the intuition, thinking, grasping, valuing, and use of the world and whatever contingent things lie within it. These schemata, which are pre-given to any particular experience, work in a united fashion and are integrated in the entirety of one's personal "world." However, redemptive knowledge can only be a knowledge regarding the existence, essence, and value of the absolutely real in all things, i.e., metaphysical knowledge.

[210] None of these kinds of knowledge can "replace" or "represent" the other. In the case when one kind of knowledge suppresses the other two (or only one of them) by claiming sole validity and mastery, there always arises tremendous harm to the unity and harmony of the cultural existence of the human being and to the unity of the vital and spiritual nature of the human being.

The exact and strict science of work and production, a science resting on measure and number, supports our collective world civilization and all technology and industry, and it supports all communication between humans across the globe. In its latest accomplishments by Einstein, this science is even prepared in its determination of the highest constants of nature to be valid for any standpoint of an observer, and eventually even for the inhabitants of other stars. It thereby strives to achieve a worldview that would be able to render and order the events of the world in terms of mathematical equations and as a consequence make it possible to direct the course of the world to fulfill the practical needs of a living and an active spiritual being. This striving is as titanic as it is successful, and its accomplishments up to this point have fully related to the existential conditions of the human being. It would be equally pernicious either to deny this project its great value or to maintain that the project could only have obtained this value if its original practical goals, which aimed to manipulate the world, were denied and it was treated as something "pure," as absolute knowledge or as the only possible type of knowledge for humans. The first is the way of a false, spiritually weak *romanticism*, and the second is the way of a false, superficial *positivism* and *pragmatism.*

If the great cultural regions have narrowly developed in their history the three kinds of knowledge, as India has done with regard to redemptive knowledge and the vital-psychic technique of the human being gaining power over himself, as China and Greece have done with regard to cultural edification, as the West has done since the beginning of the twelfth century with regard to the productive knowledge of the positive, specialized sciences, then the world-hour has now arrived when a *balancing* [*Ausgleichung*] and simultaneous *completion* of these narrow movements of spirit must be on the way.[9] Under the sign of this balancing and completion the future of human culture will be written, and *not* under the sign of a narrow rejection of one kind of knowledge in favor of another, and *not* under the sign of an absolute concern for the historical "peculiarities" of every culture. The torch, the great life-torch of the world orientation, which had originally [211] ignited Greek (Pythagorean) natural science and which during the emancipation of the cultural era of the Occident has grown to an illuminating flame for the entire world as the cultural era of the West recedes—insofar as that torch reveals itself in the "milieu" of the human being directly or indirectly on the basis of deductive thought—that torch will never be extinguished by any romanticism, whether Christian or Indian. And yet it must also be recognized that this flame will never and at no time in its possible progress give to the core of our soul, i.e., to the spiritual personality in the human being, the light—and the guiding force through life—from whose silent glow the soul can alone sustain itself: the *humanitas* and *knowledge* that it demands. The human being could still remain absolutely empty as a spiritual being after the ideal completion of this positive-scientific-technical process; it could sink back into a barbarism in the same way that every so-called primitive people was to the "Hellenes"! Because all practical knowledge serving any purpose of the human being as a vital being must ultimately *serve* cultural edification, because the becoming and formation of nature must *serve* the becoming of the deepest center of the human being, namely, the *person* and that person's effusive transcendent determination, and thus any genuine technical or practical school must serve the true cultural schooling. The scientific system supporting this barbarism would be the most horrific of all imaginable barbarisms. However, the "humanitarian" idea of cultural edification, as it has been most profoundly exemplified on German soil by Goethe, must be ranked under the ideas of redemptive knowledge and must serve redemptive knowledge in its final striving. For all knowledge is ultimately from the divine and for the divine.

If we presuppose the above distinction, pragmatic philosophy is for us an attempt to consciously and one-sidedly *reduce* all knowledge to *practical knowledge*; it is an attempt to regard the possible transformation of the world for the purposes of our willed goals as the sole meaning and value of knowledge. But our earlier distinction of the types of knowledge has already indicated that this philosophy must be false at its core, and even where it is true, it must turn out to be extremely *narrow*. Although this thesis appears to us to be beyond any doubt, we think it a very unjust procedure to dismiss pragmatic philosophy as such, to overlook its core of truth (particularly for positive science) even if this truth is very relative, and thus to throw the baby out with the bathwater.

For this reason, the attempt is made in the following chapter to *decipher what is true* and *false in the basic thought* of pragmatism. We will begin with the errors of pragmatism in order to then be able to carry out a presentation of its relative truth. [212]

3

Philosophical Pragmatism

The Two Central Principles of Pragmatism: Historical Sources and Variations of the Pragmatic Movement

William James, the person who has done the most to disseminate the word and work of pragmatism as a philosophical theory, states in his famous lecture "Pragmatism"[1] that pragmatism was first introduced in the philosophy of the American mathematician and philosopher Charles Peirce. Peirce introduced pragmatism in his article "How to Make Our Ideas Clear," which was published in the January issue of the journal *Popular Science Monthly* in 1878. In this essay, Pierce raises the central question: "*What is the sense and meaning of a thought?*" He answers: We must determine the manner of activity to which this thought is suited to lead. "The manner of activity is for us the entire meaning of this thought." James carries this point further: "And the tangible fact at the root of all our thought-distinctions, however subtle, is that there is no one of them so fine as to consist in anything but a possible difference of practice. To attain perfect clearness in our thoughts of an object, then, we need only consider what conceivable effects of a practical kind the object may involve—what sensations we are to expect from it, and what reactions we must prepare. Our conception of these effects, whether immediate or remote, is then for us the whole of our conception, so far as that conception has significance at all."[2]

Presented in this form, the Peircean principle is *ambiguous* in many different respects.

From the title of his article, we would at least initially assume that Peirce is not claiming that the "sense and meaning" of a thought *exist* exclusively in its *practical consequences*, but rather that we come to greater *clarity* regarding the sense and meaning through consideration of these consequences. However, [213] what Peirce means, or what W. James and the true pragmatists have given a *radical interpretation*, is that the practical consequences of a thought are identical to its sense and meaning, and that the imagining of these consequences is identical to the grasping and knowledge of this "meaning." How, otherwise, could James claim that the statements "matter and its movement are the original ground of all things" and "God is the original God of all things" are only different in words, and are actually synonymous in meaning if they do not posit a different kind of life and activity? If there can be no real doubt here about the Peircean proposition as understood on the part of pragmatism, then there exists a considerable ambiguity in what is to be understood by "consequences" and "practical consequences." Also mentioned along these lines is the "logical fruitfulness" of a thought. What is meant by this expression is simply that the sense and meaning of a thought coincide with the logical consequences that can be gained from this thought. There are in fact a few scholars sympathetic to pragmatism who mean nothing other than this. The unity of our worldview [*Weltbild*], the law of noncontradiction, the contribution of a thought to the confirmation of a theory or system either already proven or in the process of being proven, the fullness and quantitative precision that clarify the meaning of observed facts, are some of the criteria of this "logicai fruitfulness." Obviously, the laws of pure logic are already presupposed by *this* interpretation and are not themselves justified pragmatically. A *pragmatic derivation* of these laws as it is carried out by true pragmatism takes place where the *genetic* theory comes into play. According to the genetic theory, the laws of logic have gradually constructed themselves as the actual manner of human thought through experimentation, through the "success and failure" of acting in the world. This experimentation is not with the things themselves, but with the signs for the things. Successful ways of thinking are gradually secured through a proliferation of success and have transferred themselves according to the principle of the inheritability of psychic, functionally inherited characteristics. For William James, this proliferation takes place through social tradition, and for H. Spencer, through a legacy of kinship. Only in the case of this "clarification" of logical laws themselves is the principle of pragmatism realized as such. It is not realized when one views the laws of logic as *immanent* functional laws in human reason which are conceived as stable (as is the case with many followers of Kant), or as laws that retreat back to ontologically essential or objective insight which is independent of any inductive experience. Firstly, the statement regarding "logical fruitfulness" would coincide with theories (theories more sympathetic to pragmatism than is commonly thought) which have been put forth by the old researchers of the Marburg school, in particular Cohen and Natorp; [214] theories according to which "thinking" must execute a perpetually new "hypothesis," a new "grounding" for the propositions and theories of the sciences, due to the principle of supplying a new "account of the conditions" for the objective, logical possibility of the scientific experience; theories according to which a proposition's positioning in the system of science, its logical place, is likewise the only thing that constitutes the *sense* of that proposition. For the problem of the axioms of science, insofar as they are not treated only as pure logical axioms, but as axioms of a material nature, it appears to me, at least, that there is no essential difference whether one views these axioms as proven to be true by chance and the "implicit definitions" and their fundamental principles of use as proven to be mere "conventions" of the researchers (as is the case with M. Schlick and in mathematics with H. Poincaré and Hilbert), or whether one grants them the *distinguished* name "a priori groundings of pure thinking." This is the case if we abandon the old Kantian thought that the axioms and principles of the understanding are immanent (non-multiplying and unchangeable) and functional laws of reason itself which are not "formulated" or "derived a priori," but rather are laws that we identify only reflexively and reductively through the use of reason, laws that we must have for the scientific experience to be possible. For both cases, axioms are justified only by the force they have to derive specific meanings of propositions and theories, and thus are not examined for their inherent reasonableness.[3]

The second interpretation that can be attributed to the thought of Peirce coincides with what Leibniz had already called "*le principe d'observabilité*," a principle that Aristotle, Locke, particularly Berkeley, and also Mill have used in various ways in their writings, and which played a fundamental role in the initial stages of Einstein's theory of relativity. E. Mach and H. Poincaré have also put forward this idea on numerous occasions, and the latter made particular use of it regarding the difference between propositions that are only conventions and those that contain truths derived from facts. W. James cites this principle in the form that W. Ostwald gave it (however unclearly mixed with true pragmatism) in a letter to James: "In my lectures, I tend to state the question as follows: In which manner would the world be *different*, if this or any alternative were true? If I can find nothing that would be different, then the alternative has no sense." E. Mach [215] tends to reject with the same principle any "metaphysical" questions as "senseless," when he emphasizes repeatedly that all questions either must be demonstrated through a *possible observation* as solvable or are rendered as *senseless.*

This interpretation of the Peircean thesis concerning the sense and meaning of a thought, or rather of a word order, can be called "empiricistic," and when faced with a challenge that the consequences of a thought, when compared to the consequences of a different word order, would have to manifest themselves in a different "sensation," this interpretation can be called "sensualistic." This is not yet truly "pragmatic." However, this thesis immediately devolves into a *pragmatic* thesis when the altered experience, observation, sensation itself, and not what we use the altered experience, observation, and so on for (as when we apply a discovered law in some practical-technical manner), is regarded as the *final part of an activity* in the events of nature. "Final part" is meant here not only temporally, but also as a final part that is *caused* and evoked *by us*. Thus, for example, an *experiment*, the use of some kind of material apparatus for quantitative measurement, etc., already appears as a limit case of a technical intervention in nature through which something that did not previously exist is *brought* into existence. This pragmatic interpretation of the "principle of conceivable observation" instantaneously becomes a stringent *universal* necessity, when the *motoristic theory of perception and sensation* (which we, as will be shown, basically believe to be correct) is assumed to be true. When we assume this to be the case, any act or any impulse to act which constitutes the *precondition* for the *onset* of observation becomes an *act of verification* and a demonstration of the reliability of a "thought," and this thought itself becomes merely a kind of preliminarily sketched plan for that act. Only in this way can the "*pragmatic*" *interpretation* of Peircean thought be fully achieved.

It should be emphasized that the "spirit" of cognition and of epistemology thereby has become something quite *different* from the old empiricism and sensualism, as well as rationalism (ontological-dogmatically as well as transcendentally). Pragmatism not only attempts to break with the primordial thought that the "sense" of a judgment is something different from the act of judgment and is identifiable in the majority of individual and inter-individual acts [216], but also with the assumption that the "*facts*" to be cognized *preexist* the cognition. Both this "sense" and the "facts" are *created* through the cognizing. The world, insofar as it is not cognized, resembles an absolute "plastic" mass, a still-to-be-determined "hyle" which the human being *forms* simultaneously into a world of sense *and* facts (into a cosmos) through this indivisible dynamic process of thought sketch–activity–sensation and observation–new activity. For this reason, pragmatic thinking is not less, but rather far *more* constructive than rationalistic thinking and is thus radically different from empiricistic thinking. Because pragmatism not only rejects any *ontological* order and sense structure of the world-sphere, but also any unified, original, autonomous reason whose functional laws are to be "discovered," pragmatism is fully and deeply severed from any rationalism. It is thus only logical that W. James arrives at his radical plurality of worlds in his work *A Pluralistic Universe.*

However, in all three interpretations, it seems to us that the first of Peirce's propositions is untenable. It is untenable insofar as this proposition is proposed as general and for all kinds of "thinking," and not *merely* for a particular function which can be taken as thinking in a certain *kind* of cognition. I will characterize this kind of thinking later.

To begin, the "sense" of a proposition is not identical with the logical consequences that arise from it. This stands in direct contrast to the indubitable proposition of formal logic that the cause is clearly in no way posited with the consequences. Different propositions (in accord with their "sense") can have the *same* consequences, and this is why *one* fact which speaks against a hypothesis nullifies that hypothesis, while many facts which confirm the hypothesis can never offer a strong proof for it. If one argues that this old fundamental proposition of logic would lose its validity when one does not simply grasp this and that consequence, but every consequence of a proposition, then this claim would clearly contradict the fact that we are able to plainly distinguish the sense of one proposition from the sense of a different proposition without having to cognize "all" of the (objective) consequences of the proposition. The sense of a proposition does not change if I were to think about it in a manifold of acts, or if I were to think about it in many acts. The sense of a proposition also does not change if new consequences fall into line with its consequences that I cognize one after another. A proposition *is* either true or false regardless of whether it is proven or not, whether it is unprovable or even whether its provability is unprovable, or whether it is proven directly or indirectly to be thus or different. According to Peirce's theory, the *sense* of the proposition would have to change with every new proof (and there are always *many* proofs for a proposition), even as a proposition having [217] a fully unambiguous sense can be proven in as many ways as you would like. Moreover, absolutely nothing follows from a proposition, and something can only initially follow from a majority of propositions. A proposition cannot change its sense if it adopts functional premises together with a different proposition A or B or C or N. For pragmatic logic, there would be no "concluding" whatsoever; there would only be a reading of the concluding proposition from a collective picture that is *constructed* from the premises. This view of coming to a conclusion as a kind of construction renders wholly inexplicable how we read the conclusion directly from the constructed representative picture and judge what *"follows" from* the premises with which we work, and not from something else that can be read similarly from the "picture." From any picture, a limitless number of judgments are possible which can be "fulfilled" from this picture. How many unspeakable errors, delusions, and illusions have proven to be logically "fruitful," to be very simple and straightforwardly evident truths? They do not stop therefore being errors, delusions, and illusions!

The second interpretation of Peirce's thought regarding the determination of the *sense* and *meaning* of the world order is just as untenable. The indication that the consequences of a proposition are such that a coincidence of these consequences with a possible *fact of observation* and measurement is precluded (as it is through the currently "known" methods and measuring instruments) could make the proposition in relation to true–false highly *indeterminable* and in no way make the "sense" of the proposition clear. The laws of sense, nonsense, and absurdity are totally different from those that regulate the difference between true and false. Myths, legends, and fairy tales can be "deeply meaningful" and "rich in sense" without having to be meaningfully provable as true or false. No question loses its sense in such a manner that we could neither now nor ever resolve it. The metaphysical questions, which I. Kant held theoretically as unsolvable, are according to him "necessarily rational" questions. By contrast, metaphysical questions are, by virtue of their insolvability, as meaningless as abracadabra, according to pragmatism.

However, and this is the central point, there is a great realm of thoughts, meanings, propositions, and their consequences that cannot "alter" anything in the experienceable and observable world from its constitutional *character.* They are unable to alter anything because they mean and intend the *constant* forms of existence and the *ideas and original phenomena* themselves in which *everything* that can be observed of the world is worked into the *essential structure* of every "possible" world. A priori knowledge is defined as any knowledge that is neither obtained nor rejected through possible observation, induction, or proof. A priori knowledge is further defined as what one must already have or realize in order to carry out operations so as to prove whether something is real or whether it is only [218] the fantasy image of a "possible" observation. Everything that *constitutes* the possible world structure is meaningful (and eventually true and false) without having consequences for *changing* the experienceable world. If knowledge had determined only the possible consequences for the contingent content of experience, then it would not be a priori knowledge. That such "sense," even though its consequences do not modify the sensible experience, or should not modify the sensible consequences, is not provable either "through insight" or "blindly" would only be a consequence if all of our intuitions were identical with *sensible* intuition and if there were absolutely no other intuitions and original phenomena. Analogously, every proposition would have to be provable if there were only mediated thinking and absolutely no unmediated thinking. Yet, it is evident that, for example, the collected laws of deduction, laws according to which we make conclusions and indirect proofs, are *not* revealed and proven, but can only be shown through *insight.* It becomes clear that Pierce's principle regarding the relation between meaning and consequences, abruptly and without any concerted examination, throws to the wayside all a priori knowledge, or it hands over definition and convention to arbitrariness and mere instrumentality. It is thus entirely false when J. S. Mill asserts that it would change nothing in our experience if we were to annul in thought the existence of a substance substantiating the sensible attribute of a body and the order according to which substance is substantiated, or the "dynamism" and "tendency" taking place in every appearance of movement, or the "effect" taking place between the collision of two balls. Certainly, if we were to make these changes in our thinking nothing in our possible *sensible observation* would be different. However, in our *intuition* of states of affairs, which is incomparably more extensive and deeper than our observation, this change in thought has an extraordinary effect. This effect would be as pronounced as those brought about by pathological neurological deficits in the non-sensible elements of our intuition.

For this reason, the "principle of observation" in no way loses all significance. It is indispensable, when regarded in its second, not empiricistic, but pragmatic interpretation, for determining whether a question or the sense of a question has *positive-scientific* value, or whether it is not a question of positive science but rather something of a *philosophical* nature. For that is the specific task of all positive sciences, *to bracket out* all questions of essence, all questions regarding the world *constitution*, in order to retain from the arena of meaningful questions only those questions whose answer can lead to a specific *action* that determines whether the unexpected outcome is merely an alternative outcome or one that is utterly different. It follows, then, that if the principle of observation is given pragmatic sense which grants this principle the aforementioned motoristic theory of perception and theory [219] of sensation, it is certainly clear that the principle is incapable of limiting in general our cognizability of the world. This can be accepted if a theoretical-speculative sense is conferred upon sensible perception, as sensualism and empiricism do. If, on the contrary, sensible perception is only an index for the action of the vital center and the reaction of the world to it, then thinking that the *being* of the thing can only be reached insofar as the thing has an effect, directly or indirectly, on our possible action, would be totally absurd. To cognize something about the being of the thing is not the concern of positive science, but rather of metaphysics. Metaphysics is directed cognitively toward the essential structure, a structure that does not change through possible observation of the world or the world in its entirety. It is directed toward the condition and being type of the ground of all things (their essence and existence) which makes possible a "world as such," i.e., a world or a world structure known by a subject. Everything can be posited as being in itself (or as something different) which, when we posit it, allows our possible observation to be verifiably *unchanged*, when we posit it. This is a fundamental principle, if also only a negative one, of the freedom of metaphysics, that the principle of observability is no less remittable for metaphysics than for positive science. What it posits positively as absolute being, and not merely existentially and being-thus relative to the possible action and reaction of a vital being toward the world, directs itself singularly toward the sense and meaning of any intuition and thought which has to do with the essential structure of the world in its entirety. That is, it directs itself toward an essential knowledge about the world that would remain the *same* with any possible, practical change of the world through our activity.[4]

2. The second thought in Peirce's treatise is his new definition of truth: a proposition, whose sense and meaning have been grasped in the exactly declared manner, is then *true* if the presented activity that it gives rise to is shown to be *effective*, that is, through that activity an intention is reached, a wish is satisfied, or an expectation is fulfilled. Moreover, according to this definition, the idea of truth has an essentially *practical* sense and becomes a kind of usability and utility. Peirce's concept of truth was later developed further by W. James, and was further developed in a quite insightful manner by F. C. S. Schiller in his book on humanism.

Simultaneously, the attempt is undertaken to repudiate the older ideas of truth with this principle. Truth is not, as the Scholastic definition claims, an adaptation of the understanding to a given reality, or a "picture [*Abbildung*] of this reality." Whoever defines the truth as such would succumb to the temptation of an image wherein [220] the relation between thoughts and things is the same relation that a portrait has to the depicted human. If such a "picture" is possible, then we could never *know*, since we could never transform ourselves into the thing itself, whether the image is or is not factually identical to the pictured object. Moreover, what sense and purpose would such an *unnecessary doubling* of the world have in spirit? Would it not as a mere "world-doubling" be a vain, undignified activity? The same criticisms are valid for the theory that wants to understand truth as a mere correspondence between the relations of our presentations and the relations of the thing, while the *thing itself* remains unknown and uncognizable to us. If one declares that truth does not exist in the picture of a transcendent reality, i.e., a reality that exists independent of our consciousness (and any such relation), but lies rather in the correspondence of our thoughts and expressions with *sensible, perceiveable* facts, one has then forgotten, and is thereby showing, what a so-called "fact" is. If facts are understood with absolutely no reference to the given, then there are certainly not *constituted* facts. Facts would be accordingly any fully undetermined, fluctuating, and durationless sum of chaotic impressions in which no unity, arrangements, and divisions are found. Our thoughts in no way correspond to this "chaos," to such an extent that this chaos may only be the working material [*Arbeitsmaterial*] for the transformations we have already carried out. A "fact," so teaches pragmatism, is, in the conventional and scientific sense of the word, always already something that is somehow *determined* and *formed* through our spiritual activity. Facts arise out of this chaos and are likewise cut out from it insofar as we pose some *question* to the given whose response is then some "fact." In sharp contrast to the older empiricist epistemology and, for example, with the new sensualism of E. Mach, the pragmatists reject that the truth rests in the correspondence of our thoughts with that which is *given* to our sensibility.

Lastly, truth does not exist such that, as the neo-Kantian school claims—a school rejecting the aforementioned empiricist criterion for similar reasons—our thoughts must follow certain *a priori thought forms* and principles that construct the essence of a transcendental understanding acting within all of us, and such that our thoughts from this gain a strict systematic connection which must measure up to its *inner* logical consistency, not to an outer factual material discovered by it. The idea of such a "system," as well as the presupposition of such a [221] "transcendental understanding" which could operate independently of our human drives and needs, is contrary to pragmatism's thorough anti-systematism. Nonetheless, some analogies exist between pragmatism and some thoughts of the neo-Kantian school which I have already remarked upon. Common to both directions of thought is what we refer to as "*scientivism*" and "*instrumentalism.*" By scientivism, we understand a way of thinking that, with regard to the question of what truth and cognition are, already *presupposes* the facts of positive science, its methods and tasks, and then responds to the question by claiming that truth and cognition are the "whereto" the method leads. It is also a way of thinking that holds truth and cognition to be the answer to the question of "where" the methods of science lead. Scientivism thus responds in such a manner that the concepts of truth and cognition do not *first* need to be determined in order to then ask how far science could, with the benefit of its methods, obtain truth and cognition, what of value can be exclusively known by *science*, and how far types of cognition other than scientific cognition, e.g., philosophical, religious, and artificial types of cognition, are able to do this. By "instrumentalism," I mean any approach that, instead of letting the methods direct themselves according to the object, claims it is the method that is *creating* the determined objects. Expressed differently, this idea claims that the word "truth" is simultaneously positing the results of a "directed" thinking, i.e., a thinking conforming to particular norms. These norms could obviously not themselves, according to the definition, be called "true." In contrast to this principle of instrumentalism, the proposition states that the only thinking which may and can be called "correct" is that thinking which leads to the *truth* and which succeeds according to propositions and axioms that are *evidently true.* This is the position of a logic constructed upon an *ontology* standing in opposition to instrumentalism. A third, similar idea between pragmatism and neo-Kantianism is to be seen in the claim that anything given in spiritual activity presents a chaos of impressions, a fluctuating "mixture" of contents, a μή όν that has to underlie a determined formation through our spiritual activity. In both cases, the truth does not appear as something which we have to find or discover, but rather as a product of our mind [*Geist*].

There are a few things I would like to say about the historical origins of the pragmatic movement that originate in a more distant past. As new and original as pragmatism is in its entirety, it still has, in its distinctive features, deep roots in the history of scientific philosophy. In one respect, pragmatism shows itself to be a branching off of England's great thought approaches, *utilitarianism* and *empiricism.* Already Bacon, the father of this manner of thought, had held gaining *power over nature* to be the task of science. [222] Any speculative preoccupation, e.g., preoccupations with pure mathematics or with astronomical problems of the fixed stars of the heavens, was deemed by Bacon as a "futile" undertaking. This conviction remains active in the late circles of positivism and grounds Auguste Comte's call: "*voir pour prévoir.*"[5] Regarding the pragmatic *criterium* for the meaning of a proposition, we find the application used by Berkeley, an application also followed by Mill, who, according to James (I do not know where he states this), rejects, as I have already shown, the acceptance of a matter existing external to us. This rejection is predicated upon the conviction that the positing of this matter could *change nothing* in the experience of our senses, and therefore such an acceptance has absolutely "no sense." It is readily apparent that the pragmatic viewpoint is inspired by a spirit that is entirely in opposition to empiricism. Empiricism grasps the human spirit as predominantly passive, and its theory is that we would have to subordinate ourselves slavishly in every respect to sensibly given facts and bracket out all concepts from our thinking which could find no immediate correspondence to "sensations" of the sense. For this reason, empiricism is *anti-constructive* and *anti-theoretical.* In contrast to this position, the core of the human spirit, according to pragmatism, lies in *activity*, willing, and action from the very start. It is not a loving immersion in the facts of the sensibly or otherwise given, but rather an *active* mastering formation of the sensible chaos that leads to cognition here. It is for this reason that pragmatism offers an audacious theory of building and construction. In this latter respect, pragmatic epistemology stands much closer to a nominalistic epistemology as it was represented in England by the extreme constructive thinker, Thomas Hobbes. Hobbes is truly the grandfather of pragmatism. The pragmatic theory of thinking presents only a particular subset of strict nominalism.

With regard to the emphasis on *work* thought [*Arbeits*gedankens], pragmatism adheres to the ideas of Karl Marx. Already at the beginning of his literary career Marx proclaims to his comrades: "Until now, the intent has been only to know the world. Now let it be transformed by us!" Furthermore, not only has Marx's reduction of all economic value solely to productive labor helped to support the historical-philosophical use of pragmatism, but to a greater extent so has a second theory proposed by Marx regarding his so-called economic analysis, namely the *technological.* The technological means of production are those which also produce, according to Marx, the forms of law, artistic forms and styles, and the forms of scientific culture. On the other hand, pragmatism stands in stark contrast to Marxist theory insofar as pragmatism teaches the *freedom of the will,* whereas Marxism restricts it to any political action [223], so that the freedom of the will has to be the mere male midwife of a strictly deterministic economic development that leads to a new communistic societal order. Lately, the revolutionary syndicalism in France and England which demands the immediate, energetic action of daring minorities toward the institution of a new order has consciously based itself upon the theory of pragmatism.

Again in a different respect, pragmatism presents a further development of Kant's philosophy, and to a greater extent that of J. G. Fichte. According to Kant, the correspondence of our reason to nature exists because reason "prescribes its laws" on nature and exerts an ordering activity on the "chaos" of the given which allows it to come to the arranged unity of nature. Kant is far removed from seeing this reason itself as a result of a vital development, and from seeing reason emerging under the pressure of empirical needs and drives and the work determined through them. Moreover, his theory of the primacy of the will allows the *autonomy* of the theoretical sphere of cognition in its entirety to remain untouched, and subordinates it only in its entirety to the task of moral life. For the pragmatists, by contrast, the will interferes with the singular work of reason so that any kind of particular border between our emotional and striving life and our reason, and any border between the principles of reason and its so-called "postulates," dissipates. In this respect, J. G. Fichte could be called an idealistic pragmatist. For him, the world is first and foremost the "matter of our duty." He subordinates the idea of truth to that of the good and he lets theoretical reason be assimilated into practical reason. What distinguishes him from modern pragmatism is obviously the thought of transcendental reason, which he takes from Kant, and from the speculative method of philosophy. The German logician C. von Sigwart is very close to pragmatism through his teaching that the causal principle and other chief principles of scientific world explanation should be neither provable propositions nor empirical, nor synthetic, a priori judgments in the Kantian sense, but rather "postulates of our free moral will toward the explanation of things."

In an entirely different respect, A. Schopenhauer can be appealed to as a predecessor of pragmatism, not with regard to philosophy but rather to the methodology of science, insofar as he views the "intellect" as a mere weapon of the blind vital will in the battle for existence. As a consequence, an intuitionistic epistemic principle becomes the highest epistemic principle for philosophy and *philosophic* cognition. Clearly, with this distinction between science and philosophy, Schopenhauer is Bergson's predecessor with regard to both kinds of cognition, [224] given how Bergson sought to construct with his student Le Roy the pragmatic thought process for the methodology of the exact sciences.[6]

A new variety of pragmatism began to have an effect in Germany through Nietzsche's "will to power" (which was prompted primarily by Schopenhauer). Nietzsche's peculiar approach distinguishes itself clearly from American pragmatism by virtue of the fact that Nietzsche did not seek to give a new pragmatic interpretation of the idea of truth, but rather, holding fast to the ancient, contemplative idea of truth as the single possible idea, made the *value* of the idea of truth problematic. Nietzsche did not attempt, as does American pragmatism, to interpret anew the idea of truth. All of his comments in *The Will to Power* concerning the categories as tools of the human will to master, and above all his attempt to interpret the idea of truth as a form of the "aesthetic ideal"—and also as an idea that is necessarily connected to the thought of a spiritual divinity which must therefore fall in line with the rejection of the thought of God as expressed in the view "God is dead"—presuppose that Nietzsche still understands "truth" to be the correspondence of thought to reality. The spiritual situation in which Nietzsche dared to pose for the first time in European cultural history the most radical of all questions, "Is the truth in any way desirable?" was in no way only specific to Nietzsche's personal development, but rather was deeply embedded in the collective, scientific culture of the time in which Nietzsche was thinking and writing. But he alone had the radical audacity to pose this question, and to recognize the ancient-Christian position that there is something like a "reason" possessed by the human being and only by the human being, a reason that in its form and forces is a match for the world totality and is able to reach its subject content [*Sachgehalt*] not only as one at the core of the metaphysical position, but also as one that is historically positive and European. As support for this claim, I would like to point to an essay by W. Dilthey, who is certainly not under the influence of Nietzsche.[7] Dilthey writes: "The rationalistic position is used today by the Kantian school mainly for recognition. The father of this position was Descartes. He was the first to give triumphant expression to the sovereignty of the intellect. This sovereignty had its *support in the entire religious and metaphysical position of his epoch, and it existed in Locke and Newton as well as Galileo and Descartes.* According to this position, reason is the principle of the world's construction, not an episodic fact of the earth. No one today can evade the fact that this tremendous metaphysical background [225] is no longer obvious. Much follows from this as a consequence. The analysis of nature appears gradually to make constructive reason dispensable as nature's principle. Laplace and Darwin represent this transformation most distinctly. The analysis of nature appears to make dispensable to present-day scientific common sense[8] the relation of this nature to a higher order. Contained in both these changes is the additional presupposition that the religious relation between creator and created is no longer a pressing concern for us. As a consequence of these three presuppositions, the view which regards Descartes's sovereign intellect as merely a temporary, unique product of nature on the Earth's surface and perhaps on other stars, is no longer from the outset to be rejected. Many of our philosophers now contest Descartes's view of the intellect. However, for none of these philosophers is it obvious that reason serves as the background for the entire world relations. Thus, serving as a hypothesis or postulate for this worldview is the conviction that reason has the capacity to dominate reality."

While Nietzsche posed the radical question regarding the *value* of truth, he gave expression with cynical brilliance to the situation masterfully identified by Dilthey. It was a situation about which "many philosophers" of the time could only lie: those who lived and acted as if there were a reason and truth whose religious and metaphysical presuppositions they no longer believed in. From Nietzsche's turn of phrase arose *the German variety of modern pragmatism*, an "honest-cynicism," as I have called it. This is a form of pragmatism which disallows the cant that reinterprets the idea of truth in the sense of practical interest and use-value, and instead genuinely asks: "Why not prefer *error*, illusion, fiction, if they bring about a *better* outcome for life and its most inner nerve, the 'will to power'?" In place of the idealistic and spiritual pragmatism of J. G. Fichte, Sigwart, and others who subordinate all cognition to the idea of a practical reason and thus hold fast to the sovereignty of reason, a *vitalistic pragmatism* takes root with Nietzsche. It is a form of pragmatism which is to be sharply distinguished from the pragmatism of work and utility by its new extreme, activistic view of life.

In Vaihinger's so-called *fictionalism*, this German form of pragmatism became a scientifically constructed epistemology, when this fictionalism united Kant as seen through the eyes of Albert Langes with this suggestion by Nietzsche. An exposition of this fictionalistic form of pragmatism cannot be carried out here. But it is essential to this fictionalism that it considers the concepts of cognition and truth to be ultimately sensualistic concepts, a position developed most profoundly by D. Hume. "Truth" in ideas and in the relations of ideas is, according to this view, [226] only that which is traced back to the "copy" of an impression. Without the presupposition of this strict sensualistic concept of truth, the concept of "fiction" would no longer have any meaning. It should be pointed out here that everything which proceeds from such an approach in our fundamental scientific concepts and their defined objects regarding impressions and derivatives is a created fantasy resting upon our drives and needs; that is, a "fiction" ultimately founding our collective scientific worldview [*Weltbild*] and its objectivity upon fictions and "*res fictae*," and to a greater extent founding our religious ideas and their objects upon these fictions. It is thus characteristic of the sensualistic foundations of fictionalism that it maintains *no inner essential differences* between super-sensual forms of being, forms of effects (categories), merely helpful concepts that are in fact fictitious (ideal gas, ideal fixed bodies, juridical persons of society, "*homo oeconomicus*," etc.), "ideal objects" (as in mathematics), hypothetical assumptions of reality in the theories of matter and cells, and religious objects. Fictionalism views all of these equally as fictions, or rather as *res fictae*. The pragmatic-motoric theory of perception, the most accurate element of pragmatism, rejects fictionalism because fictionalism lets sensation pass for an ultimate pre-discovered and given thing.

The Errors of Pragmatism

I have come now to an overview of the specific errors of pragmatism.

1. The Falsification of the Idea of Knowledge

The first error that pragmatism is guilty of is, undoubtedly, its total *falsification of the formal ideas of "knowledge,"* "cognition," and "truth."

Knowledge is certainly *not* a picture (or representation) of a thing in "immaterial images" that would be, as far as these are concerned, only states of our consciousness or contents found in the so to speak box of consciousness and that would encompass, either entirely or partiwise any possible thing—yet only in immaterial form. There is no way to detect the existence of such images, images such as "perceptual images," in us that would be something different from the being-thus of the perceived object itself and that would be different than a part of this being-thus of the thing itself. The most precise inner observation seeks in vain for such "images." It is also the case that sameness or similarity amongst the contents of the images could not be compared and ascertained in respect to the existing things. The [227] thought of such ascertainment would be from the outset absurd. Other than *through knowledge*, we can in no way place ourselves in the being-thus of a thing. According to the false, Scholastic definition of truth as "*adaequatio intellectus cum re*," we would only compare images with other images. If it were possible to note any relation of similarity between immaterial images and existing things, then the intention of spirit, which is the core and nerve of knowledge, would never be presented to the thing. The "image" would be a mute, intentionless reality, as if it were a painting of the stuff of the soul; it would not signify *beyond* itself. As a painting "knows" nothing of the object which it depicts, any "image" "would know" nothing of the things. Rather, knowledge, understood as an intention and as a fulfillment of this intention in the "having" of the being-thus of the thing itself, is in principle possible *without* such an "image." Knowledge, the aim of all "cognition" as spontaneous activity, is thus not a "picture," not the thing itself, and not its relations, as H. Hertz[9] purports when he suggests that "the consequences of our images of the things" must correspond "with the images of their consequences." In the most formal sense, knowledge is a *participating of a being in the being-thus of another being* without changing that being-thus. Only the *existence* of a thing remains constantly and necessarily on the other side of knowledge and consciousness, and is as such trans-intelligible. The being-thus of the thing permits what is in principle itself, and not merely as an image, to enter into our spirit, where it becomes the object of an intention. The intention is not an image, but an *act*. For this reason, it is incorrect to declare, as so-called "critical realism" does, that not only the existence (wherein it is correct), but also the being-thus of the thing are *completely outside* of consciousness. This being-thus then could not *itself* be "*in mente*," but only an image of the being-thus. It is likewise incorrect to assert, with idealistic theories of consciousness of any kind, that the being-thus of the thing itself can not only be posited *in mente* (wherein idealism, in contrast to any critical realism, is correct) but also posited in *existence*, thereby denying any *reality that is transcendent* to knowledge and consciousness (wherein idealism, in contrast to critical realism, is incorrect). When pragmatism fails to comprehend the idea of knowledge, it has suppressed nothing less than "human reason" itself. For both theories—critical realism and the idealistic view of consciousness—*proton pseudos*[10] is the inseparability of being-thus and existence in relation to the "being *in mente*," i.e., with regard to the *relation of both* (being-thus and existence) *to spirit.* If the total intuitional phenomenon of an object and the total sense of thought of the object completely coincide, then this coinciding is the criterion for the being-thus of the object "*itself*" to beam into our spirit. The "*evidence*" of [228] knowledge is only the reflexive knowledge of this "beaming" of the object.

Pragmatism is right to harshly criticize the so-called picture theory of knowledge,[11] which it calls an unnecessary and futile "world-doubling." True participation, however, of our being in the being-thus of the world is not unnecessary and futile, even when this participation is not necessarily "useful." Participation is primarily *a broadening and increase of our ontological relation to the world* and *likewise* an elevation of a thing to its (objective) "meaning," elevated to any meaning which befalls the thing objectively, before we "mean" it conceptually.[12] Spontaneous cognition is only the *movement* of spirit *toward* knowledge, and thus not something which joins it after the fact or which would be something "more" than knowledge. Knowledge is not true or false. There is no "false knowledge." Knowledge is *evident* or *not evident,* and moreover is *adequate* or *inadequate* in relation to the being-thus aspect of the object. True or false are rather only propositions, i.e., the *ideal sense correlates* immanent to our judgments. Thus, propositions are true if they "correspond" to the evident and maximum adequate, intuitive being-thus of an object of knowledge; and are false if they contradict it.

Pragmatism fully distorts these facts. Because pragmatism correctly rejects the "picture theory," it thinks that it ought to introduce something different, namely the factual or practical "consequences" of a thought or intuition, the conceivable "change in the world" from it. For pragmatism, the "sense" of a proposition becomes in this way identical to its possible practical consequences with regard to a conceivable change in the world (Boole). Furthermore, the "truth" of a thought should then consist in whether these possible consequences are *useful* or, rather, life-promoting consequences. Analogously, our intuition of a thing is taken as an adequate, "good" intuition when it demonstrates to us the best point of attack on that thing with regard to our possible acts of movement and use of the thing.

Let's examine these theses. They are mistaken in a twofold sense. Let's imagine the case where a psychophysical organism always conducts itself with regard to any stimulus in its environment in an optimally purposeful and effective manner, and thus already approximates what the plants and lower animals certainly do *without* any "knowledge" of the objects that have initiated the stimulus. There is no reason why something like a "knowledge of the object" must be inserted between stimulus and reaction over and against their effective and typical relation! Conversely, we can posit an all-knowing being. There is no reason why the mere and pure knowledge of these things [229] would be of any use to this being, or be of use to any movement and activity by which the being is able to adapt to its environment and adapt the environment to its own desires and needs. Both cases are clear conceptual possibilities which show that there is absolutely no relation of the *idea* of knowledge *in itself* to activity, and likewise the converse. The accomplishments of absolute and "conditioned" reflexes and of the instincts, which as far as meaningful and valuable accomplishments are concerned have in many respects far exceeded the keenest, conscious technical art of human beings (with and despite all of our science), indicate quite clearly how biologically *unnecessary* a knowledge of the being-thus of the object in principle is for effective action. Indeed, quite a few entirely impractical scholars show us how powerless knowledge, mere pure knowledge, can be toward action.

For certain! We discover de facto a far-reaching *correlation* between what a being can *know* (by virtue of its functions of sense, the range and thresholds of stimulus and enhancement, and the extent and direction of the cultivation of the being's "intelligence," i.e., its ability to adapt to new, atypical situations without first testing this) and what enables that being to act in an *objectively* meaningful manner. This correlation can even be proven as essentially lawful for any knowledge of contingent reality and any possible action on reality. From this parallel correlation, three valid propositions follow, propositions that pragmatism fails to comprehend:

(1) This parallel correlation does not concern knowledge and action as such, but rather, under the presupposition of its existence (and of a particular organization of it), it concerns only the *specific content* and objects of possible knowledge and action. That is, the correlation concerns the *selection* of these being thuses' determined objects among the objectively possible objects of the subject's world. It concerns only "this or that," but not the "what" in the sense of pure knowledge *content* and the "that" of knowledge in general.

(2) There exists a true parallelism, i.e., a *reversible mutual* relationship of dependence, between knowledge and action, in the restricted sense stated above, but *not* an irreversible, *one-sided* relationship whereby the practical "resistance" determines one-sidedly the theoretical "object" or vice versa.

(3) The *collective, identical founding* of this parallelism between the content of knowledge and action is the value and love, or hate, of the objects and the function of attention and interest voluntarily and involuntarily directed through these acts. These activities of mere value-bearing as such are still *not* "practical behavior"; and in their "activity" there is absolutely nothing of some kind of willful activity. [230]

2. The Mistaken Ordering of the Reason-Consequence Relationship of Knowledge and Action

We see that it is not incorrect when pragmatism teaches that a particular practical-motor disposition, or at the very least the beginning of a psychomotor process, is necessarily connected to every actual sense perception. This is in fact correct. What is incorrect is merely the thought, which is also found in Bergson[13] and H. Münsterberg,[14] that this motor disposition is consequently the necessary ground for the sense perception; that, as Bergson has expressed it, the sense perception, understood as "pure," i.e., as freed from all "sensation affections [*Affektives*]" and all memory images mixed in with them, is only a practical selection which carries out the spirit in the manifold of objective "images"; or that, as H. Münsterberg has expressed it, the beginning of the motor nerve processes corresponding to the stimulus is conditional on the "vibrancy" of the sensation of the object. The minimum condition for the realization of a sense intuition, *besides* the stimulus process, the normal centripetal nerve process, and a psychic reception in general is rather an *accompanying act* of the psychophysical organism. The content of this intuition varies lawfully according to the direction, kind, and quantum of the sense intuition. First, sensation is indeed only *an* element in the entire structure of a *perceptual* content, an element that varies with this structure. That is, sensation is not a sum of parts, nor is it understood as something to be added to some content. Secondly, sensation is *not simply proportional* to the stimulus, and it is not proportional to the stimulus plus the nerve process and physiological conditionality of the inner and outer sense apparatus. If this were the case, there would indeed be, as W. Wundt states, a perceptual field in which there could be actual sensations and a conjoining apperceptual field founded by this field, an apperceptual field into which the contents of sensation initially enter when these contents become the object of a drive or of arbitrary attention. And yet, this is *not* the case. The spontaneous (drive or arbitrary) impulse of the vital, spiritual center is a condition of the mere realization of sensation of a stimulus which is posited as a "possibility," but not yet as reality, by the stimulus and the centripetal process. If this impulse = object, then there is *no* perception and sensation.

What is incorrect is the acceptance of this impulse as necessarily a willful impulse, instead of a value apprehension or a "choice-less" *drive preference* (and placing after) which is, as far as it is concerned, led by the direction of interest and its activity, by the so-called attention. This impulse is what *conditions* and *leads* to *the same extent* the becoming of the will and action (and the readiness of the will and action), *as well as* the becoming [231] of a sense perception. For this reason, *apraxie* and *agnosie* can very easily be separated from one another (which was impossible according to Bergson and Munsterberg), and in no way for *apraxie* in order to ground one of the possible *agnosie.*

3. The Misrecognition of the Difference between Knowledge of Essences and Inductive Knowledge

These first two errors do not exhaust the most general philosophical errors of pragmatism. The more fundamental error concerns the fact that the declared parallelism of the special content between action and knowledge is *not* valid *for all* knowledge and for *all* action, but rather only for a particular restricted region of both. This region is delineated by our knowledge regarding the "contingent" world reality and its being here, now, and thus. This region further delineating the world reality for possible knowledge of it as well as for the will and for action, delineating the world reality as merely a *contingent* world reality. However, there is also a "knowledge," and it is the highest, purest knowledge that precedes any evident and any possible inductive experience (and thus also the observation and comparison of the "cases"), as well as preceding any mediated, conclusive thinking; it is a knowledge whose sense (and possible consequences) could in no way "change" the empirical factual conditions of the world (or change any of their consequences). It is a knowledge which remains evident, when we allow the world content accessible to us through our senses and our activities in the world to vary in any manner we wish. Furthermore, we could *define* this knowledge as that knowledge which remains exactly the *same* throughout any possible changes in the qualia and quanta of our possible sense and observation contents of the world, and which fully endures and remains constant through such changes. It is the knowledge about the *being-thus constants* of any object which we call the *knowledge of essences and ideas,* or rather knowledge purely of relations among essences and ideas. From this knowledge, nothing determinant and different follows for the contingent world reality, because the knowledge is a priori valid and binding "for" any possible, contingent world reality. Analogously, there is a material *value estimation* and a "willing," grounded in this estimation, to realize this value. This willing exists as the value estimation and willing of the "pure disposition [Gesinnung]" of a person and is *autonomous.* Moreover, this willing would remain autonomous even if all the empirical actions and willful acts corresponding to this willing prove to be total failures and tremendously harmful for those who take action and for the community. It is only this knowledge that is the primary and direct bearer of the predicate "*evident.*" And it is only the judgment entering the knowledge that is the direct bearer of the predicate "*true*" (= irrefutable and evidently true). And it is only this value disposition and this willing—in the correspondence—that [232] are the immediate and direct bearers of the "ethical" attributes "*good*" and "*evil.*"

Not only does pragmatism falsify the idea of knowledge, but, as a new form of empiricism, it also no less misjudges the fundamental distinction between "*knowledge of essences*" and "*contingent-facts-knowledge,*" a distinction that relates to the distinction between "a priori knowledge" and "a posteriori knowledge." In this latter respect, pragmatism is only a new version of the old Bacon-Mill empiricism and sensualistic positivism that reduce all erudite processes of the human spirit and personality to the associative processes of sensation. Because all a priori "thought forms" rest upon new acquisitions of a priori knowledge, i.e., upon the functionalization of objective and ontological essential knowledge, pragmatism must then also fail to realize the formal *ideas* of "*philosophy*" and "*erudition.*" Pragmatism further fails to recognize that the human spirit grows and develops in the history of cognition itself in and through the activity of its cognition and not through the stockpiling of new cognitive results of contingent reality, a process of the mere "accumulation" of knowledge stuff; and it also fails to recognize that this growth, this true "evolution" of spirit itself is a *higher value* that the use of the cognitive results for practical purposes. In this manner, pragmatism is identical to the neo-Kantian school of thought which ascribes to reason a "constant" original inheritance of a priori functional lawfulness, an inheritance that would always be one and the same within any culture and era and could be successively *cognized* and conceptualized only in extreme cases.

Finally, pragmatism fails to see the strict lawfulness that exists between the practically possible *variability* of the thing and the *levels of its existential relativity.* This law states that the *more* these things are *existentially relative to human beings* and the further the levels of their existential relativity distance themselves from the levels of absolute reality and its knowledge, the *more* things are subject to variability (and "possible" variability). In my *Ethics,* I have already shown that there is similarly a law that holds for the rank order and possible levels of realization of *values.*[15] Moreover, the experiences of the satisfaction of desire and listlessness are made *less* practical and have *less* of a practical influence the more these experiences become spiritual feelings of the *personality* and the value feelings of a person. Only the feeling sensations are almost fully subjugated to our practical mastery, the feeling for the useful and detrimental to a lesser degree, and the vital feelings to a still considerably less degree. The psychic feelings, on the other hand, are a further degree less in one's control and able to be intended. The spiritual personal feelings are absolutely not in one's control; they are [233] as it were pure "grace" or "misfortune" and cannot by their very nature be in one's control. If, for pragmatism, valid knowledge is knowledge that has consequences, specifically consequences that *change* the world, then it follows directly from this that pragmatism denounces not only all knowledge of essences, but also knowledge of *absolute reality,* that is, metaphysical and religious knowledge. If absolute reality is in any way variable, it can only be variable through itself and not through a being that posits reality first existentially and whose being-thus has constituted it, a being who is absolutely dependent on *absolute reality.* Only insofar as personality is *itself a function of the divine spirit* could the divine spirit change itself through the person, e.g., could grow or redeem itself. In this manner, the divine spirit would be in need of redemption.

4. The Mistaken Axioms of Pragmatic "Logic"

Both of the logical principles which were put forward by the first logician of pragmatism, Boole, are without a doubt mistaken and quite absurd. The first principle states that two propositions are *identical in sense* if they lead to the same *action.* The second principle states that a proposition is *true* if it leads to an action that has *useful* or life-enhancing consequences.

These principles are mistaken for the following reasons. The *sense* of a proposition or of a question is in no way "identical" or "equivalent" to its *logical* consequences or to the degree of its "logical fruitfulness." Moreover, the sense is not identical or equivalent to the *practical* applicability for some real change in the world. There is a steadfast, logical rule which states that the reason is in no way unequivocally posited with the consequences, that the cause is in no way *unequivocally* posited with the effect. This rule already contains the refutation of the more moderate pragmatic definition of the "sense" of a thought, a definition that would like to make the sense equivalent to its logical consequences or its logical "fruitfulness." It is utterly false to claim that the sense of a thought is *equivalent* to its "logical fruitfulness," since it is clearly the case that entirely *different* theoretical presuppositions about the world course can lead to the exact *same* practical manner of conduct and that the exact same presuppositions can lead to entirely different practical conduct, depending on the ends whose realization our actions ought to serve, but which can never be clearly identified by pure knowledge. What is true is only that we can *never unambiguously* grasp the sense of thought in cases where we seek to derive the "sense" of the thought directing the behavior of an organism that we can immediately observe. Missing from such cases is an oral, written, or otherwise set communication of sense, or the communication that transpires in an artwork's "presentation" of the objective "sense" a thing has come to have [234] by virtue of the artistic work done to it. Rather, we depend on a range of *different* sense unities that mutually make the "behavior" comprehensible to us. It is for this reason that any question or inter-individual "uncertainty" or "problem," whose alternative or disjunctive "consequence" does not allow itself to be decided by observation and measurement (communicated directly or indirectly, i.e., through inserted mechanisms and measuring instruments), has a "sense." It simply has no "positive scientific" sense. It is for this reason necessary and ought to be demanded much more forcefully, as it is presently being demanded in mathematics and physics, that these questions should be radically dismissed from the area of positive science. Through this dismissal, the question does not lose its "sense," but rather it becomes merely a *philosophical* question or, insofar as it concerns the real, becomes a "*metaphysical*" question whose answer requires a different but no less certain and determinant methodology than the positive-scientific question. Positive science has a tremendous significance for metaphysics because positive science *circumscribes* more and more exactly the metaphysical question field, a circumscribing wherein positive science underscores with ever greater precision and certainty the *non*-metaphysical questions. The principle by which positive science eliminates all metaphysical questions concerns whether the question is in principal unanswerable through the possible observation and measurement of contingent realities and formal mathematical operations. Positive science never thereby replaces metaphysics or makes it superfluous, as pragmatism does, but it expels the problem sphere of ontology and metaphysics from its area through the increased exclusion of metaphysical questions and above all questions of essence. It does so in a manner similar to the way in which physics and chemistry expel specifically "biological" questions from the processes and makeup of organisms.

When we examine a few other logical theorems of pragmatism, we discover approximately the same fundamental errors.

Our *thinking concerning meanings* should, according to the pragmatic theory, *be* nothing other than an originally *similar* outer and inner *behavior* in different situations by virtue of the recurrence of the same stirring of drive and need, and in its highest developed form should be nothing other than the production of the same phonetic complexes in different but in some respects practically similar sensible perception complexes. To express this objectively, the thinking concerning meanings should be nothing other than the *use rules* of a *word* sign or of a sign standing for it. If I say something like "this field is green," then the word signs (which as signs are themselves already identical, recurring "forms" of a sensible, variable material, of an acoustic, optical, or musical material) [235] "field" and "green" have no inherent autonomous "meaning" which would be "intuitively" fulfilled by a perception of the green field. Rather, what we call the meaning of the words "field" and "green" would be nothing other than a drive-motoristic tendency; with regard to the perception of things that resemble the color green, the word "green" is nothing other than a merely phonetic complex; with regard to things that have similar characteristics to a field, the meaning is in the production of the phonetic complex "field." The shortcomings of this theory of meaning highlight the obvious fact that the same contents of perception of "green field" could bring about the fulfillment of an unlimited number of entirely *different* judgment sense contents and entirely *different* meanings (green surfaces, colored surfaces, grass, etc.). For this reason, this differentiation in the sphere of meaning is entirely incomprehensible, if there should be nothing other than purely factual phonetic complexes which are devoid of sense and meaning, and sensible contents of perception which are founded in specific manners of behavior. The situation does not become more promising even if levels of conspicuousness, and the kinds and degrees of accentuation of the sensibly given matters of fact through the impulsive and haphazard attention and its motoristic concomitants, are included in order to make comprehensible the "apparent" meaning differentiations of spoken language and other complexes functioning as "signs" before and independent of their occasional use. For either the attention already falls under the determination of an anticipated meaning (as is the case for any "observation" in which the meaning of the question's content obviously steers the direction of the attention) and the declared is *presupposed*, or else the impulse accentuations of attention are so blind and unordered that they would not be able to make clear to us the *constant* of meaning in the changing play of this accentuation of attention.

A. Gelb and K. Goldstein[16] have recently described two cases of "color weak" women, i.e., patients who due to brain injuries (in the second case, an occipital injury) are able to recognize colored bands as colored and either identify the actual color or recognize them as differently colored only after a long time, a time much longer than is normally needed. Initially, up to one of the specific time limits, the bands appear to the patients as colorless. For both patients when exposed to weakened color stimuli, there was no colored impression even after continued observation. "If the patient reported different names of colors, the object took on the color with the pronouncement of the correct name; with the pronouncement of the incorrect name, the object did not change. When the object adopted the color specific to the name of the color expressed, the patient regarded this as a sign [236] that the name of the color was correct. The second patient would act in a similar manner in relation to color representations." It is now very noteworthy that this effect in no way revolved around the mere pronouncement of the color name. "There is," the authors state, "certainly no doubt that one can use a word or a color name without wanting to say with this word that a specific color is meant. Hence, one can list, for example, color names in some order or upon a glance at an object of a characteristic coloring—something like a cherry—one can say, 'the red cherry.' The word is not used in its presentation function in Bühler's sense, but rather, it inserts itself in the connection of the collective situation."[17] However, for the word to have an influence on the color threshold, it is not enough that the patients could express and use the word and that the *speech* process is intact. The effect that the word has on the color of the object is only successful when when the word does not only denote the singular color phenomenon, but rather the *category* to which the color belongs, and when the word is not merely a reaction that is connected reproductively to the seeing of the color, but rather when the word serves as a nominal or presentation function for the color. These facts show us with the greatest precision the errors of pragmatic-nominalistic concept theory. First, they show that meaning and perceptual content relate to one another in an *opposing* dynamic relation even in the simplest qualities. In no way is the word meaning constructed summarily upon the finished and unchanging sense impression. Second, they also show that the categorical function of the word sign and naming and the presentation function exist *in an inseparable relation to one another*; the word already possesses *in itself* a meaning that the act of perception has in genuine functions of *fulfillment* and non-fulfillment, and this shows that the pragmatic theory of meaning is false.

In a different respect, there are a host of examples regarding a breakdown in normal psychic life that further contradict the pragmatic theory. One such example is that when the meaning of the word is not known due to amnesiastic aphasia, the sick are frequently able to declare what can be "done" with the thing in question. The stricken person describes a fountain pen as something "for writing," a meter stick as something "for measuring," and a pair of scissors as something "for cutting." These kinds of word reactions are conveyed predominantly by vivid pantomimic gestures that mimic writing, measuring, etc. However, in cases where we find particular meanings to be present but only developmentally in the preliminary stages of conceptual thought, cases such as when the child calls a thing a "bird" because the child vaguely recognizes the phenomenon of flight (as in the case of a butterfly), these meanings in no way [237] have for the subjects in question a sense that is universal, a sense that can be used as a discriminatory means to determine in which groups of things the objects belong, a sense that designates everything that flies. Rather, they describe what is there before them as something which is absolutely *singular*, and they express a "concrete behavior" of the object.[18] For this reason, those who can specify the operations that allow one to determine the specific weight of a body or those who are able to discern these operations have no "concept" of the specific weight. These different cases where a patient has "not yet" reached the conceptual stage in development or is "no longer" able to grasp concepts clearly and distinctly show how unique and *distinctive* conceptual thought is.

As E. Husserl incisively indicated, the so-called attention theory of abstraction, a theory which pragmatism renews only in crude form, cannot clarify the thinking of a meaning either in the positive or the negative sense of the abstraction procedure. The abstract parts, e.g., the being-red of a variety of red objects, retain their variety when I mentally block out all other qualities of the objects in question to the point of nullity for the attention. The parts do not grow together into a unity, as is undoubtedly meant by the word "red" or "the color red." If there is no trace of reason in our drive life, which is tempting to infer, then reason will not be able to be inferred from appearance! A sphere of meaning in general and some vague arrangement of this sphere must already be *presupposed* in every conscious moment of human consciousness. For this reason, theses which posit that a size type first comes into existence in nature when a measuring procedure and standard for it are given; that a number is nothing other than the X which I can gain through the operational rules which serve its production and identification; or that the "sense" of the simultaneity of two events is first given only when the method of its practical discovery (through a reversible light stream with the constant of the speed of light) is secured, are deeply flawed.

The correctness of the pragmatic and drive-psychological derivation primarily begins when the particular kind of *differentiation* of the subject's (or group's) sphere of meaning is made understandable, and a *choice* is realized from the objective realm of meaning. The abundance of the meaning differentiation and the exactness or vagueness of word meanings do not depend initially on the sensible perceptions of the subject, perceptions which, as we have already indicated, are under the direction-giving influence of the subject's drive and interest arrangement. Rather, they depend on what one could call the *arrangement of the subject's interest perspective.* [238] Where the interest or need is intense, the abundance and precision of meanings (as subjective intentions) are that much greater. Pets and game animals are given a surfeit of meaningful distinctions by primitive people, who describe other animals in vague generalities. "Adored children have many names." To describe a good bottle of Bordeaux as alcohol is indeed correct, but rather crude, like when one calls one's beloved a mammal, as E. T. A. Hoffmann would say! This important law, i.e., of the stock of meaning depending on the subject's interest perspective, does not concern the *origin* of meaning and the sphere of meaning in general, but only its *arrangement.* It concerns the sphere of meaning as it originally concerns the subject's perceptual world such that the "fitting on top of one another" of the arrangements of both spheres derives from the identity of these representational-differentiated *drive* forces. Pragmatism is only able to clarify the *selection* of the subjectively thought meanings from the objective, ideal realm of meaning, but it cannot clarify this objective-ideal realm of meaning, or the subjective sphere of meaning which differentiates itself in *opposing* determination and develops collectively with the perceptual sphere, but in no way develops "from" it.[19]

Just as the arrangement of the stock of meaning corresponds at first to the interest arrangement of the *group,* the *judgment* is certainly not at first a simple predicative arrangement of two meanings corresponding to the state of affairs (a purely theoretical, positive judgment), but rather a judgment concerning the object and its corresponding expression of the *ideal impact* the object has on the force center. This impact is grasped psychically and vitally, and it appears "to express" in the perceived image of the object nothing other than *expressions* our own vital ego *expresses.* The primitive person grasps the natural world surrounding him in every one of its appearances as the expression and manifestation of a "society" of spirits and demons with whom he can converse, and who have their own words and judgments. For this reason he has certain "superstitious words," and he interprets the names of things as the forces and characteristics of the things themselves. In social dealings, the judgment is not primarily the communication of a state of affairs related to a different judgment where the meaning was understood and then either ("critically") affirmed or denied. The judgment is rather an *impact* or even a "suggestion" that shared judgments of others immediately have on him. The "one-word sentence" of the child, e.g., "mama," already has the [239] sense of the expression of a need with the accompanying wish to receive satisfaction from the person "called." The place that verbal words and verbal sentences seem to have in the early stages of speech development suggests how intimately thinking and doing are *originally united.* It is a mistake for pragmatism to hold that *after* the process of distinguishing thinking from doing and after the rising individualization of the human being from his group (developments which dispel the web of suggestion, tradition, and infection, the web that stands between the ego and its being relations as a clouding medium), the judgment would have to *receive* some pragmatic character that genetically and originally possesses the sense of an after-formation and co-formation of the object, and socially, the sense of a command to the other to behave this way or that. The distinction between doing, after-doing, co-doing, and thinking is a distinction there *at the beginning* for both processes.

Similar errors are found in the interpretation that pragmatism carries out *on the categorical forms of being and thought* such as thing, causality, and the so-called expectation connections for particular sensations; in pragmatism's theory that deduction is an inner experimentation and construing with signs of the things and their relations that should pre-outline future actions; in pragmatism's theory regarding the axioms as implicit definitions of such a kind from which one can derive a maximum of propositions and theorems; and in pragmatism's theory that the sense of "*natural law*" as limited expectation and derived from limitations, which are gained in accordance with the principle of success and failure, placed on one's own practical activity. It is not necessary to linger any longer on these errors.

The Partial Truth of Pragmatism

The Pragmatic Condition of the Formal-Mechanistic Theory of Nature—Various Views regarding its Epistemic Value

Despite these deep errors, pragmatism nonetheless deserves in many respects a positive *defense,* while turning a blind eye to that which is absolutely worthless in philosophical pragmatism, as any good and healthy critique would do. The following are the central contributions by pragmatism.

First, pragmatism correctly sees that the *primary relation of humans,* as well as of any organism, *to the world* is in no way theoretical, but rather *practical;* and therefore every "*natural*" *worldview* is steered and supported by practical motives. In the same manner that the reality thesis and its primacy *prior to* any being-thus thesis about the *natural worldview* are practically co-determined, so is the thesis regarding the "empty forms" [240] of space and time (as those which come before bodies and events), as well as the natural preference, lying at the center of drive attention, to turn first to fixed, graspable things before turning to fluid or gaseous things and consequently gain the further preference in any *possible* perception to attend first to all uniform, recurring, and manageable things and appearances before attending to non-uniform, singular, and unmanageable appearances. Also practically determined is the law of the economy of the eye function. This is shown by virtue of the fact that we see that which is close to be much smaller and things that are far away to be much larger than they should appear given the viewpoint and the geometric perspective; and the fact that any natural perception of the visible thing exhibits constancy in size, form, and color and that this constancy is wholly different than what you would expect to have if there was a proportional relationship between the stimulus and sense-sensation. Furthermore, all "intelligence" related to the natural worldview is practically co-determined, the interest exhibited in the conceptual meanings a subject or group that, for instance, selects what is of interest in a particular situation is practically co-determined, as well as the impetus and direction of the type thinking that seeks to solve the practical "tasks" rooted in our basic drives and needs are practically co-determined. What is also practically co-determined the manner by which all sense qualities and all values pertaining to the natural worldview are eliminated from the world image and world consciousness, which possess no meaningful sign or potential functional sign to indicate how to make use of or manipulate an object or thing.[20] Finally, the preference of the natural human being has for the *outer* world in contrast to the inner world, preferring the cognition of what is other in contrast to the cognition of self, is practically co-determined.

From these important points, however, there is only one thing which follows: in the course of the formulation of a *purely theoretical* relation of the human being to the world, all of these practical motives effective in the formative law of the natural worldview are bit by bit *bracketed out by a particular spiritual technique*, and this takes place in particular for a "philosophical" view of the thing. The possibility of such a philosophical view does mean that there can be cognition and knowledge of the world that is not "practically conditioned."

Pragmatism has also correctly realized that the highest cognitive goals of positive natural science and explanatory psychology—to the extent that these sciences must seek to bracket out any specific anthropomorphism—are *practically* conditioned. For as (modern) science posits for its end to grasp all appearances of the outer and inner world as dependent upon the functions of a (formal) mechanism, it brackets out the specific organization of the *earthly human being* as the existence and being-thus conditions of the objects of these appearances. Modern science seeks a knowledge [241] whose being-thus correlate wipes out anything that is (as is also the case in the natural worldview) only there by virtue of *our* sensible and psychophysical constitution; it seeks a "knowledge" that would be valid for the essence of an entirely different sensible constitution than the earthly-human constitution, and it seeks, as it were, to translate this knowledge into the language of any possible organization of sense—these goals distinguish the positive sciences sharply from any anthropomorphic practical knowledge which is possible in the "natural worldview." However, and here is where the truth of pragmatism starts, modern science chooses that which enters into its knowledge according to a principle of selection that is co-determined *practically* or *primarily* through a specific *valuation* a selection determined not anthropomorphically-practically as the knowledge content of the natural worldview, but rather practically in the *essential biological* sense. There is no conceivable creature—no psychophysical organism—which can change the natural environment practically or directly, unless it be by its spontaneous mechanical movement. Therefore, the positive sciences direct their interest, their preference (of love) to that which can be moved by "any creature at all," to what can be moved directly or indirectly, and which is thus a manageable, controllable, and transformable thing in nature. In the possible and independent variations in the quantitative determination of these objects, the positive sciences seek the being-thus of all phenomena and realities of nature. Expressed more simply, science goes back to "*natura*" according to the possibility of the prototype of a formal "*mechanism*," not because *natura* in itself would only be a "*mechanism*," but because *natura* in itself, *insofar* as it is a mechanism or is largely analogous to such a mechanism, is practically *controllable and able to be directed through a living being's willing power.* Science seeks a construction plan, as it were, "for any possible machine," and not simply for the applied technique of those machines that correspond to the particular mastery goals of historical human beings, and thus for "particular" machines. Moreover, positive science calls a natural event "cognized" (at the limits of *its* knowledge goals in general) when science can declare a plan according to which the event can be *mastered* or can be *thought* to be mastered in a particular *hic et nunc* (as indicated in real experiment and thought experiment).

It would be a great error to think that the formal-mechanistic view of reality thereby *uniquely* overcomes the practical-technical motive of its knowledge goals because it overcomes any *sensible anthropomorphism*, and brackets out any human sensible intuition and any "experience" of the human being from its symbolic world image, which is mathematically formulated by equations of movement. What *remains presupposed* is not only "the physicists" as pure cognition subjects, as Max Planck states, but also "the physicists" as *mastery-willing living beings* (and that means, as beings endowed with sensibility and spontaneous mechanical movement "in general"). We could then say that the [242] "*human being*" remains presupposed, when the concept of human being is not empirically, but rather essential-ontologically, understood as "the vital being joined together with a rational spirit," an idea for which the earthly human, having the name "human being," with its particular anatomy, physiology, organization of sense, and movement, is only *an,* if not our only, "example." What formal-mechanistic science brackets out is not "life" in general, but only the human stimulus and difference threshold, the particularity of the human sense organs and modalities, etc.; it does not bracket out sensibility in general, but only the special case of the earthly human animal's senses; it does not bracket out vital directed movement in general, but only this empirical human apparatus of movement, not "homo" in general, but only earthly "human animal."

In order to make more precise the concepts concerning the peculiar characteristics of my (relatively pragmatic) view of any formal-mechanistic theory of nature, it is necessary to state which *different views of the mechanistic theory of nature* are thereby excluded. There are some such views that *overestimate* its cognitive value, and some that *underestimate* it.

I. "*Materialism*" belongs to the succession of views that *overestimate* the cognitive value of the mechanistic theory of nature. This is also the case for the absolute, realistically defined, sensitivistic association psychology and psycho-mechanical parallelism corresponding to materialism. These grant to the theory of mechanism and its presuppositions such as space, time, and the homogeneous movement of some kind of absolutely persistent "thing" (whether electrons or atoms, whether things of sensation or so-called presentations or presenting things) an *absolute reality* "behind" the appearances. Materialism necessarily fails to grasp the sevenfold existential and essential (being-thus) relativity that comes with any natural mechanistic theory.

1. Mechanism fails altogether to grasp the existential relativity of the natural mechanistic theory with regard to a *knowing subject* who is capable of pure knowledge. (That is, the materialist behaves, as W. Schuppe once appropriately said, in accord with the song of students, "I wish I were

a louis d'or, since I could buy myself beer to pour" [*Ich wollt, ich wär ein Louisdor, da koofte ich mir Bier dafor*].) Today this is readily accepted.

2. Materialism thereby also fails to grasp the existential relativity of the mechanistic theory with regard to the laws of "*pure*" logic and mathematical analysis (i.e., with regard to the object laws or act laws of the autonomous thought object and correlative thought act in general); and with regard to the laws that firstly are not *all* laws of a logos, although necessarily contained in them, and secondly, to those which could be "clarified" in any sense through a mechanical theory neither as object laws nor as act laws.

3. [243] Furthermore, the existential relativity of natural mechanical theory with regard to "sensible" intuition is not grasped. Sensible intuition is transmitted through a stimulus of whatever kind, which the lived body [*Leibkörper*] obtains, directly or indirectly, in the "that" of its realization, and thus not in the "what" that it gives. However, not every possible intuition, and not every actual intuition, of the human being is a "sensible" intuition, since there are also non-sensible, e.g., "gestalt" or "structural," intuitions whose data primarily *conditions* and makes *possible* any possible sensible intuition in its content of sensation. To this non-sensible intuition belongs, for example, any intuitive minima that lie at the foundation of the different mathematical disciplines and which ground for any discipline a particular *essential axiomatics* surpassing the purely formal and logical axioms.

4. Materialism further fails to grasp the existential relativity of the mechanistic theory with regard to the "empty forms" of absolute existence such as "space," "time," and "movement," i.e., with regard to *ficta* whose existence is not independent from either the reason of human beings or the existence of the "living being" and the "being" of humans. Space, time, and movement are (a) in themselves not empty forms, but are rather consequences of *forces* that are qualitatively and quantitatively determined as well as temporally efficacious. What concerns the lawful ordering of space, time, and movement are entirely not intuitable. In this case, space and time as different dimensions of solely and originally given "movement" and "change" (and the "exchange" rooted in both movement and change) are only different formations of the "possibility of movement," or rather the "possibility of change," which initially become through actual movement, or rather change, actual space and actual time. Space and time are thus (b) in no sense absolute but are rather *essentially relative to one another* (an insight of the general theory of relativity). (c) They do

not exist *extra mentem*, since everything which is essentially relative to one another cannot possess any existence *extra mentem*. (d) Every determinant metric "size" of space, time, and movement is *wholly existentially relative to life* and a sensible observer (straightforwardly, so that its sensible intuition is thought to be independent from any human or animal species).

5. Materialism thereby also fails to grasp the *general, vitally relative nature of any mechanistic theory* and thereby the fact that any organic "life" (as objectively physically real *and* as the vital sphere of the "psychically" conceived) essentially and lawfully escapes any recourse to a mechanistic theory. For what is existentially relative to a mechanistic theory, namely, vital-being, cannot itself be "a mechanistic" theory, even [244] if it were to be researched and studied in the method of mechanistic reflection as a bodily phenomenon and a "bearer" of life.

6. Formal materialism fails to grasp the existential relativity of the mechanistic theory and all preeminent principles of formal mechanics (and particularly its highest principle of the least effect) with regard to the *technical positing of ends* of a living being, with regard to the *mastery* of *natura* with a minimum of means, and thereby with regard to the specifically "pragmatic" existential relativity of a mechanical theory, which is only a "means" for value-realizing, end-determining agents.

7. Materialism fails to grasp that every formal-mechanistic being-thus image of a thing for the sake of this collective relativization of objects has only the value of a *symbolic* determination of nature through "signs," through which and through whose connection we humans, with the intent to master nature, make plans for our possible assault on nature and mastery over it for some (changing) purposes. This activity is essentially no different from the architect who initially makes a construction plan before he builds. Since a "knowledge" of the *real factual existence* [*realen Sachbestand*] of nature and its being-thus is in no manner given in this symbolic image, the image therefore relays as little "knowledge" of what nature really is as does an address book—a book that tells me how to track down people I want to meet, and do so over and over again, but which tells me nothing about the *essence and character* of these people. An unequivocal ordering, an ordering that I grant things through a classification of signs that I can find through pure operations, and an ordering which, through signs, can always trace, as well as divide and conjoin, specific things through pure operations and determine in advance their position in the system of "now-here-point" (i.e., the spatial-temporal co-

incidence) without empirical testing, tells me nothing about the *essence* of these objects, even if the ordering were perfect. In fact, if the ideal goal (that there is only an idea of the plan and not of the thing itself) were to be reached, I would learn *absolutely nothing* about the essence of the objects. The ordering prohibits it! Given materialism's clever and artificial *bypassing of any essence* of the objects of this world, and its bracketing-out of anything that interests philosophy or its highest discipline—the essential ontology of the world (with, conversely, the bracketing-out of anything of *contingent* existence and being-thus in the here and now)—this radical reversal of any philosophical or "pure" knowledge and its cognitive method is the goal, the sense, and the leading practical-technical value of all formal-mechanistic consideration and research. The fact that these rebukes and disparagements of philosophical and essential knowledge by the formal-mechanistic view and research [245] are presently so commonplace in different forms is a sign that (1) the formal-mechanistic worldview has mistakenly been taken as the standard of pure theoretical knowledge and as means of participating ontologically in knowing what nature is and (2) that practical intelligence, which is the only form of knowledge operative in the formal-mechanistic worldview, has been regarded as "reason" and the relativity of practical intelligence in its mastery and control of nature through vital movement has been entirely overlooked, If the formal-mechanistic view were to be measured in respect to what *it* seeks (and not in the way some researchers "want" it to employ it), to its sense and value, namely to be the grandest leader for human industry and technology, then the symbolic images of the thing that it produces are essential, crucial, and irreplaceable to such an extent that the practical fruitfulness of these images creates the *foundation* for the potential *accomplishment of the goal of "homo sapiens" in the human being*, and in particular for the accomplishment of this goal to the *greatest possible extent.*

Because materialism (of the outer world and inner world) has overlooked this *sevenfold relativity* of the formal-mechanistic view of nature and the soul, and has thereby made the theory of mechanism into a "thing itself," and as a logical consequence all qualities, gestalts, forms, ideas, essences, goals, values, and purposes of nature and the soul are only relative to the human being, then materialism's deception regarding the sense and cognitive value of formal-mechanistic science is obviously by far the greatest of all its deceptions.

The remaining, similarly mistaken, overly esteemed theories concerning the meaning of the mechanistic worldview recognize only a *limited number of its presuppositions* as presuppositions and thereby fall somewhat less into error than materialism does.

II. If only the aforementioned presuppositions (1) and (2)—that is, the existence of a knowing subject in general (which cannot be clarified mechanistically) and the validity of "pure" logical analysis as the epitome of object laws and act laws (which also cannot be clarified mechanistically)—were conceded to the mechanistic worldview, and no other presupposition were, then there would still be the mistaken view that "thinking a world would be *reduced* to thinking a world mechanistically." That is, the formal-mechanistic worldview would still be the *only "rational" worldview.* Thinkers such as Descartes, Spinoza, Hobbes, and Herbart come quite close to this theory, although there is a healthy critique of pragmatism detectable in Hobbes. More recently, this view has been quite adamantly defended by W. Wundt,[21] and also very instructively defended by M. Schlick,[22] quite extensively by the Kantian schools in both Marburg and (with the exception of history) Heidelberg, and persistently by Max Weber. Nevertheless, the above thesis is entirely ungrounded. If W. Wundt means to say that the mechanistic view of nature provides the "sole [246] incontestable" world image, then the movement, or rather the change of location, is the singular change in which what changes itself maintains its strict identity. If Wundt is indeed committed to this view, it serves as a sign that he incorrectly judges and incorrectly uses the highest "pure" logical principles. The change of state, grasped in the ontic sense, in the sense Aristotle means by his concept of άλλοίωσς, that is, of "transformation" and "creation," can very likely be partially of existence with *the right use of the principle of identity* and of the ontic principle grounding the law of noncontradiction; namely, it is impossible for the same accident to befit and not befit the same being. If these principles are, however, incorrectly grasped and used, as in cases where one fails to realize their purely *hypothetical* nature and one (instead of X = X, or rather X does not have Y, but instead has a non-Y, for example a Z) determines the being-thus *materially*, i.e., already according to particular objects (thus, for example, one writes A = A), then the determinations of a homogeneous time, of a homogeneous space, and of a homogeneous movement contain precisely the same "contradictions" as the change of conditions and so on.

It is the comparatively enduring service of the "Eleatic" Herbart to have clearly shown this. Is not any point of the homogeneous space strictly being-thus-identical with the other points (and analogously any temporal point with any temporal point), and yet still different from them? And had not already Zeno and after him Herbart sought to demonstrate the "contradictions" in homogeneous movement? Indeed, these contradictions exist when the phenomena of the intuition in space, time, movement, change, transformation, and creation are not accepted simply as "given" (and one sees only a field of application of the logical principles in them), but rather the logical principles are claimed to be above the absolutely real (for example, the principle of identity, that there is a being-thus-determined existence identical with it) and, thereby with them, the *phenomena* can then be *destroyed*, or rather proven as "deceptive phantoms." Moreover, the "one" thing with its qualities, the "one" ego with its many thoughts, and the causal dependence of cause and effect would all be contradictions. However, the logical principles state only that movement is movement, and change is change, or rather that movement is not a change of state. In no way do the principles reveal "contradictions" in these concepts. Wundt's thesis proves thus too much and thereby nothing. If it were correct, then the mechanistic principles would have to be *purely logically* deduced, as many philosophers of the Enlightenment wanted, for example, to deduce the principle of tragedy from the principle of the "impoverished ground" of the change of movement, or the causal principle from the phenomenon of the (apparently) groundless change with the principle of identity (Herbart, Theodor Lipps, H. Münsterberg, et al.).

There cannot be any discussion about any of this. The principles of "pure" logic are as amenable to a *non*-mechanical world as they are to a formal-[247]mechanical world; they would even be amenable to an absolutely chaotic, entirely limitless changing being. Conversely, if pure logic developed out of a logically completed and ideally conceptual world as idea, then this idea, as H. Driesch[23] has recently indicated, would *not* exactly be the idea of a formal-mechanistic world, but would fall under what Driesch calls the "monistic ordering ideal," i.e., under the idea of a world entirety from whose idea the existence and being-thus of each of its parts could be derived through pure a priori conceptual development (and all their relations could be derived from *a* fundamental law). It is thus an ideal whose realization makes the formal-mechanistic "in sum" world (the ώς έπί τό πολύ, as Aristotle called it).

Henri Bergson errs in precisely the opposite manner from any of those who hold a formal-mechanistic worldview for a bolstering of "pure logic." He is in agreement with those who assert that to think the world would already mean to think it "mechanistically"; that a principle of identity would only be valid, for example, where there is homogeneous space and an absolutely fixed body therein. However, Bergson does not turn to this supposed connection in support of the mechanistic view of nature, but rather in opposition to it, and not merely in the sphere of the psychic or organic, but also in the sphere of the inorganic. He uses the supposed connection to oppose *logic* by holding that the logical principles (which he recognizes only as subjective laws of thinking and not as ontological laws) come about as tools of the urge of life. By sketching a theory according to which homogeneous space, homogeneous time, substance, and fixed bodies (which he holds as a presupposition of pure logic) would be merely "practical schemas of the actions of the living being in its environment," Bergson must renounce in general the thinking for the *metaphysical* cognition of the thing in itself, and in its place support the irrationalistic cognitive means of "intuition" and "sympathy," which alone are able to directly grasp true becoming, movement (as *dynamis*), force, becoming anew, and creation. Thereby, he reduces thinking and logic in *general* to a singular kind and technique, namely a *sociologically circumscribed kind* and *technique* of thinking (which has nothing to do with pure logic and its claims). This sociologically circumscribed kind and technique of thinking is precisely the kind and technique that is relational and anti-substance in nature and is particular to the later development of "society" in the West, which is a further manifestation of the formal-mechanistic ideal. The reason for this reduction of all thinking to a specific kind and technique is to strengthen his fight against "the" thinking in general. Bergson correctly recognizes that the formal-mechanistic cognition of nature possesses a symbolic and practical *co*-conditioned value, and that philosophy and metaphysics first begin where these end. Nonetheless, he fails to see that this mechanistic cognition of nature is also "true" and "correct" [248] with regard *to the objects that are ontologically relative to life.* By further regarding the "concept," in an entirely nominal and pragmatic manner, as simply an impulse of movement sequences of image representations and "fixed" signs, which demonstrate the way of our actions, and by presuming all categories to be clarified as mere practical-economic unified images to which our actions can be attached,[24] and also by identifying the causal principle with its particular *mechanical* form in the exact same manner as Herbart and then returning to the principle of identity, Bergson falls into the same error as the above-mentioned researchers, but along the opposite path. In the concept, Bergson sees only an immaterial "tool"; in the "conclusion," only an "experimentation of ideas" (a thought experiment) tested according to the principle of success-failure and thereby hereditarily fixed; and in "*Wissenschaft*" ("science") *only* a consequence of the vital will to dominate nature which realizes itself in technology and industry. The "intelligence" of the human being is, for Bergson, a consequence of the fact that the human being is "*homo faber.*" We have already criticized these errors in earlier in our text.

Although Bergson holds a mistaken and untenable position regarding the merely practical meaning of "reason," he is correct, on the other hand, that philosophy and metaphysics are essentially different from science, and their contemplative and apractical ideal of cognition exists *next to* and *above* the ideal of science. Secondly, Bergson correctly sees that the formal-mechanistic method of explanation is *practically* and *biologically* conditioned and therefore "life" cannot be explained mechanistically. It is primarily in his positive theory of metaphysical cognition through "intuition" as the higher synthesis of intelligence and instinct, and in his theory of life and its development, where Bergson's real errors begin.

III. A third type of theory regarding the sense of the formal-mechanistic view of nature, and indeed of this view of nature on the level of Newtonian science—a complete formulation of which has not yet been given—can be found in Kant's philosophy and the neo-Kantian schools. This third type gains its peculiar characteristics distinguishing it from the second type through its theory of apriority, subjectivity, and the existing, objective ("transcendental") validity of the forms of intuition, space, time, and movement (on which Kant only wavers as to whether they are "pure" or "empirical" concepts), as well as through its conception of a synthetic, transcendental logic—which is different from a "pure analytic" logic—as the epitome of the conditions of possibility [249] for our experience of the objects of nature, and thereby for the objects of nature itself. (The so-called Copernican revolution: "The understanding prescribes the laws to nature.") If a pragmatic motif is not already seen—though easily seen from a historical perspective—in Kant's all-encompassing thought that rational cognition is one of synthetic *forms* and of spontaneously and lawfully bound images of the objects of nature (as connections of experience), and is not a mere receptive grasping of the being-thus of the objects, then Kant fails to understand that the mechanistic worldview has a practical-technically conditioned meaning, and metaphysics has a purely theoretical meaning. He fails to understand this relation so completely and so radically that he in fact entirely *reverses* the relation. For him, the mechanistic theory of natural science (and associative psychology) is "*purely theoretical*"—even if in the sense of the entire reconstruction of the concept of "cognition" through the new cognition concept of "form"; and metaphysics can only support some of these theses (e.g., God, freedom, immortality) insofar as they are constructed as "postulates" based on the moral law.

In connection with this, it is only important to us that Kant realizes, first, that pure logic as such allows for an entirely *different* worldview, namely the formal mechanistic worldview—this is undoubtedly progress—and second, that the "thing in itself" has absolutely no cognitive value for this natural worldview, since the three central data of "space," "time," and "movement" would be only "human" forms of the intuition of the things, forms that would not be brought to the things themselves—and this is certainly a further step of great progress. Without question, we hold as unsound Kant's proof of "transcendental logic," his, in many respects, untenable theory of space and time, and his conception (supported by nothing more than the *proton pseudos* of an unordered chaos of sensation) of a synthetically formed thinking bringing forth the objects of experience and his conception of a particular science of them. While he, as Newton did, understood space and time to be "independent" empty forms which precede the things and their relations, or rather precede the events and their relations, Kant made these forms (which existed *in themselves* for Newton) into mere "human" forms of intuition—unlike Newton who, in his teaching of space as "*sensorium Dei*," made them into divine forms of intuition. Rarely does the birth of a different theory of space and time prevent the birth of a correct theory of space and time, of a theory which has to proceed from the cognition that space and time, independent of things, events, and their relations, are nothing other than phantoms of human drive fantasy. By overlooking the fact that space and time are to be understood primarily from the more *originary* and simpler data of dynamically grasped "movement," "transformation," and ultimately from "change"—and that movement, for example, does not presuppose the existence of space [250] and time, Kant significantly stifled the emergence of a correct, philosophical grounding of theoretical physics.

There are two reasons why Kant was able to grasp the limits of the formal-mechanistic worldview in its entirety, which in itself is a noble project, only in so far as he was able to contest the metaphysical validity of this worldview. First, Kant was able to use his transcendental idealism and empirical realism to contest any theoretical metaphysics—the empty constructs of his theory of postulates do not constitute a genuine metaphysics. Second, due to his dogmatic conviction, presupposed in every aspect of his philosophy, regarding the validity of the formal-mechanistic worldview (in Newton's sense), he held this theory of empirical reality to be "fully valid" for both *life* and the empirical *theory of the soul.* Nonetheless, Kant has *secured* more than any other philosopher the dominance of the formal-mechanistic worldview over the spiritual.

With regard to the sevenfold relativity of the existence of objects in the mechanistic theory of nature, Kant has only clearly recognized the *first three* kinds of this relativity and has overlooked the *four* other kinds of it.

IV. It has been the great service of the *positivistic* and *pragmatic* movements of thought, in fact, "to go above and beyond Kant," though still in many ways remaining behind him. The service rendered by these movements regarding the clarification of the meaning of the formal-mechanistic theory of nature is not diminished by the inherent philosophical errors of both movements. It is not diminished by the fact that positivism defends the sensualistic theory of givenness (in part, Kant's *proton pseudos*), and maintains that what is given is merely sensations proportional to the stimulus. Thus, positivism has *not* seen what Kant had *already clearly and effectively seen*, namely, that the structural relations of experience, in whose empty place the sensations enter and alone can enter, are really "*pre*-given" to the sensations—a fact that Kant only mistakenly clarified when he traced them back to their origin according to the a priori functional lawfulness of reason. Pragmatism and positivism are not diminished by attempts such as those undertaken by Avenarius and Mach to reduce all logical laws of thinking to the principle of the economy of thinking, rather than to laws of being (the correct undertaking). Edmund Husserl has conclusively refuted these attempts.[25] Pragmatism and positivism are not diminished by pragmatism's attempt to do the impossible, to give a new interpretation of concepts such as "cognition," truth, and evidence. Some of these errors, which are of a general philosophical kind, are merely false generalizations of correct insights into the essence of cognition, insights which have been acquired by the cognitive practices of the exact natural researchers (and in particular of the theoretical physicists). The mistake here is that the [251] kinds of cognition (the exact and philosophical) are not distinguished and not derived from the highest principle of "knowledge," namely, the participation of a being in the being-thus of the being of another. Consequently, knowledge *in general* is reduced to the sense of cognition which has been gained in the cognitive praxis of *formal-mechanistic* research into nature.

In contrast to the typical theories regarding the cognitive value of the formal-mechanistic theory of nature (which I have dealt with previously), the true positivists without a doubt *go too far in their relativization*. They not only make their image of nature (and the soul) biologically relative and relative to the practical task of seeking to dominate nature by the use of technology, but they go so far as to relativize *historically* this natural viewpoint. Not only do they not see the particular difficulties in the realization of this, but they also tend to make the mistake that the formal-mechanistic theory of nature (which posits no absolutely constant, moving, extended "things") shares with the older *material*-"mechanistic" natural view of the Galilean-Newtonian school, which wanted to make in a very strict sense every discipline of physics, chemistry, and biology into an application of "mechanics," an attempt fully accomplished today through the theory of electricity and optics; the mistake that the formal-mechanistic view of nature is a theory that *goes beyond* anything up to that point in the history of science.

Along these lines, Ernst Mach, particularly in his works on epistemology and the history of physics, and Pierre Duhem have criticized the ideal of the mechanistic theory of nature as an ideal of cognition in order to replace it with the ideal which Descartes had already imagined, an ideal which has gained even greater support through Einstein and Minkowsky; namely, to replace the ideal of cognition with the ideal of a pure and thorough *mathematization*, or more precisely, with a *geometrization of physics*. This ideal would be reached if all forms of force-activities, i.e., of causal concepts, as well as all types of substance concepts, were discarded from physics and nothing would be considered as "cognized" other than mathematical and analytically determined *functional dependencies*[26] of changes of observed appearances. While, as a philosopher, the realistic and Aristotelian-oriented P. Duhem accepts in the deepest manner a *metaphysics* of nature that is entirely independent from this "mathematical" physics, E. Mach, who contests any outer-sensual reality and regards any metaphysics to be trivial, holds this mathematicized ideal of cognition to be the *only* ideal that we possess of nature. What, then, was the mechanistic view of nature in relation to this new ideal of cognition? It was, understood *historically*, merely a transitional point to reach this ideal. E. Mach's opinion, succinctly expressed, is as follows: "To clarify" is nothing [252] *more* and nothing *less* than to render nature in the form of mathematical lawfulness. It is not to recognize the "causes" or the appearances (i.e., the reasons for the being-thus and effective factors of existence), but rather, this word "clarify" has only a subjective mentally-economical meaning; namely, to lead a relative unknown back to a relative already known as a constituent part of the known things, or rather as a lawful modification and alteration of the known things. It may also then mean, as it has been recently formulated by M. Schlick with scarce consequence, that cognition is only to find something else in a complex that was given before in a perceived complex, and as clearly as possible point to it with the use of signs. Because, in the inherently contingent "history" of Western physics since Galileo, the phenomena of the motion of ponderable masses were, temporally-historically, *first*, then if these phenomena and their laws were "known," one sought to lead all natural appearances that were less known back to the fundamental concepts and principles of *mechanics*, intending (though falsely) "to clarify" them ontologically through this process. If this process had "by chance" gone otherwise, and if the phenomena of light and electricity, for example, had been the "first" to be studied, or acoustic phenomena had been initially examined, then the phenomena of the movement of ponderable masses would have to be clarified with the aid of whatever presented analogies to these in physicalistic optics, the theory of electricity, and acoustics! However heuristically valuable such "analogies" have proven to be in the progress of science,[27] which follows the principle of the economy of thought and images, it would require that these analogies were weeded out in the final construction of science, since they became harmful to the progress of science. This would hold true primarily for the "mechanical analogies" and "models" by which the appearances are intended to be "clarified" ontically. Thus in the finished construction of science—away with all supersensible "hypotheses" and realities, substances, causes, and forces! And there then would be the reduction of the known to measurable sense-data and mathematical similarities, i.e., the so-called "natural laws," which "limit our expectations"!

Mach's theory contains difficulties and contradictions in great number, as they have already been presented at great length.[28]

Where do the objective dependencies and independencies of the complex of elements come from, if everything that our spirit possesses is reduced to "elements" which, in the context of the organism and its changes, are called "sensations"? Relations are not [253] sensible elements like blue, hard, and sour! If we spontaneously create them, how could these relations grant truth regarding objective being? If we "discover" them in intuition, how is atomistic sensualism able to maintain itself? Is there not, thus, a *non*-sensible intuition? Do the "elements" and their complexes, in the manner that they are in the perceptual event, truly possess among each other a strict "lawfulness" of change? Is it not rather the case that the *real and conceived relatively constant objects* and preceding unities possess this lawfulness, in explicit contrast to the inconstant, cursory sensations that are never proportional to the physical stimuli?[29] Does not the acceptance of a natural lawfulness presuppose the trans-conscious, intentional *objectiveness of nature* (which "appears" in sensations, but is never indentifiable through them) or even the *trans-conscious reality* of nature?[30] Both of these contradict Mach's theses. Has not Mach thereby only been able to claim, in a similar manner to Hume, that the substance idea has to lead back to the fact of relatively constant elements = complexes of sensations, since he has already substantialized and objectivized the pure qualities and sensations *themselves*?

Moreover, in the manner that Mach operates with his "principle of the economy of thought" there is not only the mistake—a mistake which at present is totally rejected (by E. Husserl and in a different way by the Külpe school of cognitive psychology)—of denying unintuitable meaning intentions and their objective correlates in the things themselves, and of regarding a concept like law as merely a "place holder" for possible sense impressions, but there is also a peculiar contradiction hidden in the *use* of the principle by Mach. If the acceptance, for example, of a trans-conscious reality of nature (which we gather from its other bases) is an economic acceptance, and if the principle of thought economy itself is the logic of the highest principle—then why does Mach contest these? And is it not the same for substance, causality, and for the formal-mechanistic reduction of appearances? Insofar as Mach allows his economic principle to fall prey to these fundamental questions, he shows a deep skepticism regarding his own principle—you could say that he undermines his own project. He shows that he himself would like to think the world not "*only*" economically, but also to think the givennesses themselves adequately and purely "logically." However, this logic cannot then be immersed in the economic principle, and thereby a "pure logic" is already in principle recognized.

[254] Concerning nature and the ontic presupposition of the economic principle itself, Avenarius and Mach find themselves in a peculiar deception. There is no doubt that this principle itself is a thoroughly *teleoclinal*[31] principle. If you grant the psychophysical organism a "tendency" to persist through a minimum of means and use of energy, then you have already fully *abandoned* a mechanical view of life and the organism, as well as a strict associative-psychological explanation of the spiritual experience. In other words, you are, in some sense of the quite ambiguous word, a vitalist. Both thinkers show in their writings no hint that they were conscious of this "crypto-vitalism" in their philosophy. Henri Bergson was the first, in a fully *conscious* manner, to make this connection explicit. It is initially here, where the merely practical sense of mechanism in its extreme form is claimed, but simultaneously where an apractical, *purely theoretical* worldview is consciously striven for (obviously under "*sacrifizio dell'intelletto*"), that the formal-mechanical lawfulness becomes a subtype: one that is "roughly" valid for only a cross-section of the world process (and not for the becoming or development of the world), of the teleoclinal-directed vital tendency of the "élan vital," and of the relations that demonstrate the character and type of concrete, historical-developmental causality. Neither for Mach and Avenarius, nor for Bergson is it conceivable how it is in any way *possible* to think the world according to the economic principle without the presupposition of *ontic or real constants* in the given of nature. A great line of thinkers during the seventeenth and eighteenth centuries, for example, Leibniz, Maupertuis, et al., had accepted and sought an ontically real principle of economy that would ultimately account for (in at the very least an orderly, conclusive manner) the "wisdom" and "goodness" of the creation of the things. Leibniz's "*principe du meilleur*," which enables God's creation and the process of nature to proceed, according to the principle of a maximum of compossibilities, in incontestable things, is truly the most abstract and

purest ontological form that this ontic principle of a *lex parsimoniae* has found. Only particular varieties of this principle were for mechanics and physics the ontically conceived principles, principles such as the principle "of the least effect," the principle of the "smallest constraint," the principle of the "virtual displacement," the principle of tragedy. At this time, the teleological character of these principles was readily apparent. From this "'God' or the 'nature of the thing' proceeds so," the modern positivists made "the human being thinks so." Is this justified? I believe not! I am wholly of the opinion that Max Planck's thought[32] that any natural law divides into inert accidental laws and into those things which express a [255] dynamic necessity, and that the highest principles, those which determine any "dynamic necessity" according to different courses, are reduced, as Planck has already indicated, to the "principle of the smallest effect," is to be granted philosophical merit. In this approach by Planck, I not only see that this reduction is possible, but I also see one of the probability proofs demonstrating that nature, understood as *all that is non-spiritual in its entirety* (which would include that which is not necessarily an organism), is *amechanical*. For the principle of the smallest effect as the most profound support of the principle of mechanics and simultaneously of the life laws is not itself a mechanical principle, but rather a thoroughly teleoclinal principle, and consequently it turns everything which happens in accord with mechanical principles into the technical means of a causality of a teleoclinic kind, and thus is not yet necessarily of the vital or organic kind. The subjective principle of the economy of thought, the attempt to ground all principles as simply as possible, is merely a special case of this cosmic teleoclinal principle. It is itself only an adaptation of the ontically valid principle of the smallest effect. This principle should obviously not be confused with the "psychological economic principle," the principle that our soul tends to reduce the unknown to the known, since the fundamental grounds for what is true are for the most part psychologically not discovered first in time, but rather later, at the end. In this respect Aristotle's law is valid, the "thing in itself" is not what is most originally known to us, but rather known "subsequently."

If we look more closely, with these prefatory remarks in mind, at Mach's judgment regarding the cognitive value of the mechanical theory of nature, then we notice that he far overshoots the goal. If he had been right in his view of the "historical contingency" of the old tendency of the seventeenth and eighteenth centuries (and also the nineteenth century up until Helmholtz and Lord Kelvin), a tendency making physics, chemistry, and so on in their entirety into special cases of the mechanics of extended matter, a tendency abandoned by present science, he would certainly have been mistaken about the formal-mechanistic view of the *world in general.*

The formal-mechanistic view has in no way been abandoned through the classification of the mechanics of ponderable masses in the theory of electricity or through the special and general theories of relativity. It presupposes neither the acceptance of a specific, absolutely constant "thing" nor a specific law of movement, and it presupposes nothing other than the essential connections which ground themselves in space, time, and movement as final givennesses. And yet the "formal" mechanistic theory of nature found in contemporary physics is to be called "mechanistic" insofar as the measurable coincidences of the natural appearances in space and time and the laws of these coincidences determine whether the phenomena are to be considered dependent. Hence, it is the measurable coincidences and the laws of these coincidences which constitute the existence and nonexistence, the contingent being-thus and being other, [256] of the natural phenomena, and never the essence of these phenomena. Time, space, and movement, however they are understood, have a certain *precedence* over all the qualities, a precedence not necessarily of being (in the sense of a theory of the "subjective" nature of qualities, forms, gestalts, values, aims, and purposes), but rather always a precedence in the cases under consideration in the direction of research. Mach's sensualistic theory of the elements is unable to clarify this precedence, since space, time, and movement are only able to be given as blue, sour, and hard.

Furthermore, the historical course of things does *not* confirm Mach's thesis regarding the "historical" relativity of the mechanistic theory of nature. This thesis of his does not explain, for example, why the formal program of a mechanistic explanation of nature could in fact be so incredibly *far out ahead* of the actual execution of this program. Certainly this was not the case because the phenomena of movement were "known" to them in particular through empirical study; these phenomena were entirely unknown to them in the sense of positive science. Democritus and Leucippus had already developed in antiquity a universal program for a mechanistic theory of nature. Also, ever since Galileo and his predecessors (who have been brought to our attention through P. Duhem's research), the program and the *schematic form* of this worldview have been continually way out ahead of their actual execution in the specific disciplines of physics, chemistry, biology, and the theory of the soul (as associative psychology). So it is just the reverse of what Mach understands it to be. The appearances of movement, initially of the ponderable body [*Körper*], were necessarily first known and studied, in the historical sense, because the logical gestalt schema of the mechanistic worldview lived, *from the beginning*, in the founders of modern dynamics and physics—this worldview was already an encompassing proto-thesis, and was even becoming a particular hypothesis—and had been demonstrated long before its empirical feasibility was demonstrated in the particular disciplines (and thus there came into existence in successive fashion a mechanistic acoustics, thermodynamics, optics, etc.). The stubbornness with which this cognitive ideal—an ideal of experience, observation, and measurement serving more as a defiance than as a genetic process of experiences—would firmly hold to an audacious *act of the will* in the times when "proofs" of it or even mere demonstrations of it were still minimal, indicates that Mach neither sees the great course of things correctly nor sees it *historically* correctly. Given the extremely *sudden*, when taken in its entirety, coming-into-being of this schema of world cognition in contrast to the 1,500-year-long dominance of the completely opposing "organological" worldview of Aristotle, a worldview that conferred every original phenomenon, form of being, and form of becoming of organic life upon the dead and spiritual world, it is unclear why it suddenly occurred to some (coincidentally) [257] "to study the appearances of movement more precisely"! If the mechanistic worldview is neither summoned alone through logic and mathematics, nor results from "pure," apractical, irrefutable experience and observation, then this worldview must possess an originary ground and originary possibility that has its roots far more deeply *in the things and in the human being in general* than Mach recognizes with his theory of "historical contingency."

Certainly, Mach has concretely demonstrated in his historical presentations, more so than anyone else, the right way to a historical understanding of the origin of the mechanistic theory of nature in the modern West. His works continue to show that most of the foundational experiments resulted from actual *technical* problems and tasks, not from the experiments themselves. What this approach has demonstrated is that a *new will to dominate nature* and a new *belief* in the restless feasibility of this will to control exists *at the start* of the origination of any thought-schema. The origination of this stubborn "belief," namely that nature must be so and so and thus also thought so and so, that nature is absolutely manageable, controllable, and determinable through the will and movement of the human being, is in fact what clarifies the sudden emergence of any schema: a new ethos and a new drive structure of the human being which *consequently* have a new thought type and form. Mach was, despite any pragmatic substratum of his theory, not enough of a "pragmatist" to integrate his various singular observations of this kind regarding the technical conditionality of knowledge progression into the *principle* cognition that it was not the rule "to clarify" the unknown through the known, but rather it was this new will to dominate nature, or more precisely expressed, this new valuation of the human being's control over nature, which sacrificed the organic-contemplative worldview of the Middle Ages.

This sovereign thought of control appears in theology (the voluntarism of the Scotists, of Protestantism, and particularly of Calvinism and Puritanism with their embellishment of the power will in God), in the theory of the human being as psychology (associative psychology), in the theory of the state and society (Bodinus, Machiavelli, Hobbes), and in politics (mercantilism and the cultivation of the absolute state and of the concept of sovereignty, the theory of balancing) *as originally* and *contemporaneously* as in the mechanistic theory of nature. Moreover, the formal atomism of the to-be-dominated object and the disintegration of the "objective form" idea appear contemporaneously in the natural cognition (thus nominalism), in views of the state and society (atomistic singularism and atomism), in biology (Descartes), and psychology (associative psychology and mosaic theory).[33]

[258] Let's suspend any historical investigation and investigate the broader reasons for Mach's epistemological errors.

There is a quite significant, but concealed, root of the formal-mechanistic worldview (and of the cultivation of its levels) which is not grounded in a specific circumstance of the history of research and in what is "first known," but rather which is grounded in the simultaneous *general-biological and practically* conditioned law of the cultivation of the *natural worldview* of the human being and thus grounded in natural perception. This root is historically constant, not variable. This root lies neither in the nature of the absolute thing itself, as naive materialism asserts, nor in pure logic or in transcendental logic and pure mathematics (Kant); but rather lies in the most universal laws according to which the *milieu structure* and *natural perception*, or rather, the natural thinking of this structure, are formed and must be formed for any possible living being, that is, any living being that possesses a natural perception and an environment. We could also say: the mechanistic worldview and its "schema" are *not the result of the experience* of our human meaning of chance, but rather are "*a priori*." However, they are apriori only for any possible experience that is "important" for the instrumental, spontaneous movements of a living being and thus are *motor-practically significant*, and are in no way apriori for *any* possible knowledge, for any possible intuition and thinking of the world in general. The mechanistic worldview is no rational apriori, in the manner that Kant means it, nor is it an apriori of the human being in general. Rather, it is *only* a *biologically relative* apriori, and is a "universally valid" apriori only in the limits of the relativity of the existence and being-thus of objects. It is likewise no apriori for the human being in general, and especially not for the ultimate and essential features that make the human being a "human being" (*animal rationalis*); rather, this apriori exists only for the human being as "*homo faber*" or as a practically intelligent animal. The mechanistic worldview is thus an apriori of the "practical intelligence" and the drive structure conditioning it, which simultaneously conditions the cultivation of our natural world of perception. The mechanistic worldview can become a conscious program not for the "natural" worldview but only for the scientific-artificial worldview when the dominance over nature is consciously and spiritually desired—as well as the most highly *valued* goal—and when the *principle determining the technical objective* constructs the *selection principle* for objects according to existence and being-thus, which should be recognized as independent variables of natural phenomena.

Let's clarify each of these statements in particular:

E. Mach overlooked the fact that the sense content of the physical-formal-mechanistic worldview and the realization of this sense content are inexpressibly far [259] removed from the meagerness of the facts that comprise the natural environment of human beings and their perception, and he subsequently overlooks the fact that the *laws of cultivation* and *order of foundation* of the givenness in *both* kinds of worldviews are exactly *the same.* He further fails to see that the schema of formal-mechanistic objectivity is nothing other than the *idealized* and *absolutized* law of the order of givenness of the natural worldview—but with the withdrawal of anthropocentrism and thus with the withdrawal of *specifically* human meaning organization and all of its specific characteristics and contents that are dependent *only* on it. This can be shown for the basic data, reality, value, time, movement, substance, force, and uniformity of events, and can also be shown for the role of the qualities, relations, forms, and gestalts here and there. It was E. Mach's principal error, which he shared with D. Hume and I. Kant, to hold that "elements" and "sensations" have a genesis and order in the origination of experience wherein they are first "given" in a purely "receptive" manner (i.e., in a manner wherein there is no impulsive attention that is directed to a particular schema and conditioning its coming-about), and only after this initial passive reception would the elements and sensations be processed and "united" into a gestalt-thing and other types of complex unities. The opposite is actually true: sensations and individual qualities are always "given *after*" a *schema* that is typically *pre*-given through spontaneous acts of the *impulsive attention*, a schema that is not sensible, but rather "intuitable." Sensations and qualities are given after a schema only insofar—in the case of identical stimulus conditions and strictly identical nervous centripetal processes—as they are the means "to fill out" this schema concretely, to occupy the schema's open or empty places; and only insofar as they are signs for the existence or nonexistence of the reality of this or any special schema that belongs to the *milieu structure* of an animal.[34]

Closely related and necessarily tied to Mach's aforementioned errors is another mistake: it is the data of direct intuition or direct "having" which grant fulfillment to the fundamental concepts of the mechanistic worldview, which are *subsequently* culled from the "elements" or are themselves such elements (e.g., Mach's space sensations or movement sensations). This is what on occasion he meant by his criticisms of the well-known lecture by Du Bois-Reymond regarding the "limits of natural cognition" (which was philosophically an entirely worthless discussion of outstanding physiologists and great rhetoricians); one cannot avoid responding with the epithet "Ignoramus" to the question: How do sensations like blue and sour come from brain molecular movements? [260] The only meaningful question is how we would come from our sensations to the concept of movement or, yet further, to the manifold concepts of the material unities. We would not be able to "climb up" to the concept of the movement of the smallest material elements to our sensations, but rather must "climb down" from this concept to our sensations as an ultimate given. In its intention to reject DuBois-Reymond's dogmatic mechanical theory of nature, this spiritual reversal of stating the problem by Mach has meant tremendous progress. However, when Mach in the same sentence discerned a way in which we would be able to go from pure "elements" (in his sense) to the phenomenon and concept of movement and to the remaining fundamental concepts of physics, he fell victim to a deep error.

To have to overcome these errors is the meaningful service of the pragmatic method, a method to which I will turn now.

4

The Pragmatic Method

The Methodological-Pragmatic Standpoint and Its Meaning for the Philosophical Interpretation of the Mechanistic View of Nature. The Kinds of Knowledge Concerning Nature.

Regarding Mach's element of sensualism, as we characterized and criticized it in the explication above, a host of physicists have proceeded along the lines of the formal-mechanistic natural view, physicists who are not philosophical pragmatists, but merely *methodological pragmatists*, and initially only for their special science, *theoretical physics*. Among these physicists, I would include Maxwell, Boltzmann, Lord Kelvin, and perhaps Einstein in the first period of his research, a period in which he discovered the special theory of relativity drawing from the Michelsonian attempt ("simultaneity").

The difference between this group of researchers and E. Mach is rooted in the fact that this group considers the formal-mechanistic reduction of natural appearances as a *necessity* and a *constant* necessity—and thus this group does not simply want to get rid of this reduction in order to have nothing left other than the facts of observation and measurement and their formulation in functional equations. But in stark contrast to the older rationalism, they do not view this reduction *as indisputable.* On the contrary, the reduction can grant, in accord with its standpoint for any epitome of natural appearances, an unlimited number of different "mechanistic models"—Maxwell's favorite word, through which anything could be "explained" equally well. Only their simplicity, force to stimulate discussion, and capacity to cause the strictest unity in the physicalistic worldview [261] could thus serve as a selection principle between these "models." This *methodological* and *epistemological standpoint* shares the constructive spirit with the older rationalism and realism, a spirit that dominated the epoch from Newton to Helmholtz, but with Mach and the positivists of the sensualistic kind the viewpoint shares the conviction that it does not assign the meaning to its "models" to depict a specific *reality* behind the natural appearances for which clarity would be necessary. The important tenet that is necessarily presupposed here is that the construction of a mechanical model for the clarification of natural appearances must *always be possible.* E. Mach cannot accept this tenet since, according to him, the primary qualities have no priority, neither an ontological priority nor a priority of givenness, over the secondary qualities, and the mechanical natural view should be only a historical accident. In relation to the theoretical-physicalistic theory of principles (and likewise the mathematical axiomatic), this new view of the validity of the formal-mechanistic theory of nature shares the general standpoint of the *philosophical* pragmatists that no clarity following from *factual* connections comes to the principles and axioms, and no "truth" for itself comes to the propositions formulating them, but rather that they would be cleverly chosen "implicit definitions," so chosen that the logically simplest "incontestable" connection comes to the discovered propositions and theories by virtue of the derivation from them. The same holds true for the supposed finalities [*Letztheiten*] of the "material" and "forces." They are and always remain relative to the explanation of the particular area of appearances with which chemistry and physics have to do. According to this epistemology, there is no "absolutely" final component of material. It is not our still-incomplete research that is responsible for the fact that we can declare no such "absolute" finality. Rather, "indivisibility" is itself a concept that is essentially relative to specific lawful relations and forces (molecules, atoms, positive and negative electrons, etc.).

The still little-understood *philosophical meaning* of the standpoint described above would indeed come to be known if *three questions* were answered, questions which the aforementioned researchers, who were actual physicists and not philosophers, in no way answered.

1. Why is (in contrast to E. Mach) a formal-mechanistic reduction of the natural appearances *always necessary*?
2. Why and how so is it *always possible*?
3. Why can it *never* be *clarified*?

Ad 1. If the *motoristic theory* of sense perception and of thinking is true, then we could *eo ipso* perceive and observe no state of affairs of nature [262] without the same object in that state of affairs determining some movement in our corporeal organism (i.e., it is in the broadest sense a "stimulus"), but this movement at the very least is the initial beginning of a "*counter-movement*," i.e., a motoristic behavior counter to this movement. Only then does this entire circular process, movement *and* counter-movement, correspond to the content of perception. All of the merely possible thoughts that we construct about nature for ourselves could therefore affect in a lasting manner only *the* movements and their possible connections that such counter-movements, or rather intuition and thought pre-sketches and schematas, are suitable to give rise to. Only as possible direct and indirect stimuli for our motoristic behavior can nature (as the state of affairs *hic et nunc*) become known as contingent being as such [*Soseiendes*].[1] The thought would thus not be in a direct *intentional* relation to the real in-itself [*Realen*] and real being-thus of nature, but would stand in a *causal* relation and in a relation to our voluntary and involuntary *motoristic behavior* to all movements that make any perception expected from the present perception possible. Whether the thought "corresponds" or does not correspond to the real which appears in the perception is totally irrelevant for this *output value* prompting us to such spontaneous movements through which we are able to master any possible stimulus movement effective for any exchangeable subject (and indeed to any variable purpose). The *necessity* of a formal-mechanistic natural explanation would have the *consequence* that we could perceive nothing and grasp nothing which does not give rise to a possible *impulse to movement* in us and which does not allow the expression, independent of its being and being-thus in itself, of a movement that gives rise to some impulse. The mechanistic reductive necessity of the natural appearances is fully secured in this double condition under which these objects of a *possible* experience alone could become for us. To grasp nature according to perception means, according to the presupposition of motoristic theories of perception and intelligence, nothing other than the invention of a mechanistic model according to which we can either bring forth or think as brought forth the natural appearances as strictly identical appearances.

More precisely and clearly than Maxwell, Boltzmann has laid out the same thoughts. In an essay on the methods of theoretical physics,[2] Boltzmann distinguishes between three central methods: (1) the empirical-inductive method [263] in which one proceeds from the facts of observation and so determines a concept, for instance the concept of mass, which excludes from a given body any successive characteristics that do not come into question in the research of the relational laws (e.g., the body's weight in changing heights over the earth in free fall); (2) the "Euclidean" method wherein one performs deductions from principles that are taken a priori as self-evident and cogent; and 3) the methods used in mechanics wherein one makes use of *arbitrary* presuppositions which do not need to be a priori and self-evident, but which are selected so that the known theories and facts become deducible as simply as possible. Accordingly, Boltzmann judges, "neither logic, nor philosophy, nor metaphysics ultimately decides whether something is true or false, but the *act* does. For this reason, I don't believe the achievements of technique are the irrelevant refuse of natural science. I take the technique to be the *logical proof.* If we had not obtained these practical achievements, we would not have known how one must conclude. Only those conclusions which have had practical success are right." Just as much to the point, the same view of physics is expressed in the following, a sentence cited by W. James from the physicist W. S. Franklin: "I think that the sickliest notion of physics, even if a student gets it, is that it is 'the science of masses, molecules and the ether.' And I think that the healthiest notion, even if a student does not wholly get it, is that physics is the science of the ways of taking hold of bodies and pushing them!" (*Science,* January 2, 1903).

The big difference between this theory and viewpoint and Mach and Avenarius's theory is already obvious from what has been said. While no sensualistic epistemologists are able to provide an account of *why* and how the fundamental phenomenon of *movement* has become the ultimate independent variable of any modern formal-mechanistic natural explanation—their final answer to this question is merely that "it was a historical coincidence"—the above view is capable of doing so. For movement in this view is not, as it is to E. Mach, a content of sensation, or rather an "element" under remaining and different sensations and "elements," but rather it is objectively (like stimulus movement) and subjectively (like motoristic innervation and like intellectual schema of movement) the highest and necessary *fundamental condition* for the entrance of merely *possible* sensations and perceptions.

However, it becomes readily apparent what the difference—and preference—of this view are from the old rationalism, a rationalism which holds a purely logical motive responsible for any special position of the appearance of movement and claims that it is one and the same to grasp nature *incontestably* and to grasp it *formal-mechanistically.* Instead of certainly falsely applied logical [264] principles, this view concerns a law conditioning the accomplishments of any possible perception on the part of some perceiving *living being,* which assumes that perception and no less the "intelligence" sketching the schemata of movement are *between acts,* acts between the *action* of nature upon a psychophysical subject and the *reaction* of this subject on nature.[3]

This theory has one important principle in common with I. Kant, namely, that the conditions of the *experience* of nature must contain in themselves the highest laws of *its explanation* through science. It is the most fundamental aspect of the *origin* of our experience of nature, and indeed of the *essentially lawful* origin (which is independent of any individual particularities of the experiencing subject), with which the explanation of nature as the *object* of this possible experience, and not as the thing in itself, has to comply. What is new is merely the insight that this experience is *motor-practically* conditioned in the given double sense of direction and that this is also the case for perception, the intuition of space and time, as well as for thinking; and this insight is new to such an extent that the ultimate meaning of the theory of any of Kant's principles finds a fundamentally new use. Also new is the *behavioral* determination *of the movement regarding time and space.* For Kant, and so too must Newton be considered here, the assumed movements of nature and their laws are to be thought so that the a priori synthetic judgments, which are possible through "pure" spatial and temporal intuition, are absolutely preserved. According to our theory, namely that space and time originally *derive* from the phenomenon of movement, that is, from the different dimensions of the epitome of possible movement, space and time must be thought in the reverse so that the assumed movements and their laws hold and remain thinkable.[4]

Ad. 2 According to this view of perception and thinking, it follows necessarily from the formal-mechanistic view of nature that there is *always* the possibility of finding some mechanistic model for the explanation of an event in nature. For this possibility must necessarily exist if the outer and inner phenomena of movement, phenomena in which all sensible data presents itself, possess no primacy of being, but rather possess a *primacy of givenness* or a primacy in the *order* of any remaining possible perceptual givenness. This primacy exists in a double sense. On the one hand, we know that temporal and spatial stretches, whose types are filled in through sensation datums, are no longer separable and differentiable for us, but are still given as courses of *movement* (or rather as changes), and are [265] given as such within *any* modality of sense. We also know that comparisons between such stretches, which, as dormant stretches yield no further experience of difference, are still able to yield differences, when they are given as courses of movements.[5] What is thus required for the sensation of movement is much, incredibly much less than what is required for any other impression that we can receive from nature in general. Secondly, the motoristic theory of sensation and perception maintains that the experience of a changed motoristic approach (in the form of a *drive* impulse) precedes, as a *condition*, any new perception, and furthermore, the order of this drive impulse precedes the purely sensual, modal, and qualitatively determinate material of perception (the order of the simultaneity and succession of the sensations, which is independent of the *content* of the sensation, makes it possible to *separate* the spatial position from the content of the sensation and the constant order of this spatial position from the content of the sensation—a *separability* that is constitutive for the becoming of any spatial intuition). That we must go back in principle to the natural appearances of some element as independent variables (of its possible experiencing), which in the order of givenness are *pre-given* in the *most unconditioned* and strictest lawfulness with any natural appearance, is obviously the case, since, in general, the essentially lawful order of the possible cognition and experience of nature—but not the order of the being of nature, which is always unknowable to us through possible observation—has to determine the goal and course of our *natural explanation.* A formal-mechanistic model must therefore *always* be *possible* as a cognitive ground for some natural appearance, since the phenomenon, from whose material all formal mechanisms are constructed with the help of relational thinking, namely the phenomenon of the appearance of movement, is *pre-given* in all other possible phenomena in the order of givenness.[6]

Neither an ontic "underlying" of the movement in relation to all other appearances, nor a supposedly better logical and mathematical "apprehensibility," nor "historical coincidence" and arbitrary "analogies" (Mach) make this formal-mechanistic explanation continuously possible; rather, it is *the law of the order of givenness* that makes it possible, the law that would remain in existence as nature would be created in itself and through itself.

[266] Ad. 3 The third thesis runs as follows: despite the necessity and absolutely guaranteed possibility of a formal-mechanistic natural explanation, this explanation could *never* be *indisputable*—only things such as the "unity of world image," and the simplicity, economy, purposiveness, and logical explanatory force of the chosen principles for the most irrefutable principles and theorems, i.e., for the ontic *factual* truth [*Sachwahrheit*] of entirely meaningless standards of the cognitive value of theories, allow and demand a choice among logically, and *similarly* good mechanistic models. This third thesis becomes reasonable, and even essentially and lawfully necessary, only from this view of the formal-mechanistic explanation of nature. This fundamental *non*-indisputability, the fact that any mechanistic model is replaceable by an infinite number of other models which accomplish *the same* explanation, would obviously be a priori excluded if the movement did enjoy an *ontic* or purely *rational* privilege, a privilege of "conceptuality," over other appearances in nature. Then the formal-mechanistic explanation would have to actually be a strictly *indisputable* explanation. Nevertheless, the matter is entirely different when the formal-mechanistic explanation demands and simultaneously makes *possible* a necessary and steadfast, but still *only* one "order

of *givenness*," an order thus not of nature as in itself of real objectiveness, but of nature "only" as an *object of possible experience* for any living being in general. Then it must give for any natural appearance *in concreto* not *one* mechanistic explanation, but rather an unlimited number of imaginable mechanisms which must be able to ground it; this is in principle no different from the fact that for the same technical goals, an unlimited number of "machines" could conceivably be *produced*. The ambiguity of the task of a mechanistic natural explanation is in this case the consequence of an *essential law of the order of givenness*. This law is not only valid for any enduring perception of a natural process, but is also the *chief reason* why the mechanistic model is able to be construed by thought; this model can from its onset be used to intervene in nature in such a practical manner that our conceived expectations constructed upon this model are fulfilled and satisfied through future perceptions. According to this theory, the mechanistic model is not and should not be a depiction of a *reality* extant outside of our consciousness or of a structural relationship of a formal kind, a reality whose "place" would be occupied by our human contents of sensation only in the subjective sense. The same model would be translatable in the languages and sensory systems of organs and the functions of organic beings, but would identically and clearly correspond to a formal-mechanistic structural relationship existing *in itself*. The mechanistic model is rather a pure *thought construction* which claims meaning not for the reality of nature and its real being-thus, but *only for its correspondence to our* [267] *expectations* and their accompanying future perceptions. However, what remain identical in the succession of models through which the same natural appearances can be construed as their consequence are the same *functional equations* which dominate all these models collectively and which enter singularly as abstract numbers in the space-time-movement quantities of any type. Only for these equations, and not for the formal-mechanistic models, does the demand for clarity exist as before.

The very same is expressed, only in different form, by this proposition: *no singular* natural appearance in its intuitive fullness of the being-thus can be determined indisputably by virtue of the givenness of an ideally complete formal-mechanistic explanation of nature, an explanation which allows us to dominate nature as we wish. There could still be an unlimited number of *fundamentally different* vivid natures that would be sufficient for the same ideally complete formal mechanistic natural explanation. The famous Laplacean world formula would make indisputable so few "of any" natural appearances that it would make indisputable *not even the simplest* of them. The formula contains only a compromised description of the position and point of nature in its concrete entirety which our spontaneous free will and movement would be able to channel as we wish, i.e., to avoid or give rise not to nature in itself, but rather to those *appearances* of nature which are in principle *accessible* to us.

Yet, does this theory, which at first glance appears bleak with regard to present-day theoretical physics' search for an *indisputable* natural explanation, mean something other than some essential aspect of what theoretical physics currently calls the "general theory of relativity"? Certainly, the point of departure for Einstein's theory and its specific mathematical-physicalistic accomplishments is fundamentally and essentially different from the tasks that any English researcher had taken up, and this different approach is in no way of the only *philosophical contribution.* What then does the proposition regarding the absolute relativity of any extensive or intensive measures of space, time, and movement from the "standpoint of the observer" in the four-dimensional space-time system mean other than what has been expressed differently and much better in the words: "Any natural appearance can be explained through an infinite number of mechanisms"? Only the Lorentz transformations bind these world images under one another into a *logical* unity which is itself obviously an absolute unity.

However, in still other respects, the above-mentioned view of the formal-mechanistic theory of nature reshapes most dramatically its *epistemological value.*

The formal-mechanistic theory fully and immediately disposes of any *ontologically* meant difference of the so-called primary and secondary qualities, but retains the difference (in [268] stark contrast to the sensualistic theory of Hume, Mach, and Avenarius) as a *difference in the order of givenness.* The extensive quantities (and the intensive-dynamic quantities, as far as they return to the direct, singularly measurable extensive quantities) possess no absolute constant. An extended "material" becomes increasingly irrelevant as a result of this different approach. Only a metaphysically dynamic construction of the material, a construction striven for by Leibniz, Kant, and von Hartmann, remains a speculative possibility.[7] The spatial and temporal gestalts, which the ancient mechanistic theory of nature disposed of (in contrast to Aristotle and the Scholastics, for whom the gestalts were genuine forms of *being*) and had to burden the "soul" with a productive force in order to account for the intuitable, phenomenal appearances of the spatial and temporal gestalts; the *ideel meanings* of natural objects, which modern nominalism in like manner attaches to the productive force of the human subject; and lastly the so-called *sense qualities* (insofar as their simplest content and their ideal lawfulness come into question): all of these reacquire their *ontological* validity. It still remains *a very significant philosophical problem* whether one sequesters all of these and the "primary" qualities together (as do Berkeley and Rickert) in the retainer for "consciousness in general," or whether one grants the given and possible "bodily images" in all of their phenomenal determinations an (ideal) existence beyond any "consciousness," an existence of the "objective appearance" of *forces*, forces that, no matter how one determines them speculatively, manifest themselves in these images in an existential relation to the living being.

This problem's resolution depends above all on whether one accepts or does not accept a *unique, super-individual,* and *super-species life agent* (in the sense of the problem of biology). If one is convinced that the old mechanistic biology is once and for all invalidated, and that the new "physicalism" of W. Köhler's, a physicalism that seeks to introduce a super-mechanistic gestalt lawfulness of being and happening into physics, is incapable, despite its valuable and partly successful critique of "vitalism"—insofar as the latter claims (Driesch) to introduce particular form-constructing factors (*Entelechien*)—of clarifying organic life according to its objective and subjective side, then one cannot avoid having to accept not a form-constructing life agent, but only a *functionally determining* life agent. If there are, however, pressing facts that compel us to accept a *super-individual and super-species unity* of this life agent classified richly in itself, a life agent that not only affects the life of the species, but also "learns" in the course of its manifold [269] production—the experiences of the organism whose structure develops its temporally newer and newer usefulness—then the *"images" of the body* must be granted an *existence independent* of human consciousness. This is an existence that is attached to the relation tying the inorganic "material" dynamic factors to the universal agent of life.[8] Thus, one thing ought to be certain: the intrinsically irreal, extensive bodily images undeniably require a vital, and not a "spiritual" or "conscious," subject to whom these images appear. This is the case since relative space, relative time, and relative movement are not relative to reason, but rather, as intuited image contents (refraining from their "*fundamentum in re*" in exclusively the "real" dynamic factors), are relative to the vital-soul and its ordered *goal-oriented drive-impulses.* Analogous to the manner in which the image of a meal arises before a hungry person in that person's fantasy, it would be to think that the universal urge [*Drang*] of life allows the bodily images to develop from itself by virtue of the immanent *productive forces of the imagination* belonging to every vital soul, when actually the inorganic force factors dynamically motivate it to that end. Although these "images" with all their determinations in this case would have an independent and lawfully ordered, although only "ideal," existence distinct from the human subject and consciousness, they remain vitally ontologically relative, ontologically relative even to the one universal life itself. Our and all animal perceptions and representations of these images would be only inadequate *side*-views and *partial* contents of *this objective, ideal image* world and would be dependent on the specific psychophysical organization of our or the animal's kind, and would correspond to the particular vital function and drive bundle that universal life transmits into our species and our particular organic being, so to speak.

Relative existence with regard to all-life [*Alleben*] ought to be ascribed to *space, time, movement,* and their lawfulness, an existence that is only an objectively ideal and not a real existence, but one independent from all organisms, including the human being. They exist as the *forms of the productive looking* [*Hinschauung*] of all-life. Space and (relative) time as dimensions of the *possible being* of movement and changes, or more precisely expressed, as dimensions of the possible being of the phenomenon of the *ordered image-change,* would be hereafter neither absolute and real existing things—as they were for Newton, who, as a metaphysician, viewed them as God's forms of intuition [270] ("*sensorium Dei*")—nor merely transcendental forms of intuition of the human being, as was the case for I. Kant. For space and time are not in general ever forms of intuition, but are rather primarily *forms of activity* whose outcome becomes intuitable after the fact. They are "forms" in which the *image-appearances* of forces and drives manifest themselves. Furthermore, space, time, and movement do not have an *absolute and real* existence; only the *forces* (force centers and fields) and the dynamic relations, which are the objective phenomenal forms of space, time, and movement, have an absolute and real existence. God's forms of intuition, in the Newtonian sense, can certainly *not* be absolutely and truly existent, insofar as God should be a spiritual and *merely* a spiritual being, as the theist Newton suggests. This is the case because forms of intuition (positive) are not spiritually relative, but are rather vital and drive-relative, and because (negatively) a purely spiritual subject can have no "sensorium" but rather only "essences" and "ideas," but not "images," as its correlates. A sensorium (and motorium) belong essentially to a, and *only* to a, *living being,* i.e., an "animal." However, space and time cannot be *merely* "human" forms of intuition, since the animals and most likely all living beings already "have" some kind of spatial and temporal, changing and moving environment (although the "being in the environment," as an ecstatic grasping or "having" of the environment, must still not mean a grasping as knowledge, much less "consciousness"). Not the human as human, i.e., by virtue of what *distinguishes* the human from the animal, but rather the human as *living being* has a spatial and temporal intuition, no matter how differently formed that intuition is from any of the animals. However, a form of intuition as exclusively a *subjective* form of intuition of the organism cannot be the space-time system, since following this presupposition the real forces, which posit inorganic nature as image-world, would not be derivable from the movements and their laws or from merely "subjective" data conditioned solely through the human organization; "a thing in itself" in its essence or being-thus is nonsense. The Leibnizian determination that space (and relative time) are a "*phaenomenon bene fundatum*" thus continues (contra Kant) to remain correct, despite how little Leibniz's idealistic-spiritualistic metaphysics is valid.

However, it should also be noted that any final form of pragmatism of the formal-technical view of nature with its three main principles of necessity, possibility, and the ambiguity of the mechanistic explanation, absolutely *demands* the existential relativity of the mechanism to a living being. This means, then, that a *mechanistic* explanation of the *living being*, of the life process, is *necessarily impossible.* Since the ambiguous mechanical models are only "construed" in order to make nature controllable and directable through a spontaneous vital movement, but are not "known" as ontic (and [271] clearly absolute) reasons and "causes" of the natural appearances, the collective epitome of these models, of the collective formal mechanism of nature, is in general existentially *relative* and its cognition is knowledge-*relative* to the possible (and relative) *free mastery of a living being.* Moreover, the order of givenness, namely the *pre*-givenness of movement and of the space-time system, which make this contrsuction possible, is existentially relative to the being of a living thing. Since it is an absolutely evident tenet of general epistemology that the X, to which an object A is existentially relative and its cognition is consequently cognitively relative, is never explainable through the same ontological and knowledge principles as the object A, but that, on the other hand, a cognition of X must be possible if the existential relativity of A to X itself should be still cognizable, it is then clear that "life" to which the formal nature-mechanism is existentially relative *cannot itself be clarified mechanistically.* The construction, which life executes for the sake of its spontaneous movement of mastery, cannot itself be further applied to life. This would only be possible and meaningful if the mechanism were only relative to a *rational, spiritual* subject, i.e., if logic and analysis necessarily demanded it. If the mechanism, aside from this existential relativity obvious to it, is also still relative to a sensory-motoristic vital system in general and to its "position as possible observer," i.e., if the mechanism is also still practically and biologically relative, then a mechanistic explanation of life is impossible. Life, however it is regulated according to autonomous biological laws, is *free and spontaneous movement* in contrast to the nature-mechanism.

If the metaphysical hypothesis of a super-individual life as an independent agent of at least a functional kind is rejected, then the formal nature-mechanism is a purely *subjective, human* construction for human, practical purposes. It is wholly different if the hypothesis is *accepted,* however. Then there is irrefutably no formal mechanism of nature that we are able to cognize in the ontological sense. Yet, (objective, ideal) formal-mechanistic systems are to all-life what physicalistic functions and organ systems are to the entire life of the organism. These systems construct only the *technique* of *natura naturans, neither* its *logic* nor even less its *teleoclinal* and teleological *sense*; they construct a middle-world by which image-creating life preconsciously creates and construes its corporeal images according to the stimulus of the inorganic force-factors. Nonetheless, the actual mechanisms are not indisputably absolute.

The *laws of nature of the formal-mechanistic structure,* insofar as they are actually "laws of nature" and not purely formal-mechanistic and kinematic essential connections [272] or derived from such connections, or are static and dynamic genuine laws which prescribe the conservation of certain system structures to the formal-mechanistic lawfulness of the event, are in this case only *laws of a statistical character* (laws of the greatest number, of the ώς έπί τὸ πολύ in Aristotle's sense). They are objective possibilities of the event regarding the *rules of probability.*[9] This result, which present-day physics has already meaningfully approached at the very least in relation to any "natural law" of a formal-mechanistic character (i.e., in relation to any law which has structurally the immediate temporal consequence of the appearances and spatial contact of the event), corresponds quite closely with what *pragmatic* epistemology teaches about the origin of our belief in formal-mechanistic "laws of nature." It argues that this belief is justifiable neither deductively nor empirically (Mill), and is not a condition for an objective sequential order of appearances in accord with the deduction of the principles from the idea of "possible experience" (as Kant would say), but rather is a mere consequence of the *selection of the uniformity in time* already co-determined through the needs of the *living* being and its drive structure, a uniformity in time according to which *environment*-things can be formed out against the world and can be there so that they may be a possible perception for the living being. Only the *essential connections* of mathematics and kinetics, as well as the physical (static and dynamic) *gestalt* laws are then purely *rational.*[10] Everything regarding what was called a remunerative "law of nature" in the classical time period (Descartes-Newton-Helmholtz) is a law of the "objective *coincidence.*" If one rejects the hypothesis of all-life and is content with a subjective, idealistic pragmatism, then the "laws of nature" obviously mean even much less. They are then nothing more than *subjective restric-*

tions [273] of expectation constructions in the form of practical "principles of work" according to which nature is to be grasped with regard to certain perceptual givennesses in order to experience [*erleben*] certain other perceptions.

Finally, it is clear that what is *philosophically* most important, more important than what has already been said, is that neither the formal-mechanistic laws of nature nor the laws of nature of the formal-mechanistic structure have an *ontic* meaning. They are simply that which is *biologically and practically relative* [*geltungsrelativ*]. They simply allow, by virtue of an ideal knowledge [*Kenntnis*] of any possible law of nature of this kind, a *playroom* of an infinite number of *different* "natures" based on content, essence, image, and gestalt, and they determine not a single one of these natures indisputably. *Pure,* apractical, and biologically nonrelative "laws of nature," if they are still to be called as such, are exclusively (1) the formal-ontological laws that found pure logic, (2) the laws of analysis and (perhaps) the laws of geometric topology, (3) the physicalistic, chemical, and biological *gestalt* laws of nature, and above all the dynamic gestalt laws (since the static gestalt laws are likely clarified from the dynamic gestalt laws), and (4) the *material essential connections* (connections of ideas and original phenomena) that *restrict* the *possibility* of the contingent and arbitrary "images" of the concrete body [*Körper*].

Nonetheless, these things are the genuine objects of a natural philosophy, i.e., of a purely apractical natural cognition. Without the addition of these objects to the formal-mechanistic construction of nature, which is in principle *not* irrefutable, our knowledge can *never* become *certain.*

But the addition of natural philosophy (which already is found in much of present-day theoretical physics) still does not make our knowledge of nature utterly indisputable. Two things must be brought into natural science and natural philosophy in order to complete, at least ideally, their indisputability.

The first is the *study of nature,* which concerns itself with the contingent *individual image contents* themselves, image contents which are given to us from the objective-ideal images and which can only be known [*kennen*] in different degrees of adequacy without "grasping" or "understanding" them, without being able to "clarify" them. Obviously, every single electron is an individuality, [274] a unique "image" just as the earth or Germany is. However, for the human being a "study" of the electron will be forever impossible. Of the stars, there is a genuine study and, apart from the planet Earth upon which we ourselves live and which we "study" in geography, there is to a greater extent merely the study of the Moon and perhaps even of Mars. Although there is for every star a *possible* study, this is for us humans still unobtainable. The world of the stars appears to us ultimately only as an "example" of general mechanistic, physicalistic, and chemical lawfulness. Our study of nature is quite restricted, since it is conditioned by location in an entirely different sense than natural science and natural philosophy are. The person who always regards the bodily-images as objective-ideal existents, and not simply as mere symbols of unknown stimulus-sources for conscious human sensations as "idealism" and "critical realism" do, must also concede the objective possibility of a study of every electron and every particle of the furthest nebula.

Nevertheless, even with this, nature would still not be indisputably grasped. Entirely beyond any natural science of a formal-mechanistic character, beyond any natural philosophy and any study of nature, lies a fourth knowledge relation, and grounded in this knowledge relation is a relation between the human being (and every living being) and nature as "*natura naturans.*" This fourth type of knowledge is a purely dynamic and emotional *understanding* of nature as a field of *expression* of image-creating all-life—image-creating on the basis of dynamic, material factors and of the eternally *singular* "urge," an urge of which these "factors" are but partial functions and which is nothing less than all-life itself. The eternally generating, dynamic originary ground is disclosed exclusively to human feelings [*Gemüte*], to *sympathy*, and in the highest cases to *empathy* and *shared activity* with their forces as forces (not their conceived determinations) through the "characters" grasped in the images. Neither reason nor sense, neither the grasping of ideas nor the display of the original phenomenon can become aware of it.[11]

Nature is or can be *clear* to us only through the ideal cooperation of having, knowing, consciousness, cognition, grasping, essential intuition and idea thinking, explaining, recognizing, and the comprehending, understanding sympathy with nature as a pan-physiognomic field of expression of the eternal urge and its characteristic fundamental directions.

[275] In order to complete our list of the different kinds of cognition of nature, we would have to add the metaphysics of nature, which has only recently come to life again, to this list. Its task would be first to give a *synthesis* of all the other aforementioned kinds and manners of knowledge of nature and, based on the material essential ontology of nature and its two main areas, namely living and dead nature, to investigate which attributes are to be granted hypothetically to the *ground of all things* for the sake of *nature.*

Two questions would be central here. First, how do the *force-centers* and force fields, which we come across as the ultimate real subjects of any physicalistic judgment, behave, and how do the gestalts and essences that we find realized through them relate to the *ens a se* as the ultimate ideal and real principle of nature? Second, how does the *one universal driving force of life* relate to the *ens a se*, the universal driving force that the philosophy of the organic world impels us to accept? The possible answers to these questions cannot be fully developed here.[12]

Important for our purposes in this problematic is something else. We would like with the above enumeration of the four different kinds of "knowledge" of nature that fully differ from the formal-mechanistic natural explanation—namely (1) the philosophy of nature, (2) study of nature, (3) understanding of nature, and (4) metaphysics of nature—to indicate *here* that the more and more precise *limitation of the validity of the formal-mechanistic explanation* and the very gradual, growing insight of the *existential relativity* of its object (up to any final form of its restriction that we have put forward) have opened our eyes to the independent being of these four different cognitive tasks that we have of nature. This has become quite clear.

The formal-mechanistic view of nature has assumed from the outset of its arrival in the modern era an *absolute and metaphysical interpretation* of what is of cognitive value and once this interpretation was disclosed (for which I. Kant deserves tremendous credit) there has been an increasingly underestimation its cognitive *relativity*. The direct consequence of this mistaken interpretation regarding what is of cognitive value was that during extensive periods in history the four different kinds of our knowledge of nature would no longer be of concern and to a greater extent considered to be of no genuine value. This mistaken interpretation of the formal-mechanistic view of nature was that it had fully closed any path or footbridge to the philosophy of nature, to the study of nature, to the understanding of nature, and ultimately to the metaphysics of nature.

Who would want to strive for *pure natural cognition* of an apractical kind, if any *gestalt* or form of nature, and even [276] the entire realm of *teleoclinic* behavior in nature, is regarded as what is originally *brought into* nature "anthropomorphically" through the production of the "human" soul—as every metaphysical-absolute interpretation of this view of nature believes it to be, and as Kant still believes it to be, despite traces of better insight?[13] And how are you to investigate in a material *essential ontology of nature* the intuited *primordial phenomenon* and the non-intuited *ideas*, ideas that are realized in the process of becoming natural through the general technique of the formal mechanism for our experience, when you—by virtue of the mistaken ontological or purely rational interpretation of the mechanism—believe that these essences and ideas are only made by human beings as inductively obtained concepts or are dependent on the organization of the senses or the brain? And how are you to do this if the natural laws of the formal-mechanistic structure are regarded not as static laws, but rather as factually necessary *real laws* preceding the creative event—in truth the exact opposite is the case—laws whose alleged forces realize only "contingently" this or any gestalt, this or any originary phenomenon and ideas? Neither an *ideal-genetic morphology of nature* nor an *essential ontology of nature* will have to reckon with some kind of understanding or interest. How is it possible to come up with the idea of autonomous vital laws if the existential relativity of the formal mechanism of the living being and its spontaneous self-movement are overlooked and "non-things" (Leibniz) such as absolute, infinite space, absolute infinite time (already in physics), and absolute movement are held to be real—instead of recognizing the life-relativity of these objects?[14]

How is it possible to muster the earnestness for a genuine and lovingly devoted *exploration of concrete nature* if concrete gestalts such as landscapes, and any quality, color, tone, and smell are regarded as peculiar "effects" that an absolute natural mechanism triggers in an entirely mystical manner in our nervous system or in a so-called "soul," and if all concrete unified constructs of nature are regarded as merely subjective human syntheses? For if the imagination, supported by not a single argument, is abandoned, nature would be nothing other than the "reality of laws" (W. Windelband, H. Rickert) and the reality as an individual thing would already be an object [277] of history.[15] The entire realm of the *individuation levels of nature* and the very different existential relativity of different inorganic, organic, ensouled, and spiritual "individuals," which are fundamental problems of philosophy, completely disappear under the presupposition of an absolute mechanism. The same holds true for the *levels of freedom* and the degrees of freedom of the event up until the human willing act. The *study of nature,* i.e., the adequate cognition and description of the objective, ideal, consciousness-independent images of nature and their concrete relations, is no mere "preceding" task with the aim of the cognition of laws. No image and not even the minutest aspect of an image is clearly determined through natural laws of a formal-mechanistic character. The idea of the Laplacean world-formulation is not only unable to be realized; it is an *absurd* idea and rests on an *absolute* interpretation of a merely relative, formal-mechanistic natural explanation. Moreover, it is not the case that the study of nature is merely anthropomorphic cognition. Rather, the minimal knowledge [*Kenntnis*] and study that we can possess of nature is one of the most lamentable limits of our human cognition.

The same also holds true for the *aesthetic values and forms of nature,* which are not merely "subjective" or gifts of our emotive heart. Rather, our sense and our feeling are still small and narrow for this objective, truthful, extant, ideal beauty and natural art, even if they could be broadened through conscious culture and edification. The non-consideration of these aesthetic values in natural science is fully understandable,[16] just as understandable and necessary as the non-consideration of the *goal*-laws of the event, of the *images* and *gestalts* and the so-called secondary *qualities*. The cognition of any of these object determinations does not help the human being to have *mastery* over things! However, for pure and *philosophical* natural cognition, all of these determinations are equally very ontically existent. Within the world-ground—not in the grotesque-comical and exaggerated "filling" of the human bosom—there must be something that makes these value and our [278] limited sense and our so limited feeling for them—their perfection *and* our limitation—understandable to us. The dreadful *alienation from nature* of the human being, an alienation which has given rise to the ontological and absolute misinterpretations of the formal-mechanistic view of nature, has above all prevented a true cognition of the *objectively aesthetic and constructive laws of nature*. "Ethics," no less, which is specifically human and spiritually divine, is not something that hangs there freely in the air without basis and foundation in a "value-free" nature. An ethics has its basis in a *universal axiology* and characterology. The ethical values are only the highest peak of the objective value order known to us, an order that reaches back just as deeply as the order of being itself, however little it is identical to it.

Moreover, the "determination" and the *end* condition of the temporally formed, rhythmatized world-event is, as quantum theory suggests, determined for the course of the event in the exact same way as is the *beginning* condition. Furthermore, it is only the *practical* motive of modern human beings, resulting in the domination of nature, which has led us to regard (for the sake of clarity) events exclusively in the direction of a beginning → end condition. Hence, we can obviously control nature for the sake of the directionality of the flow of our life only insofar as nature is determined in its course through the practically directed, graspable *causa efficiens*. And insofar as nature is *not* so determined, we must patiently wait to see what happens! Nonetheless, who wants to "demand" or "postulate" that nature obeys this practical need of ours? If we accept forces in order to grasp the realization of the laws of this type, as quantum theory must demand it, then we must effectively imagine the same vertically with regard to absolute time. For this reason, there in no way exists an absolute difference between the ontic, inorganic elementary event and the elementary, functional vital event which modern form-vitalism, e.g., that of H. Driesch, appears to accept. The predominant mechanical impression of the inorganic causality is just as anthropomorphic as the predominant teleological impression of the vital-event. Nature in its self-being [*Selbstsein*] probably knows nothing about the mechanical or the other teleological impression. Nature knows *neither* purely mechanical, effective causes *nor* purposes. What distinguishes the vital realm from the inorganic realm lies in a different direction than in the ontic lawful structure of the elementary event. If the *"determination" of the human being* may always be a determination elevated above all other finite things, then *every thing* also has *its determination,* its "becoming what you are." The absolute and ontic interpretation of the formal-mechanistic view of nature has so completely lifted human beings out of nature, has so completely *uprooted* [*entheimaten*] and alienated them that they, as if drunk, begin to waver between a ridiculous materialism, which reduces them [279] to animals, and spiritualism, which is just as ridiculous, and rips them from any brotherhood with nature. Already for Descartes, human souls are fundamentally pure, spiritual thinking-souls [*Seelendenkpünktchen*] which are dropped down from "above," as if by rope, from a purely mechanical everything, from God! Is there a more grotesque, a more naturally adverse representation?

An *understanding* of nature, a theory of expression and character, and a *pan-physiognomic of nature* obviously become an utterly absurd beginning if the conditionality of the formal-mechanistic theory of nature is not recognized, if one, some, or all of its conditionality is overlooked. For a formal-mechanistic theory, then, any expression, i.e., the (proven) *first*-given of what we experience in all things, what the primitive and the child experience exclusively "at first," is clearly nothing but "appearing" [*Schein*], it is merely the projective empathy of our human bosom [*Menschenbusenfülle*] and our drive-impulse in the being of the thing. There is only one possibility: we could reach back to this "appearing" in its original place, our omnipotent heart, and distrust the entire sense and sense-laws of our *heart* [*Gemütes*] (which would include the total underestimation of all intentional feelings, of all kinds of fellow feelings, vicarious feelings, and affective union [*Mit-, Nach-, Einsfühlung*] and its cognitive authority). Instead of precisely investigating the limits of this capacity of ours as well as its efficacy [*Leistungskraft*] in comparison to the different types of things (types of animals, plants, inorganic matter) and their inner being [*Innesein*] and being-for-itself (which everything that is "real," i.e., which is more than a pure "object" for another thing, *must* possess, whether or not we humans are able to recognize this quality in its "expression"), instead of investigating the elementary *essential laws of "experience"* (inner-condition [*Innenstand*]) and *"phenomena of expression,"* which are no more specifically human and inductive than the elementary, biologically essential connections, but which certainly have a far greater *ontological* breadth of validity than the static laws that we call "natural laws" of the formal-mechanistic type, any direct expressive understanding by virtue of these laws is not thought to be an understanding, but is regarded as an apriori *mis*understanding and *delusion*. There is no concern for a culture, for a broadening or an education of our empathy and our understanding. Or it is thought that the projective affective unity of our real experiences, or conclusions by analogy, which still *presuppose* the alien-soul-sphere and these laws as material premises, if they are not to end in emptiness, lead us to the acceptance of the existence of other souls. The contradictory possibility—which is obviously not going to be accepted without very specific reasons—that all things and also the so-called dead things in principle possess comprehensible inner-conditions [*Innenzustände*] and only our force of understanding rejects this for the sake of the myopia of our aforementioned heart (already in the [280] plants)—can never be genuinely taken into consideration by a theory as mistaken as the formal-mechanistic theory of nature. It is so readily obvious that what has led to these particular opinions has nothing to do with investigations or reasons, but rather originates from non-epistemological causes of a historical and social nature, that there is no need to mention this. What consequences this radically skeptical disposition of the heart (*Gemütshaltung*) has brought forth and what this skepticism must mean for the relationships between humans, and between humans and the whole life of nature, is a matter I have dealt with elsewhere.[17]

Finally, a *metaphysics of nature*[18] would have to become entirely superfluous, if the formal-mechanistic-technical view of nature claimed to capture the absolute being of nature or to be the only possible means of cognizing nature. Or, as Kant had mocked Haller and his "innerness of nature": nature exists from nothing other than "outer relations" which open themselves up to "mathematical analysis." This is quite the opposite of Goethe's question, "Is not the core of nature the human heart?" Mathematical physics is regarded as the prototype for any cognition of nature. The practical-formal-mechanical construction of ambiguous models (for the purpose of dominating nature), which poses itself as "cognition" of the being of nature, can and must reject any metaphysics of nature simply because this type of construction regards itself as already occupying, inappropriately, the position of a metaphysics of nature. Where it did not do this, the old view took refuge in a consciousness-idealism of a very different kind and in an abstruse epistemology which surrenders the meaning of the words "cognition" and "knowledge," and desires "to make" any cognition into one that is creating the object (Cohen), forming a formless material of intuition (Rickert), creating from *ficta* (Vaihinger), or is a clarifying naming of the already cognized (Schlick). If one is, however, clear about the different, *irreplaceable kinds of cognition* of nature and about their order of validity in the definitive metaphysics of nature, if one is above all clear about the exhibited limits of all formal-mechanistic explanations of nature, their origins, and their reasons and motives, and if one is clear about the existential relativity of their object to a spontaneous, practical living being in general, then suddenly *greater free space* is opened up *for a metaphysics of nature.*

[281] This completes the analysis of the *relative correctness* of pragmatism's epistemology, which has also shown how pragmatism has *philosophically* been overcome.

According to everything which has been said up to this point, the knowledge of nature has become fruitful and powerful for the *practical* life of the human being and for the realization of the human being's higher *vital* values[19] and of the *biologically conditioned* objectives derivable from these values only *insofar* as it organizes itself in a formal-mechanistic manner.

However, two questions still remain open: Is this fact itself only a *metaphysical coincidence*? And is it a metaphysical coincidence that, conversely, the knowledge of nature becomes *purer* and more theoretical *the less* it is able to accomplish this mastery goal, this eternally pressing need for power and life for the "orientation" of the human being in the time-space system? Is it a metaphysical coincidence that any purer or purest knowledge, any "*theoria*" in the sense of the Greeks, primarily begins when the pure, spiritual soul of the human being, or better, the pure, spiritual subject in the human being, begins to turn resolutely away from the power drive and the valuing and deliberative assessment of any domination over the thing and turns, in a wholly "indifferent" manner in respect to that which is practical and that which concerns the vital values, to the *pure love* of the world and any possible fact-content [*Sachgehalt*] and value content (*amour pur*), or to speak with Leibniz, "*Je ne méprise presque rien*"? Are we to answer these questions by suggesting this metaphysical direction in thought to be mere coincidences of the human organization, or are these questions grounded in the *ground of all things* and in the *ontology of the kind of being itself*?

Whoever desires to ground this highest and ultimate problem of pragmatic science *and* of apractical, pure theoretical philosophy must raise a question that is perhaps one of the most enigmatic in any or every philosophy: the *question regarding the essence of* "*reality*," or the particular and undoubtedly unique and peculiar kind of being that we humans indicate by the word "reality." If it were to be shown through the investigation of this question that *being-real* is *originally given in the resistance* that some inner and outer factual complex asserts against our striving (drive and desiring) impulse, that the purely theoretical knowledge relation to nature does not convey the *original experience of the real* and the experience of the actuality of the thing, but rather only our fighting and *dominating relation* to nature does, then our pragmatically conditioned knowledge of nature would be *founded* in an *original phenomenon* of the ontic world. And then a *theory of the essence of reality* and of the *having of reality* would make possible the technique and method of spirit through which we [282] can complete what E. Husserl has called the "phenomenological reduction." The phenomenological reduction is a spiritual disposition that Husserl himself knew how to carry out exquisitely in his investigations, but he was totally unsuccessful with the descriptions and theory because they led him to an utterly unclear and, insofar as it is given, a certainly incorrect theory of reality: a being-real that was defined as having a place in time. Only by disconnecting from the acts and psychic functions which give the reality-moment is it possible to introduce a *refraining* from reality, a leaving-open and bracketing-out of the being-real, which Husserl viewed correctly as the precondition for any cognition of essences, as the purest theoretical disposition in general. It thus requires two completely different things: (1) a *technology* of the cognition of essences, and (2) a *methodology* of the cognition of essences. The technology, however, which I have developed thoroughly in a different work, demands not only the *disconnection* of the acts giving the reality-moment, but also the bracketing-out of any impulsive love of the being and value-being of all things which replaces the mastery relation with a new and *spiritual* fundamental relation to the world (*amor intellectualis*). It also demands a spiritual and soul technique of transitioning the energy of activity that was anchored in the mastery relation to nature (which is ultimately always the drive energy, since acts and functions are in themselves not calibrated activities and primarily obtain a calibrated energy or "activity" through attachment to the drive impulses)[20] to the *loving relation* to nature, i.e., the highest condition of any pure objective behavior devoted to the thing itself, a condition first and foremost of "pure" theoretical behavior.

In this respect, the theory of reality is just as much the fundament of any pragmatically determined kind of knowledge as it is of pure and, in a very specific sense, *philosophic* knowledge.

Before we say anything more about this point, we should first turn to the question of how the philosophical problem of *perception* and *sensation* relates to the results that we have obtained in this chapter regarding the interpretation of the *meaning of the mechanical view of nature.*

5

Concerning the Philosophy of Perception

The drive-motor theory of sensation and perception, which as a comprehensive theory was first worked out in different forms and under different presuppositions by *pragmatically* inclined philosophers such as Maine de Biran, Bergson, and Münsterberg, [283] contains a series of incontestable *elements of truth.* This theory could be proven to be true quite extensively in the multi-branched positive sciences which occupy themselves with the animal and human perceptual worlds and the conditions of their origination. For us, the proof depends on selecting a few characteristic *examples* from a whole host of the particular facts that phylogeny, ontogeny, comparative sensory physiology, the physiology and psychology of animal and human sensory functioning, and the pathology of perception have collected, still with little standardization. These examples are able to illustrate any element of truth, and simultaneously demonstrate the *coincidence* of the results of fundamentally different types of research taking place independently of one another in the *theory of the drive-motor conditionality of sensation and perception.*

The fundamental attitude with which any theory of the drive-motor conditionality of perception must begin can be summarized in the following sentences: the sensory functions and their accompanying organs are not instruments of an interested, theoretical knowledge of nature, but are regulatory and modifying procedures of our *actions* with them. Furthermore, they are not isolated or separate from the entire organism and its collective physiological economy of life—these sense functions, in contrast to all other organs and functions of an organism, do not impart a "knowledge" of nature that is fully indifferent to and uninterested in the organism, its preservation and unfolding self and kind, a knowledge of nature unusable for its reactions—rather they serve, just as *any other* organ and function and in the innermost functional *unity* and connection with them, the exact same *teleoclinic entirety of meaning,* the *optimal life course* of the organism. The so-called "content" of perception as a functional, unified act, in contrast to the sensory functions (seeing, hearing, smelling, touching, etc.), is neither an immaterial positive "reflection" of the being-thus of the environmental thing, as Aristotle and the Scholastics accepted in their theory of "*species sensibilis*," nor is it a distinct and proportional causal consequence of physical and chemical stimuli that exist in the brain or in the so-called soul-substance. It is never a mere "complex of sensation," but rather, it is nothing other than an ever-changing, specific aspect brought about by physical acts; it is nothing other than a *partial content of the intuited being-thus of the thing itself.* However, a being-thus, existential, or effect-relative objectiveness belongs to these things only insofar as they are "environmental things" (or "environmental processes"), i.e., they belong to the existence and being-thus of the organism's type and individual being-thus. This objectiveness is fundamentally and completely different from the objectiveness of the physical world. [284] However, perception takes place through some degree of the involuntary-spontaneous behavior of the organism, behavior that appears psychically in passive *attention* and in *drive* impulses that adjust attention, and it appears physiologically in *motor* innervations, always co-determined and never merely proportionally, which are indisputable consequences of stimuli and are not simply linked to some sensory process. Without some degree and some direction of *drive attention,* without *value*-grasping, and without the beginning of a *motor* process, *a perception,* no matter how simple it may be, *can in no way take place.*

These statements stand in stark opposition to the traditional view and theory of perception in the whole of Western philosophy. Rationalism, as well as sensualism, had for centuries regarded sensation as something only "receptive," thought a stimulus *effect* had to be proportional and qualitatively similar to the *stimulus,* thought the perception and its content *had to be composed of sensations*—but also simultaneously saw a "cognition capacity" and also "the underlying cognitive capacity" in the sensation.

In what follows, let us attempt, without calling upon ontogeny and phylogeny, to lay out the penetrating *changes* that our theoretical view of perception and sensation has discovered.

Perception and Sensation

The insight that has led to the most meaningful reversal in philosophical thought—and is also recognized for its far-reaching consequences—is that as phenomenal constructs, there are no "pure," i.e., strict stimulus-proportional, sensations; there are no additional "isolated" sensations, i.e., sensations beyond the functional, unified perceptual act; and the particular content of a perception has nothing to do with the "sensations" that are simultaneously present. We will begin with the last point.

1. Perceptual Content, Sensation, and the Trans-Conscious "Corporeal-Image"

There is no doubt that what are called "sensations" in ordinary language are particular changing, experienced conditionalities that we experience as modifications to our *lived body* and what is directly related to it. These sensations are the so-called organ-sensations and feeling-sensations, and the sensation of touch is the earliest of the types of sensation; this type is originally related *objectively*, because natural consciousness accepts on the basis of vague experience that the touched object stands in strict spatial and temporal contact with a part of our bodily organism. [285] Everything else, what philosophy and psychology still call "sensation," is not experienced as sensation, but rather is a *hypothetically* posited thought construct. To call a tone, a color, and even the taste or smell of a fruit a "sensation," or to accept that these qualities, which are given to us initially as characteristics of the thing, must be sensed in order to be had, are claims which are totally foreign to natural consciousness. *Sensed* sensations are thus something other than sensations *invented* according to the sensed sensations and according to their "exemplars."

But what led to both the hypothetical and conceptual *expansion* of the original concept of sensation? Strangely enough, it has never been made clear that what gave the primary impetus for this expansion was not particular experiences, or experiments of either a physiological or psychological kind, but rather a metaphysical hypothesis about absolute and "true" natural processes taking place outside of our consciousness, namely the *mechanical view of nature in a metaphysical setting.*

The first figure who thought up a hypothesis of this kind, who first put forward the theory of the subjective and secondary nature of qualities as a consequence of his metaphysics, was Democritus. He rejects that there is an original *remote perception* [*Perzeption*] of the thing and of its visual being-thus; that is, there is without a doubt a sharp *distinction* for the natural being between how the *perception* of the being-thus of the thing is experienced and the sensation. Democritus insists that we must understand and explain the "apparent" remote perception of the thing in a manner analogous to our understanding of how tactile impressions occur, impressions having—apparently—a content that is identical to both the thing determination (such as softness, hardness, smoothness, roughness) *and* the related bodily sense organ, but which is merely a peripheral layer. Thus, the original act of seeing experienced as distant perception "should" be thought here *according to the analogy of the tactile* process; and this ought to be the case because the specific qualities that the metaphysically real entities, the "atoms," possess, such as absolute firmness, rigidity, hardness, and impenetrability, are only idealized tactile qualia. The atomistic materialism and the rejection of a spatiotemporally distant perception of the imagistic being-thus of the thing, the reflective expansion of the concept of sensation regarding color and tonal sensations, etc., and the theory of secondary qualities are thus original logical connections and have still to this day never been separated from one another, thus allowing the reappropriation of the atomic-mechanistic theory of nature in modernity.

Serving as convincing evidence for the power of a mere thought *tradition* is the fact that the sensory physiology and psychology of today are so rarely aware [286] of this origin or its concept of sensation and stimulus. The cloak of this tradition continues to conceal the *philosophical problems* of perception and sensation, despite tremendous change in our physicalistic, physiological, and psychological notions. Our physics has long ago thrown on the scrap heap notions such as "extended substance," the distinction between primary and secondary qualities in the ontic sense, as well as absolute space, absolute time, and absolute movement, i.e., sheer things that are logical presuppositions for this view of perception and sensation. Psychology has shown that between objective space, whether it be Euclidean or non-Euclidean, and our phenomenal perception of space there exists nothing other than *indisputable* ordered relations. This intuited space is just as *alien* to physics as are color and tone. Psychology has also shown us that all modal sensual qualities [*Sinnesqualitätenkreise*] carry in themselves the phenomenal distinction between "actual" and "apparent," which was earlier only made for gestalt, distance, and duration; and that sensation content and object quality at no time conceal themselves phenomenally, not even in the simplest touch where the given hardness or weakness of an object (e.g., one grasped under a paper whose surface we touch) is always phenomenally *different* and *simultaneously* different in a single experience from the tactile sensation that is a limit case of a sensation organ. The manners of appearance that D. Katz has demonstrated for the colors are demonstrated in analogous manner for tactile phenomena (Katz), tones, and smells (Henning), and it is not possible here to distinguish between the central and peripheral condition factor.

Despite this and other refuted cognitions, the familiar thought schema of Democritus is still so powerful that an entire series of *prejudices* is still quietly held to be true:

(α) "Red," "hard," etc., are *merely* the contents of our senses and are not *similarly original object determinations*. They are constructed from the same elementary, psychophysically indifferent, simple qualities and are constructed in such a manner that the experienced content of sensation *never* corresponds with the simultaneously experienced object determination.

(β) The qualities themselves are "subjective" and are "produced" by the nervous system, by the soul, or both together, where the *sensing* of the quality (hearing, seeing, etc.) is only dependent upon the nervous functions.

(γ) The corporeal object image in the objective filling of its intuited being-thus, the object of intention of perception as a functionally unified act, *exists* from "sensations" or from qualities that are *only given* as contents of sensations and *are* only such. [287]

(δ) The physicalistic stimulus processes would be related to these conceptually expanding, merely sensational qualities principally as *real, effective* causes relate to effects and, since the corporeal images should "exist" out of these qualities, the physicalisitic stimulus processes would also be related to the corporeal images *themselves*. As a consequence, that which is beyond our conscious-having would in no way exist as objective appearances *independent* of their becoming perceived, but instead would be replaced by movement processes of a different kind (air vibrations, air waves, etc.) that we would falsely consider as such to be something real.

Of these peculiar prejudices, not a single one is valid. Let's attempt to resolve them.

One of the first mistakes is to let the corporeal image or the imageness and thus the intuited being-thus of the physical body be assimilated entirely into the perception or into a "possible" perception. The corporeal images are, however, in their fulfillment of being-thus thoroughly *transcendent* to human "consciousness of something"; they *can* only inadequately, partially, and *also* "*in mente*" exist as objects [*Objekt*]. Certainly, anything and everything which can be represented and perceived in a body is *merely* "image" and image-determinateness. This holds for extension, spatial and temporal characteristics, gestalt, color, hardness, etc., in fully the same manner. Movement as the transformation of place or change of place of an identical being-thus is *only* an image and nothing other than an image.

We speak of an "*image*" or "objective appearance" for the purpose of making two distinctions. In contrast to singularly real—i.e., what is not an appearance or image—"forces," the images are their manifestations (and are the same for metrical, spatial-temporal relations as well as for extension and gestalt); "images" are thus accordingly *transcendent of consciousness* and are fully *irreal*. In contrast to the contents of perception, the "images" are their *transcendent of consciousness objects*, and thus never assimilate into such contents of perception. It is still a much greater error to regard the "images" only as objects of possible consciousness and to reject (as does "idealism") their real foundation in forces. a concept that the resistance we experience to our will and striving grants us and which is no purely intellectual operation; or to regard the images (as is the case with all forms of "critical realism") as effects of movement on an organism, its nervous system, its "soul," or its "consciousness." That these images could be founded in forces is a notion that can only be conveyed through the resistance the will and striving experience and is not graspable by any purely intellectual operation. A great deal of the philosophical discussion up until now has been preoccupied with these two errors. The conviction of natural consciousness is that the inkpot standing before me *continues to be* and to be in the fullness of its thing-determinateness *ceteris paribus*—i.e., without my having any specific reason to accept the opposite; that my perception grants nothing to and takes away nothing from this inkpot, [288] and that it as an object [*Objekt*] is continually richer in fullness than any possible perception. This obvious conviction is as a phenomenal datum shaken by nothing. I "expect" to have again the same image, whether it is in perception or in the form of remembering, under certain conditions, or rather to have again this or any aspect of the image, since its being and being-thus are already set for me by virtue of *a single* perception. The adoption of this being and being-thus does not mean something like a "possibility of perception" in the sense that Berkeley, Mill, Cornelius, and others mean it.[1] Thus, the image cannot be an "effect" on our subject because conscious-being is *ideal* being, and all movements and stimulus processes are ideal being—even "images" themselves are ideal—and since there are only causal relations *between real being*, i.e., forces and force centers. Conscious-being = conscious-having always exists with *what* is conscious *only* in an *intentional* and never in a causal relation. The "images" are the identical, unified objects of intention, and in part they are the contents of perception itself, but they are not its "origins," they are not the starting point of the causal processes (stimuli) that "give rise" to perception—"perception" as something that would be different from the images themselves (immaterial image, stimulus sequence, etc.).

These multiple ambiguities have come to exist by virtue of the fact that the *three fundamentally different concepts of stimulus*, namely (1) the biological concept of stimulus (stimulus as environment-thing), (2) the physicalistic-chemical concept of stimulus, and (3) the metaphysical concept of stimulus, have not been clearly distinguished.

If I hear the ringing of my alarm clock, then that stimulus can be called the ringing bell itself, i.e., that *environment-thing*. I can, as Pavlov had first systematically done, examine the changing *behavior* of the organism and the physiological processes in that organism in accord with the environment-things or their changing attributes, and can secure lawfulness. Analogously, I can investigate the change of color appearances and physiological processes in the retina and the nervous system and the dependencies of this change, just as Hering had first done in contrast to Helmholtz, who used the physicalistic concept of stimulus.[2]

I can speak further about stimuli, e.g., the air waves for tones and ringing, the ether waves, or more cautiously about light waves for the eye. These things and their movements are obviously "images," or rather they are *formal-mechanistically* images that have been stripped of any attribute of primary environmental things.

[289] Let me make myself clear: I do not allow these two concepts of stimulus to get mixed up. Air waves do not come out of the environmental thing, the ringing bell, and hit my ear; ether waves—if there is indeed an "ether"—or light waves do not come from a "blue ball" and hit my eyes. Such discussion is nonsense! For in the stratum of objectiveness (concerning existential relativity) in which there are ringing bells, there is only the remote perception of this ringing bell, but there is not in this structural relation a phenomenon "air waves." Where there are air waves and light waves or even radio waves, there are no longer the environment-things "ringing bell" and blue ball, but rather, there are very complicated systems of molecules, atoms, and electrons. These complex systems correspond to these environmental things "motivating" the subject in the objective and abstract space only as their formal-mechanistic model and then also *continuously* associated with its surroundings and to the entire formal world-mechanism. Furthermore, in this order of objects, there are no "eyes" or "ears" which are themselves unities with all of their partial unities, which anatomy and physiology attribute to them; there are merely environmental-things.

Finally, there is that non-intuited order of forces, which, according to a dynamic theory of matter and movement—as it is imperiously claimed to be in some form by present theoretical physics—underlies *all* these "images," including the formal-mechanistic "stimuli." In this respect, the discussion can be about "causal" efficacy, since "reality" first begins here and everything else is already some image and nothing other than an ideal image.

The relation of the aforementioned "metaphysical" concept of stimulus to the other concepts of stimulus is now entirely different than what it is generally thought to be. The force center and force fields, which *causally* give rise to some image and its gestalt, its extension, its spatial and temporal order, are actually the *collective* causes of the environment-things, i.e., of the stimulus in the primary sense, *and also* of the formal mechanistic "stimulus process" in the secondary sense. What they have an effect on is not the corporeal organism, which is itself an *image* among images, but rather the system of dead and eventually vital *force factors* and *drive factors* which underlie the organism. In no way do the formal-mechanistic stimuli (in the sense of the second concept) determine the appearance of the environment-thing "blue ball" or "ringing bell." These formal-mechanistic "stimuli" determine logically (but not causally)—and this only when their movements from the starting point of the stimulus are *taken together* with the *entire* centripetal *and* centrifugal nerve-process in the organism as far as the cortex and further out to the periphery—*only the functions of sensing,* of seeing, hearing, etc., and eventually in its entirety [290] the "*perceiving*" of the environment-thing: there is thus *not* the "image" as objective appearance, but rather the *contents of perception* of the image, contents that give partially always merely inadequate and mutually expectant aspects of the environment-thing. The image *itself preexists* the selection that unified psychophysical functions such as seeing, hearing, sensing, and perceiving (as the leading overall function) implement with their distinctive intentional character found in the image content and found in the content's uniform fullness, which in the modal seen-heard-touched thing remains *un*broken.

This relation is presented in the schema:

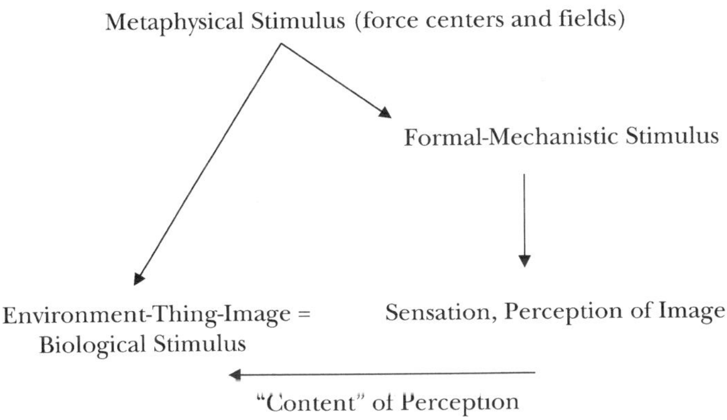

This schema concerns the four *well-differentiated levels of being* of the being: (1) forces, (2) "objective appearance" and "world image," (3) formal mechanistically reduced image, and (4) phenomenon of consciousness. Accordingly, there are three errors to avoid: (1) to claim that the formal-mechanistic stimulus process explicitly determines the *content* of perception, and not understand that the *functions* excise and sequester this "content" from the fullness of the image, of the objective appearance; (2) that the formal-mechanistic process fully determines the *"image" itself* as an objective, trans-conscious appearance; and (3) that the formal-mechanistic process posits the *centripetal, physicalistic part* of the *entire* circular process—i.e., the part which takes place *centripetally* and *centrifugally* between the starting point of the stimulus and the collective reaction of the nervous system—*in explicit proportion* to the psychophysiological functions of sensation, seeing, hearing, tasting, and ultimately perception and *indirectly* to the "aspects" of the objective image defined through these spatial-temporal distant functions. This explicit assigning of stimuli to the functions and to particular partial contents of a perception—partial contents *different* from other possible partial contents of the perception—which makes the "image" possible in the objective-ideal sense, is *not* the work of the physicalistic stimulus, but rather is only accomplished when this stimulus assumes *the addition of* the entire chain of centripetal, central, and centrifugal processes followed by it. We will examine this in greater detail a bit later.

[291] The quite mysterious, mythological belief that the *physicalistic* stimulus and the *centripetal* process along with the cortical process solely determine a sensation in a "terminus" "in" the brain or in the "soul" or "in" consciousness, and furthermore, that the perception is the sum or some kind of complex of such sensations, that the corporeal image is only, though falsely posited as "existent," an ordered group of perceptual possibilities, and that beyond consciousness all that exist are merely air waves and radio waves, etc., contains such a web of the deepest and most serious falsehoods that it bridles the horse on the tail end. Already, the view that the sensation comes into existence in some kind of "terminus" of the nervous process posited through the physicalistic stimulus, e.g., a red sensation (or that the spiritual soul brings about such a sensation through a *qualita occulta* of "arrangement"), is, no matter how it is phrased, entirely mysterious and unacceptable.[3] This view has also led to all sorts of impossible constructions—e.g., that of a "projection" of the sensation; to the acceptance of an original, merely "punctual" sensation; to the acceptance of an "unconscious" end-function through which the object (e.g., a red ball) ought to be given as the *cause* (Schopenhauer, Helmholtz); to the acceptance of a "concretizing" function of the "originally" merely ego-conditioned sensation; to the myth of a genesis of that which has extension from that which has intensity—in other words, to an accumulation of wholly opaque and in every sense wild and untestable hypotheses of which several are refutable and contradictory.[4] It could not be clearer that nothing in particular takes place in any so-called "terminus," given that the latter is merely the conversion of the centripetal nerve process into a motoristic process. Or better expressed, there is no such "terminus," but

rather only more and less preferred, circumspective, physiological fields of functions of a particular functional unity which is at the same time a continually centripetal process, transverse process, and centrifugal process, a procedure corresponding explicitly to the psychic, i.e., a specific, act of seeing (like the seeing of red). Red is the determination of a seen thing as the aspect of some visual thing that is freed from the concrete corporeal image through the psychic function of seeing. The concrete corporeal image is and remains the primary object of intention of the unity of perception, a unity in which the act of seeing partakes. This unity remains when there is a change in the contents of what is seen, contents that for their part possess a substantial permanence in the case of changing optical contents of sensation.[5] There is nothing mysterious here. Everything is fundamentally clear. The [292] fact that the accompanying unity (accompanied according to the over-function, the under-function, etc.) of a psychic functional accomplishment and of the physiologically functional accomplishment belonging explicitly to it (whose constitutive parts continually obtain the above-mentioned three aspects of the process) is only rarely bound to a circumscriptive functional field in its arrangement; and the fact that, to a great (and earlier seldom suspected) degree of disturbance of the normal functional field, other organ parts of the nervous system can overtake this field character, but the *structure* of the appearance still remains the same,[6] indicate that the specific, circumscriptive, "localizable" appearances and the functional fields conditioning them are primarily *created* through the accompanying functional complex unities, at the very least in the root development. A further fact which closely relates to this point is that the structure-imagining force of the function is nowhere as strong as it is in the nervous system and in the human cortex.[7] According to this view, the discussion cannot genuinely be about some explicit ordering of the contents of appearance of our perceptions and of the primary perceptual *appearances* and secondary representational *appearances* according to brain parts and brain functions, since *only* psychic *functions* and physiological *functions* are always explicitly linked, but these are strictly explicit and strictly parallel. This is a linking that is, in our opinion, ontologically and metaphysically rooted in the identity of the psyche and its functional constructs with the functional hierarchy of the nervous processes. We have thereby psychologically laid the foundation for a functional concept that has only seldom been recognized.[8]

[293] Just as misguided as the talk of the "termini" and the coming into being of sensations as qualitative, thing-like blocks is the theory that *perception is a complex of sensations.* The error of this theory can be easily seen, if one recognizes *beforehand* that neither intuited being-thus of the

body nor the "corporeal images" have indeed *any trace of reality*, which is only granted to the forces underlying them, but rather they have a *trans-conscious existence* [*Existenz*]. The error of this theory is further demonstrated by the fact that the being-thus of the body and body images are not *mere* contents of perception or "possible" perceptions, just as the content of perception is not a complex of sensations.

What is then meant by "image" or "objective appearance"? A *corporeal image* is a specific and unique *constructed ordering of being-thus-determinations* (gestalts, qualities, etc.) lying at the limits of the essential regulations, and is *not* rooted in the organization of the subject, but rather is ultimately rooted in a particular constellation of *dynamic factors*. The corporeal image is thus a constructed ordering, which is neither a mere "sum" nor simply, as Hume and Mach maintained, a summation of *sensations*. The *qualities*, which in privileged positions form the lining of the always pre-given spatial and temporal gestalts of the "image," are not sensations. They can only *become*, for any organic species in limited number and type, the *content* of the *function* of the senses because they are psychophysically indifferent ideal contents; but they always remain, when they become this content, *objective determinations of the image itself*. The functional bundles of our perceptions *decompose* and dismantle the concrete images into a great manifold of subjective types of appearance and aspects, but they allow them to remain intact in their characteristic ontic condition. At the very least, they create and generate them.

In the trans-conscious *being* of nature, the following series of *levels* of being can be demarcated.

(1) the force factors that alone determine the real [*Reale*] of nature;
(2) the space-time system and one (to be chosen) of the formal mechanisms;
(3) the transcendent ideal "images" and their essentially regulated ordering of construction;
(4) the related environmental structure and the environmental images.

[294] In the sphere of knowledge, the demarcation is as follows:

(1) the possibly essential perceptions;
(2) the actual and real "possible" perceptions;
(3) the sensible appearances.

In no way are the images only "effects" of the force factors, or of the mechanism first posited from them, upon the psychophysical subject. If we see the content of perception as *part of the disassembled image itself*, then obviously this proposition only gains meaning when we distinguish the *levels of existential relativity of this image* more precisely, and in particular distinguish between the "*environment image*" and the "*world image.*" The moon, as astronomy and selenography regard it, is a part of the world image and is itself an "image" [(image 1)], an "objective appearance" of certain force factors. It is not initially accessible to our perception with regard to its essence, but only to our earthly-human perceptual apparatus (the moon's stimulus threshold, difference threshold, etc.). Only through mediated thinking, with the help of geometrical, formal-mechanistic, dynamic, optical, and chemical (spectral-analytical) laws, can we construct concepts of the moon and attempt secondarily, through fantasy, to visualize and summarize these meanings. Our factual perception contains no *part* of this image, but rather only a part of the moon's environmental image, which demonstrates great variability: at one time the moon is a gold ball and then a crescent, at one time it is hidden and then present; it has this or that position in the night sky, and is at the pole something different than at the equator. However, this environmental image is nothing other than a mere perception, or an "epitome of perceptual possibilities." The image is only existentially relative to our psychophysical organization and our position with regard to a particular part of the "image" earth. This existential relativity has nothing whatsoever to do with the "immanence of consciousness" and still less with subject-relatedness, if by subject we mean the epistemological or the psychic "ego," and not rather the entire psychophysical organism. Furthermore, the environment image is not a psychic appearance, like a "complex of sensations," which would be produced in us by image 1 of the moon and through a stimulus process proceeding from it, or from which we can make "causal inferences" on that image.[9] From all of this, there is nothing in the concepts of the relativity of being-thus and existence. The environmental image is an "objective appearance" which is explicitly bound to the actual relation that exists between the dynamic factors, which are foundational for image 1, and the position and state of the [295] entire psychophysical species' living being (i.e., only the *species'* characteristics, not individuals' characteristics). As a mirror, the image is "existentially relative" to the mirror and the mirrored body, and the environmental image is existentially relative to the real being of the moon *and* to the real being of the earthly human being (with both regarded in the thing-in-itself sphere). The *environmental* image does not first come into being by virtue of our consciousness, our perception and sensation of it, but rather it preexists these functions of having and knowing no less and no differently than image 1 of the moon does. Nonetheless, the environmental image disappears if we annul the existence and nature of the earthly human being—although image 1 in no way disappears. The *structural forms* of the *possible* environmental image are, through the functional-dynamic species organization of the living being (its functional constructing laws), no less originally secured than the morphological construct of the *body* of the organism (of the living body-physical body [*Leib-Körper*]), which is merely an image among images. The environmental structure is thus in no way directly ontologically relative to the living body-physical body as image. The construct law of the living body-physical body, i.e., the formal morphological law of the organism in the stationary and genetic sense, and the environmental structure are, however, continuously in *reversibly opposing* lawful relation, which can be called "fitting in." They are, however, both explicitly determined through the special species-hierarchy of the structural-imaging dynamic functions which have the physiological and psychical components. Thus, we can examine entirely for themselves the changing physiological processes in the organism and the changes of its "behavior" through the changes of its environmental thing and "image" and their attributes and relations to one another in the sense of a broadened physiology (Pavlov), and we can research the laws of this dependency. We can do this *without* thereby introducing the physicalistic and chemical stimuli (in the sense of the second stimulus concept) which can affect the processes defined and definable physicalistically and chemically, processes in which a physiological unity of function and course of events (which are as such never reducible to the chemical or physical) *presents* itself and is realized for our experience; and we can do it without including the eventual conscious and psychic functions in the investigation, functions that determine the observable change of behavior.

The decisive argument demonstrating the objective consciousness-transcendence of the image, as well as its absolute existence, namely that perception (in the essential meaning of the word) can not only reach and grasp its decomposed aspects, but can consistently reach and grasp its being-thus "itself," is fundamentally—as I have already said—*the ontologically valid and essentially lawfully ruled construct ordering of the image from its being-thus determinateness.* That every physical body is extended, takes up space (whose axiomatic structure is posited therein), has duration, has [296] a determinate form, is infinitely separable as a spatial and temporal being, has colors that are determinable according to the quality system of colors, and that at the very least *these* qualities come to it as fulfillments of its characteristics, which are *also* given as the simplest contents of our normal sensations; that the body has a location, position, and distance from other physical bodies and has temporal positions and temporal relations, that it can change its location and still much more; these are all not determinations that are attributable to inductive experience. They constitute the *ontic being of the body*, and *one* body is enough to establish these being-thus determinations forever. It is not only the case that the designated, constitutive determinations of the body or the "image" are not simply constructed upon one another or "founded" upon one another, but also, as multifarious as they can be in their specific differences, they have an *ontic constructive order in genere* that cannot be dependent on our human organization, an organization that has itself being-corporeal as one of its essential determinations. This ontic constructive order corresponds exactly to the essential lawful order of *givenness* of the constitutive determinations of the corporeal object or "image." The ontic constructive order determines the order of givenness, or determines the framework for it, out of which it is able to fall out. The order of givenness surrenders the framework for the contingent, factual order according to which the specific determinations of the appearing being-thus-affair of a real or effective subject (as the foundation of the corporeal image) *become* and are determined in the becoming. The essential order of the construction encloses equiprimordially the order of givenness and the contingent existential order of the corporeal world and binds them lawfully to one another. Such an ordering makes it quite clear that it is entirely independent from the frequency of our experience.

Here are a few *examples* supporting these claims that concern the *founding order of the corporeal world* (which cannot be investigated here). (1) The (nonhomogeneous, changing from quale to quale) "*extension*," grasped simultaneously as condition and act of the self-extending, is the *ultimate founding* being-thus factor of any corporeal image. (2) It follows the appearance (original phenomenon) of the "*change*" of such being-thus determinations. (3) The change becomes, when irreversible, pure "*movement*," and when not reversible, "*change*." (4) "*Spatiality*" is the pure possibility (i.e., possible being) of movement, and "*temporality*" is the pure possibility of change. (5) Change and movement are ontological and, according to the order of givenness, are *prior* to the spatial and temporal qualitative point fulfillment "between" which they take place. (6) Change and movement "found" this "space" and "time" and their contrary [297] relation in a four-dimensional or now-here point. (7) The "*distinct from one another*" of the being-thus determinations of the body is independent from and prior to the particular forms of the "*after one another*" and "*next to one another*" (amorphous temporality and amorphous spatiality), and the laws of change decide what is after one another and next to one another. (8) If the spatially and temporally amorphous determinations of the body are given, then the next determination to be founded is its "*space-time gestalt*," which is also the core and basis of its *spatial gestalt* as well as the *rhythmic gestalt* of its possible changes. (9) The spatial gestalt grounds all of the *qualities* (color, tone, warmth, coldness, taste, odor, etc.) in ontological and givenness ordering, and thereby originally determines *which* sensations are "possible" (as also in the case of any change of the psychophysical apparatus of perception and sensation). Analogously, the temporal gestalt, the rhythm, grounds all possible changes of qualia which *can* assimilate in themselves an experience of change. (10) The *primary* qualia, which fulfill some limit point of the spatial gestalts and temporal gestalts for our possible intuition, are the (possible) colorings, and are thus not, for example, the qualities of touch, tone, odor, or taste. The colorings for the body are "more essential," or at least "more fundamental," than are tones, tactile qualities, odors, and tastes. Coloring also subsumes, for instance, mirror images, shadows, rainbows, fata morgana, sky-blue, etc., which are only surface layers, not "superficial" fulfillments, of bodies. It is much easier to think of a non-tactile, toneless, odorless, and tasteless corporeal world than a non-colored world. Everything that is hard or soft, everything that makes a sound, also has a color, but not the reverse. (11) Under the coloring, the qualitative difference of the *black-white series*, which yields with regard to superficial colors the appearances of *bright-dark*, has a *specific* priority of being and of givenness. A colorful color can only be and be given if its specific brightness is given, i.e., pregiven. Thus, since the X that determines the change of the bright-dark value of a possible body (the so-called "light") is predetermined for any remaining, sensibly perceivable, objective content of appearance, this unknown something has a *constituted* character for the place and temporal difference of possible sensible appearances of any kind, including possible, sensibly perceivable bodies and their spatial and temporal physicalistic character. Thus, if space is merely the epitome of the possibilities of "pure" movement and time is merely the epitome of the possibility of "pure" change, then the movement and change prevailing as the "fastest" (at a particular stage in science) are the measure and sense of the formal determination [298] at least for all possible qualities and even more so for the possible sensible experience of these qualities., The possible axiomatic formal determinations can only obtain secondarily the universal essence of spatiality and temporality (that contains nothing other than being next to each other and after one another).[10] The possibility of different types of exposure determines not only the simultaneity of sensibly perceivable natural events, but also determines the possibility of differences in general between sensibly perceivable spatial extensions. (12) To examine the other qualities, which can become determinations of the body, in their order of becoming and order of givenness is not our intention. Rather, these other qualities, in particular qualities of temperature and the amount of warmth; the quality of vibration, which we grasp prior to the tactile quality; the acoustic quale as the particular tone of things which we grasp prior to the other acoustic qualities; the tactile qualities; and the probably equiprimordial scent and taste qualities, have an essentially lawful development that is in no way grounded in our psychophysical organization (or that of any animal).

It appears to me to have become altogether clear with regard to *one* of the being-thus determinations of images that *trans-conscious existence* [*Existenz*] is particular to the images, while perception *only breaks* the images *down, but does not bring them forth*—that is these images' *gestaltness.*

The gestalt as *object-determinateness* had saddled Aristotelian and Scholastic philosophy with the ontic factor of "*forma*" (the "*forma sensibilis*" as image-form), a factor that together with the *materia prima* should constitute any physical body. Meaning and gestalt were, as we clearly realize today, united together in a mistaken manner in this ambiguous concept of "form." They are united in such a manner that the meaning determines the form and that the meaning creates originally in the hyle of sensible material the limits (ὅροι), which characterize the gestalt (Plato). In every case for these old philosophies, the gestalt (as gestalt of space, time, movement, change) was anchored *ontically*, and not in the human subject in the sense that this subject would bring forth the gestalts. The new mechanistic view of nature, in the most severe form of Descartes's geometrism, not only *disputed* that the meanings, the value-being, the goal-directedness, the purposiveness, and the qualities had an ontic character, but also disputed that the gestalts have an originally *ontic* character. Descartes [299] did this explicitly. He is the genuine father of gestalt theory, which is currently called the "production theory of gestalt" (V. Benussi), a theory that primarily enables the gestalt phenomena to emerge from pre-given impressions through an unconscious psychic process. Only the points and lines, which form a triangle and quadrangle, have thus physicalistic stimulus correlates. The *soul* gives rise to new appearances of the "gestalt" with their new characteristics. Since then, whenever the gestalt concept has claimed ontological validity in the movement of positive science, it has initially battled with tremendously antagonistic prejudices, e.g., in stereochemistry, in crystallography, and in biology. Ostwald's "gestalt energy" was immediately rejected by the physicists as a particular type of energy. Kantian philosophy taught the subjective origin of the gestalt in the "secret depths of the force of the imagination," even though Kant had recognized—in the profound chapter of the *Critique* on the schematism of the concepts of the understanding, and in contrast to Hume's sensualism—both the *pre-givenness* of the gestalt determinateness prior to the sensible qualities on the one hand and the categories of the understanding on the other, and also the outstanding meaning of *temporal* schemas prior to the spatial types (the temporal gestalt constructs the mediation for "sensibility and understanding").

Under these circumstances it was a deeply incisive reform, going back to the ultimate questions of natural philosophy, theoretical physics, physiology, and perceptual theory, when the representatives of *gestalt psychology*, in the final phase of its rich and diverse experimental research on gestalt perception and presentation, and following suggestions by C. von Ehrenfels and H. Cornelius, no longer felt compelled to ground gestalt perception in a purely psychological (productions theory) or merely physiological process,[11] but rather to ground that perception in particular kinds of *physicalistic stimulus processes themselves.* These processes do *not* follow the lawful results of the individual processes producing them. The old hypotheses of gestalt perception had a very simple and fundamental problem that was long overlooked, and which I myself had already thrown into sharp relief many years ago. W. Köhler[12] expresses this in the following statements: "We say the inkpot depicts itself in the eyes, the specific processes of sensation that correspond to its superficial parts would further be led into cortical areas, [300] and then the inkpot would be seen. According to this idea, we mentally hold together every assumed elementary process and separate their collectivity from the elementary processes that correspond to the surrounding of the inkpot, entirely without thinking about it, so that according to our fundamental presupposition there is no real belongingness to any inkpot element. Thus the related cortical end processes have as much real connection under them as the neighboring cortical elementary processes. There is no event corresponding to the "inkpot" created that would be some kind of separate unity in the somatic field, but a great number of single processes that are as indifferent to one another in the same degree as they are to their neighbors, e.g., the singular processes that correspond to the adjacent visible table surfaces. Yet, the seeing of the unities of things such as an inkpot and a rock, as well as the seeing of the ink spots on the table, etc., is for us such an obvious state of affairs occurring almost every second that we do not notice how every natural unity *disappears* from our fundamental physiological hypotheses and how we apply the hypothesis in such a manner that according to the hypothesis these unities *can* in no way exist."

Accordingly, it cannot be the mere frequency of complex experience, as Hume and Mach thought, which determines the arrangement of worldly things of sight in independent image and thing unities (and this so much the more imprinted the more developed the psychic life is); thus, it is not the case that specific singular stimuli and sensations proportional to them are found together very frequently. Max Wertheimer has shown through numerous experiments that Hume's and Mach's assumption is mistaken. These experiments have demonstrated that these arrangements materialize clearly and distinctly in *first* seeing of the thing and indeed in explicit *opposition* to the complex experiences that have taken place frequently. It also does not suffice to draw upon the experiences of different modal sense functions, of tactile sensations, of kinesthetic sensations, to make the arrangement of the seen things understandable. W. Köhler[13] is absolutely correct in his judgment when he says: "If a thousand points of sensation (of something like the inkpots) do not together make conceptual in and for itself the characteristic 'round' of the whole thing, then it is not created through continual repetition of the same perception. If I were to use as help a different sense area, e.g., the tactile or kinesthetic area, in order to import the character 'round' from these sense areas, which have had reproduced experience of touching or feeling of the inkpots, into the optical area, it would be of no use to me. I would be dealing with a deferred task to grasp such characters in different sense areas. However, if the inkpot did have specific formal qualities that are not directly seen optically, how could the inkpot reproduce particular tactile [301] kinesthetic formal conditions, since the optical form is the most essential 'reproducing moment' through which at best the 'correct' 'aftereffects of experience' are roused from the other sensible spheres. If the inkpot is optically only a particular number of black sensation elements, then it correspond perfectly, according to this view, to the raven, the black pencil, and the briefcase, if I observe these things only from a suitable distance. It is furthermore entirely not clear why under this presupposition the 'incorrect' experience from other sense areas should not continuously be reproduced. This explanation proves itself to be circular. The gestalt problem in perception does not allow for any empirical reduction."

The *already given* gestalt experience probably has an influence, and indeed a very powerful one, on the *remote* gestalt experience. I express this fact thus: gestalt experience, like the experience of forms of being in general, tends to "*functionalization*" and then determines more far-reaching possible gestalt experiences. In this elementary process, which is still to be studied in depth, I see how to make it understandable to us that what Kant had called "categorial function," and whose psychological-genetic emergence he correctly rejected vis-à-vis Hume, is in no way a super-historical constant, as Kant had held, and is further not an explainable facility of human "rational capacity," but rather comes into being through *functionalized initial intuitions* of forms of *being* and gestalts. This "experience" does not explain gestalt perception altogether, but it does allow us to understand complicated gestalt perceptions in terms of simple laws[14] of the composition, and to be sure to understand them in terms of laws that have *from the outset a common* and thus a genuine *ontological nature* for the physicalistic, physiological, and psychological areas.

Furthermore, in a different respect, W. Köhler's theory of the physicalistic conditionality of the organization of the optical visual object field prohibits it from being excessively one-sided. This in no way rules out the possibility that there are for different types of animals (including the human animal) *different* rudimentary gestalt laws for their perception *and* environmental structure, and that these differences are *grounded* possibly in physicalistic differences, *but not exclusively. They are also possibly grounded in biological* differences (that are always psycho-physical). If the most deeply rooted differences are found in the spatial structure of the environments of different animals without the amorphous spatiality of the formal comparison being treated as identical, and [302] if it is probable that the highest animals, the apes, do not refer a tactical thing, seen thing, smelled thing, heard thing (partly because of the absence of erect posture[15] as a particular frontal brain function, but certainly not for this reason alone) to *a* concrete thing as does a human being of similar development, height, and maturity, and if the animals possess other systems of orientation experiences, e.g., systems bound to smell and taste, and if the directional difference between right and left in all animals is missing, then the differences of environmental gestalts particular to a species and the differences of corresponding perceptual composition are shown in these analogous facts, which we would describe as "*preference gestalts of a milieu that are different for a species.*" These gestalts certainly have nothing to do with mere adaptation, to which Spencer reduces them, and even less to do with the morphological structure and the physiological function hierarchy of the organism in general. The ontological meaning and the physicalisitc reality of the gestalt stimulus in no way become superfluous through the existence of these preference gestalts, in the extreme manner that Henri Bergson maintained, in the sense that first this, and then quickly a different pattern would be stamped on an entirely non-formed flowing continuum of changes by virtue of the species' organization. It is certainly true that fish and animals that fly do not have, for the demarcation of a concrete thing, any preference for the solid aggregate state over gaseous and fluid states, a preference that is particular to human beings and all land-bound animals.[16] But to conclude with Bergson that the arrangement of things in the environment is only extant where there is a preference order for fixed objects, to conclude that we humans would bring a particular arrangement of things in the environment, by virtue of our drives and needs, into a flowing continuum of impressions, are grossly mistaken ideas. *What* the unity of a thing becomes for different species' organizations is an entirely different question than the question concerning the arrangement of the environment in general.[17]

For us, the *drive structure of the organism type* is decisive for the *preference gestalts* as the *choice factor* out of the physicalistic possible gestalts—this in contrast to Köhler, who fails in his attempt, according to our view, to explain the life processes as a special case of physicalistic gestalt lawfulness. *However, a different factor is selection as well as generation and creation.* Within an unstructured spatiality—i.e., of still [303] undifferentiated being next to and behind one another (as a kind of "comparison" of homogeneous extension in general, which circumscribes the amorphous temporality, the one after another)—is, according to our opinion, an *essential* ontological and intuitional form which is *pre*-ordering all sensible and motor organizations for *any possible* living being and its possible environment, and which is neither logically derivable nor replaceable by the ordering experiences of different spatial sensations. Within this unformed spatiality, three-dimensional space and the level space of the measure of curvature show only a *particular preference gestalt* of the amorphous spatiality *for the human species.* This was misunderstood for so long because, in the concept of Euclidean straight lines, an analytically determined concept (= the spatial shape determined clearly only through two "points"), a dynamic concept of direction (= the shape whose generating movement shows at no time in any such phase a change of the direction of movement), a metric concept (= the smallest connection between two points), and a *genuine gestalt impression*—the impression of straightness—were collapsed into one and the same object. This is, however, neither logically nor intuitively necessary, and is also not established through observation. A line that gives the impression of straightness is thus not less of a "gestalt" than an isosceles triangle or a quadrangle. This impression is just as indefinable as any genuine impression, and in that sense the concept straight = gestalt fully *distinguishes* itself from any preceding definition.

A *universal* biological law, which holds true for the spatiality of any possible structure, is now understood as follows: animals' *kinds of movement* and their *perception of the space structure* of an environment *correspond* exactly to one another, and this space structure itself contains the *simplest* spatial type form, which is sufficient for the above-mentioned dynamic concept of direction and for this reason sufficient for the metrical concept of straight lines. An ontological law holds that in every space-type manifold there will be a form that is clearly determined between two points, i.e., two points are necessary and adequate in order to determine it clearly. This final, purely analytic definition of straight lines indeed presupposes an intuition, but only the intuition of amorphous spatiality; this intuition can nonetheless ground all expanses, such as the ones grounded by positive and negative curvature measures, as well as by constant and inconstant curvature measures, The spatial form in one of the expanses will be "straight" in this (analytic) sense only if the spatial form has the *same* curvature measure or the same change of the curvature measure as the corresponding expanse. This form can thus be its *gestalt* with regard to, for example, a circle or ellipse; for these are determined clearly through two points. It is hence an error to hold that the analytic definition already defines the Euclidean [304] straightness. It by no means does that. For in all three cases, straight line, circle, ellipse (which is determined through two focal points), the addition of an absolute gestalt character (straightness, circle gestalt, ellipse gestalt) is required in order to gain representationally the thing, i.e., the addition of an essential indefinability. In the same way, circle, ellipse, straight line are sufficient for the dynamic and metric definition, according to the organization and space structure of the environment of the living being which are always set in opposition to each other.

That which is absolutely *contingent,* and thus not logically, intuitively, or sensorially necessary for *human* space intuition and not necessary for the spatial environmental structure corresponding to this intuition, can be precisely and distinctly characterized: the forms that come into being through a movement without change of direction (and consequently with the smallest expense of energy) are such that they (1) are sufficient for the analytic definition, (2) but also simultaneously give the impression of the straightness gestalt. Moreover, the *straightness gestalt is a preference gestalt of human space,* a preference gestalt of the space of the natural human worldview-milieu. This is entirely and absolutely *not objectively necessary.* That this is not at all objectively necessary singularly constitutes what we call (in relation to the measurement of curvature) the *Euclidean nature* of our spatial intuition and the space of the milieu thing, which are both elemental and uniform. If an a priori of a *species* is subjective and *biologically* related to things in the environment, but has no trace of an objective a priori befitting Euclideanism, then this Euclidean nature of the human species is in no way binding for *geometry* or for *theoretical physics.* Euclidean nature must give preference to the geometry that corresponds best to its laws of time-space coincidences of the being-thus, and ultimately to its dynamic *laws of movement* and the coincidences of maximum covariance of similarities through which it presents this—a point Einstein had corrected, insisted upon, and worked out. Physics has nothing to do with the environmental space of the human being, but rather with the spatial type structure of natural events independent of this milieu. Thus it is not at all precluded that there are animal species which combine *other* preference gestalts with their dynamic and metric "straight lines," e.g., the gestalt that we call angularity. According to Buytendijk, mice, by virtue of an instinct, will go around the corner at the end of a corridor, even where doing so contradicts their frequent training experience of finding a particular fodder in the maze. It is not out of the question, but rather likely that their dynamic and metric "straightest" has the gestalt impression and their environmental space has the gestalt quality that we call "angle," and they perceive "around the corner" by virtue of the strict correlation of the drive system of movement and the sensorial system of perception in relation to preferential direction, when they perceive in general. If these mice were in a position to propose a physics of [305] light, then they would need to ascribe with exactly the same accuracy (and inaccuracy) to every stream of light a band that is constructed from angles. The old physics had to do the same thing when it adopted that light moves in a "straight line" in the Euclidian sense of the coincidence of the metrically dynamic definition with the gestalt character of straightness. The preference for the straightness impression over other possible gestalt impressions, which we attribute to the human species' spatial intuition (and spatial environment structure), means only that we humans possess the inclination, which exists independently of the modal sense sphere and its accompanying thing world, to see a straight line in any curve as long as it is possible and even where it is no longer possible, i.e., where the stimulus prevails *over* our biological species-determined inclination at the very least to think *as much as possible* the curved image as composed from constructs of the impression of straightness. If our sensible thresholds for *minima sensibilia* are so arranged that there is no conceivable gestalt-bend that could appear to us not as a piece of a different gestalt—if this bend is determined to be big enough and a change of its possible non-constancy of the bending from point to point to be *close* enough—but could appear to us dynamically as having an identical direction, then no sensible experience of a qualitative kind on its own accord, or for that matter any sum of all possible inductive experiences of this kind, can overcome this human inclination.

It was a significant *error* of sensualism (Hume, for example) to equate the "point" with the minimum sensible of the sensible area and assert that we would have in the intuition only an extended colored surface, so that the geometrical point would be merely a fiction; or to say that we would always have a sensible characteristic line or stripe with some kind of bumps, and the straight line is only a fiction or a conceptually idealized something by which we "learn" of stripes and bumps from forceful negative abstraction. The old rationalism of Descartes and Malebranche playfully contradicted this error. At one time in this bumpy line "the" straightness is absolutely not there; it exemplifies it truly for the geometer, but it does not "contain" it. If we learn only "negatively" from the bumps, etc., then we get something or nothing, but not the intuition of it or the concept of straightness. Furthermore, the "idealization" or, as others say, the "fiction" is meaningless, since in order to give the direction of the straightness to the "idealization" or to the fiction, this intuition must already have the straightness! And, as Descartes and Malebranche asked, is the finite line, which we should "make" into straightness, a straightness in general, if it is not grasped as part of an infinite straight line? Perhaps the lines, which appear to us as parallel, intersect, or perhaps they are parts of a very big circle, if one were only to proceed further [306] in order to lengthen them! Above all, the sensualistic position does not hold up phenomenologically. Rubin[18] has recently and impressively shown through very precise experiments of visualization that the matter is just the reverse. Moreover what as stimulus (in the sense 1 of the stimulus concept) is a color speck is for a very short exposition time a truly colorless point for our *intuition*; and the bumpy color line is "initially" a thing with a gestalt of straightness. If railroad tracks which are in fact parallel intersect in the purely optical space and progress as if they would cut each other off, then an experienced conflict of this appearance to the parallel gestalt arises—as a result of measurement or approximate scanning of the similarity of distance between the contrasting appearing points; the appearance is to us a deviation from the gestalt of parallelism in the same sense as the figure  appears to us as a "rectangle with trimmed corners."

Still, this is no proof whatsoever for the old rationalistic and Kantian proposition that Euclidean space is absolutely "the" space. These facts of our intuition prove only that the preferred value of straightness as a gestalt is not at all rooted in the modal sensual spaces, which are not Euclidean, but that it is a *super modal*, elevated above the difference between perception and representation, as with all genuine laws of preferred gestalts. This super modality in no way means that this preference is grounded either "purely" geometrically or entirely physicalistically in the *human* species' organization alone. It is a "human" characteristic—relating to the perceptual *and* objective environmental structure in their entirety—and thus not a merely subjective or psychical form. Yet it is not *more.* Euclideanness is in no way rooted in an actual essential insight, as H. Driesch explains in his writing on the theory of relativity.[19] However the physicalistic space might be formed, we humans with our species organization would *always* maintain the gestalt straightness for the "straightest" shape in the dynamic and metric sense.

There are other laws of preference gestalts that are clearly more biologically contingent than those already mentioned. If, for example, three points are shown in temporal intervals on some spatially perceived sense area, so that in the case of a distinct optimal temporal value the impression of movement arises, and in the case of a still smaller optimal temporal value the impression of a stationary curve arises, then a *circle* gestalt arises in both cases, rather than, for example, the gestalt of an isosceles triangle arising. This law is independent from the modal sense circles of seeing and touching. When Aristotle, in his physics, declared all movements [307] of nature to be either straight or circular (sub-lunar straightness, supra-lunar circularity), he was not doing physics in our sense, but he had ingeniously discovered—in accord with his biomorphic worldview in general, a worldview wherein all opposites in the environment (high-low, hot-cold, bright-dark, slow-fast, cause-effect) also hold true for physics—both of the central laws of gestalt preference for the human being in the environment (milieu) and perception.

Whether gestalts as such befit the *images of the object of perception themselves* (which must then also, of course, be conditioned physicalistically in this respect), as we maintain, or whether, as W. Köhler[20] thinks, there is only the physicalistic process described at length by him, a process in which the prevailing condition of every system-field co-determines the event in every other field, the phenomenal gestalts are nonetheless *only* contents of perception, which are causally called forth through the transmission of this process onto the nervous system. None of this in any way depends on the interpretation and view which has, since the first gestalt research by C. von Ehrenfels, H. Cornelius, E. Mach, and F. Krüger, been referred to as the *transposability of gestalts.* It is a very peculiar, though positive fact that the same exact gestalt of an object can be grasped by us through sense perceptions of fundamentally different modalities, e.g., through seeing, touching, and kinesthesia. In fact, the gestalt is grasped by these different modalities with the same level of certainty at the very least of the general possibility and of the original expectation, which is gained by experience, of a genuine and strict *identity* of that which has been grasped that, in my opinion, it completely rules out a clear classification, adopted first through association, of those elements of qualitatively different limit points.[21] Hence, where the positive experience yields differences in the gestalt impressions of different senses, we push this originally and instinctively onto changing subjective factors, and thus presuppose the principal and strict identifiability of the gestalt. If any specific recognition of gestalts as "the same" were only to take place within a single modal sensible area, then one could perhaps, following this line of argumentation, avoid the trans-conscious existence of the images and their gestalts. It would be otherwise if the identification was, so to speak, working throughout the modal aspects of the objectiveness. "Even the transmission of simple, spatial stimulus forms [308] from optical forms to the tactile area allows the most general gestalt characteristics of perception like 'oblong,' 'straight,' etc., to remain more or less unchanged," says W. Köhler himself. He remarks further: "All (optical) sensations and place values can be exchanged with radically different sensations and values as the observed object is colored differently and portrayed in an entirely different retina position of a nonetheless homogeneous field. If the primary stimulus effects are all different, according to the mechanistic view, then no primary relationship whatsoever can exist between the first and second perception—which stands in direct opposition to what has actually been found, which shows that both perceptions in gestalt characteristics would be virtually identical."[22]

Yet, there are still a great number of facts regarding the *preference gestalts* that have been neglected and are of much interest. Both the stimulated skin position and the stimulated retina point make, in accord with the choice of speeds, a circular movement and dormant circular gestalt. This gestalt formation is entirely independent of the differences of the sense organs *and* modal functions. The word "gestalt," as I have explicated elsewhere, is strictly speaking one and the same in motoristic, optical, and acoustic word images. The same gestalt of the change of place carries over from qualities of the temporal form into the spatial form. If, as A. Gelb and V. Benussi[23] have shown, three points A, M, and B are presented in succession with the same distance between them, but the time difference between A and M is different from the time difference between M and B, M does not appear to be in the middle of A and B. But B moves closer to M when the time difference is faster after M than between A and M. When the difference is faster between A and M, the opposite takes place: M moves closer to A and further away from B. I understand this to mean that the same gestalt of the "separation-between" identically shared by our spatial and temporal manifolds transposes in this case from a "one after another" to a "next to one another." An appearance like this is, for me, a proof that there is an intuitive separation-between *prior* to the intuition of space and time and a proof that the *phenomena of ordered "exchange"* which contain no trace of movement and change, are in identical fashion at the *root* of both of these appearances just mentioned. I do not agree that in these latter appearances, it is solely a matter of identical effects of an invariant, perpetual "real-psychical side of the whole process" (Köhler) which determine the appearances as mere consciousness appearances. Certainly [309] this is the case, but it also concerns something *more*; it concerns the *identical image gestalts themselves* which turn our sense functions primarily into *partial aspects*. Köhler's physical gestalt processes are truly the conditions for the becoming of these images and their gestalts, but they are not only what is trans-conscious. These identities are for certain *being-thus* identities, not real identities. Yet they are not only an identity of immanent consciousness being-thus, but are also transcendent consciousness being-thus. *Reality* does not in any way have "images," but rather only the force factors which bring them about. What is important to note here is that the biological species-specific preference gestalts are absolutely not transmitted from the perception to the representation, memory, and fantasy, but rather prevail *as originally* as all of our image perceptions.

There is yet one more thing. If only straightforward classifications of the gestalt phenomena took place, but these phenomena did not reproduce the gestalts of *the same* trans-conscious corporeal images themselves—however inadequate—then there are two possibilities. Either the classification would come about through and by virtue of growing experience, which was the old view of sensualism and the theory of association that Köhler rightly criticizes; or the classification would be "factually" conditioned in Köhler's sense, i.e., through the same physicalistic stimulus constellation. In the first case, we would have to expect a *developmental* direction (ontogenetically or phylogenetically) which would at first be in accordance with the gestalts recognized and identified very poorly, but then better and better. In the second case, we would have to expect a rough, but general *tendency* [*Konstanz*] during the life process of the child to adult, of animal to human being, of primitive to civilized. As is well known, the facts of the incremental developmental laws, which have been discovered in abundance by developmental psychology, do not demonstrate either of these conclusions, neither increasing nor constant, but rather a conspicuous *decrease* in the direct identification of gestalts. *Dissociation*, disassembling, and analysis are all accomplished by increasing experience, not by growing classification, and this all the more so as physiologically higher centers of the nervous system take part. What is important to note is that the soul or consciousness almost never creates the primary gestalt phenomena from isolated impressions. Rather, the reverse is much more the case. The same stimulus-determined phenomenon X that is *given as* gestalt in the developing periods *is* indeed gestalt in the less-developed periods, but is not given as gestalt, but rather as a "relatively simple impression." Most likely, it is the subcortical nerve functions relatively far from the physiologically ontological conditions of the more highly awakened consciousness that correspond physiologically to the gestalt phenomena.

That a rich *development*—but in the reverse direction that sensualism stipulates it to be—takes place, speaks against Köhler's [310] all too one-sided physicalism and against the underestimation that he has lately bestowed (which incidentally is in opposition to Wertheimer's theory of the cross process) on the physiological and central *reshaping* and utilization of the physicalistic gestalt stimulus—especially when there is such a stimulus. Therefore, because the conscious gestalt phenomena (as the facts of the preference gestalt indicate) are so strongly physiologically self-conditioned that such a development is possible, a far-reaching, but secondary and more or less voluntary interpretation of different gestalts into the same stimulus-defined sensible material appears to be the case (gestalts that give rise to the theory of production); and, according to our opinion, there must be, nevertheless, "physical gestalts" as transposable, dynamic structures of the collective process. This is why the theory of association which Köhler has developed is not the case. There are trans-conscious images with *gestalt structures* that are intentional trans-conscious objects of our lived gestalt phenomena as changing "decompositions" of each, and which in Köhler's "physical gestalts" have only their (as yet only provisional) physicalistic correlates.

The simple existence next to one another of dynamic "connections" which comply with the laws of results, and physical gestalt laws, as Köhler adopts them for physics, may not be incorrect for the description of the momentary state of this science. The *demand for a unified explanation of nature* is, however, not quieted by this. We maintain for many reasons not given here that *all genuine, ontic, and concretely valid natural laws* are only and *exclusively gestalt laws*, and that these laws are not for static gestalts, which is how Köhler treated them in his investigations, but are laws for the gestalts of *events* (as quantum theory treats them); and that all other natural laws of formal-mechanical structure possess no dynamic and concrete meaning, but *only* a *static* meaning. Köhler's "physical gestalts" are the same as what we call "images" (objective appearances), not concrete, effective causes, which are ultimately to be sought solely in the *forces* and their constellations which we have taken as the basis for any material in space.

There are two final facts that neither Husserl's phenomenology nor the gestalt psychologists have acknowledged in their full meaning: (a) the *pre-givenness of gestalts* prior to any *sensual* contents of modal and qualitative determinateness which merely present and likewise line the gestalts, and the corresponding ontological and becoming *priority* of the image gestalts prior to the qualities founded by them; and furthermore (b) the *pre-givenness of the modally defined functional spheres of sensual things* (seen things, heard things, touched [311] things, etc.) and of their functional and appearing lawfulness residing identically in perception, representation, and fantasy.

We know (a) that the slenderness of rectangles and the gestalt differences of angles are given quite differently when the individual shapes consist of these simple spatial gestalts; otherwise this is not the case (Bühler).

Analogously, this holds true for the apprehension of movement (Exner, Wertheimer) and of change (W. Stern) in relation to point distances and qualitative intervals. Furthermore, we know that we still grasp the gestalt of a shape as the time exposure becomes smaller and smaller, and can identify it in memory when we no longer grasp the varied colors and the shade of the shape. We also know that we experience the phenomenon of movement, for example, in the palms of our hands, when it is no longer possible for us to determine the direction of the movement (Külpe)—and this is also the case irrespective of the modal sense area. This clearly demonstrates two things: that the laws of becoming of our perception are in direct *opposition* to what sensualism and Kant, with his presupposition of an entirely unformed, non-related "sensible stuff" which is formed through synthetic thought function,[24] had in mind. Moreover, the fundamental concept of the Meinong school, that of the "founded object" or the object "of the second order," as well as Husserl's concept of the categorial intuition "founded in simple acts of perception," are concepts that are not able to meet the demands of the above-mentioned facts. These theories show, in contrast to Hume's old sensualism, the newly gained insight that the gestalt-apprehending function, in contrast to the senses, is its own and particular lawful function and is distinct from the sensing; however, the theories give absolutely no account of the *pre*-givenness of the gestalt phenomena *in species* (and thus not related to a particular body, where without doubt, e.g., in the case of relative gestalt blindness, thoroughly constructed gestalting can fall away in view of less thoroughly constructed gestalting). Conversely, these theories, with their concepts of "founding," completely turn the matter on its head. What is "founded" or pre-given is simply the *gestalt* phenomenon and not the sensual contents whose stimulus correlates are merely objectively present. In addition, the *ontological, reciprocal*—and thus not one-sided—*shared identity* of gestalt and foundation obviously exists, as in the case of a movement with an identical something (=X) which moves. It does not follow from this that there could be no appearance of movement without an immediate and foundationally experienced identification of the subject of movement (which is what, for example, Lincke, in contrast to Wertheimer, claims). In limit cases, it is the other way around. The appearance of movement leads [312] secondarily to the acceptance of an identical subject. Furthermore, the law of the pre-givenness of the gestalt, which holds just as true for the formation of a memory and a fantasy image as it does for perception, remains incomprehensible if I do not assign a gestalt to the *images themselves* and if, moreover, I do not accept that in the case where the images themselves as objective appearances of the force-factors *become* ontological, the gestalt is *pre*determined prior to the qualities of the body (and prior to each of these real parts or pieces).

It is only in the same manner that the other point (b) becomes comprehensible. Every seen-thing, for example, is (1) already a genuine *thing*-givenness (a shadow that moves, a mirror image), and in no way is thingness given when seen- or touched-things, etc., are related to the same concrete thing; and (2) every modally sensible thing bears an intentionality to the *entirety* of its givenness in the same sensible sphere. The seen thing is always given as the "partial being" of an *entire visible thing*, and those parts which are not represented qualitatively in the seen-thing (as in an interior or a backside) are *co*-intended as non-filled-out empty or still empty areas. This holds true for *all* modally sensible things that demonstrate the same levels of "manners of appearance," which D. Katz first established for the colors. It is, however, no less the case that all sensible things are related primarily and originally to a concrete thing. A preceding *experience* is not required in order to anticipate a tangible or tactile quality from intended, visual things, as the theory of "perception possibility" contends, but a particular *disappointment* is required when I am *not* in a position to anticipate the future experience from some seen things: for example, a dog runs behind the mirror in order to find the thing that he saw; or an infant tries to grasp every optical appearance that pops up in her optical field. (According to Schilder,[25] this primitive grasping reflex is awakened again in adults when certain brain injuries occur.)[26] It should also be added that, as comparative sensory physiology teaches, the corresponding patterns of function and appearance of the anatomical and other organizations of sensible *organs* are in a very broad sense *independent*.[27] That these should concern only inborn, fixed connections and forced processes of the nervous system and [313] physicalistic gestalt stimuli, seems rather improbable, since these structures functionally turn out to be very malleable, and everything that we know about structural formations confirms that they have *come into existence* phylogenetically through the function. If modally sensible things already have for themselves a material gestalt which, intentionally given, meaningfully motivates the *progress* of the specific act of seeing, and if this gestalt is not transferred from a sensible area to another area (such a transfer has been assumed since Berkeley!), then under the assumption of some physicalist gestalt stimuli, it is still very unlikely that these stimuli are re-formed in the different sensible lines and centers so *similarly* that they are covered—*ceteris paribus*—by the *one* gestalt of the concrete thing.

Is it not much easier to assume that *the "images" have their gestalts* and every perception merely breaks down the images into different aspects by virtue of a great series of dissociation forms that correspond to the drive structure of the living being? And is it not much easier to assume that many individuals, when they perceive a thing, have the *same images* of the object of their perception, only in *different aspects*, different levels of sufficiency, and different levels of being-thus relativity? And would this also be the case where there the *stimuli* were not merely the same for each individual?

There are still further reasons why images have been *confused with the "contents" of perception* and the "possible" contents of perception:

So long as bodies, which as concrete things are only *images* and nothing other than images, are taken as *real* things, as the naive worldview does, and so long as an extended real substance, as the "bearer" of the image impressions and characteristics, underlies anything that can be the image of them, then so-called critical realism and, to a greater degree, the *idealism of consciousness* (Berkeley, Hume) are justified in their opposition to and fight against such a bogus idea of such a "substance" and choosing rather to understand the image content entirely or partially as a subjective determination. For whoever believes that what is *not real* must therefore be "subjective" (in the sense of consciousness determination, production of the soul, etc.) must then consequently ascribe every imageness to the subject of the human being. Certainly, images are *not* real. All of their characteristics change, not only the so-called secondary ones, but also their size, gestalt, temporal relation, and distance change according to the standpoint of the observer, and this is also the case when we completely bracket out the psychophysiological apparatus and what it alone is responsible for; mass, electrons (positive and negative), etc., are and remain functions of movement. As concrete images, bodies are only the *constructing order* [314] of their modally sensible things, but a constructing order that is absolutely *objectively* grounded, and is not grounded in us or in the possible biological organization of a finite being. The so-called primary and secondary determinations are certainly on an *equal footing* in relation to consciousness, and thus one is not subjective while the other is objective, as the opportunistic teachings of "critical realism" maintain. We only claim to be able to show that they are all *objective*, i.e., *transcendent* of consciousness and the soul, and not, as Berkeley and others maintain, immanent to consciousness. It is certainly not out of the question that these determinations have different levels of the *priority of becoming* and are to be differentiated not only by primary and secondary levels, but by *various* levels of becoming. What exists behind the images and the construction order of their (abstract) parts are not images, which none of their determinations befits. they are *forces* which bring about and create these pseudo-substances, these images which are transcendent to consciousness. "How" they do this is a question which does not interest us here.

A second and fundamental reason for the same error leading to the aforementioned confusion is that the possible (optimal) perception was *underestimated*, mistakenly regarding perception to be what perception is not, namely a genuinely objective, being-thus-conditioned grasping. *Tradition, fantasy*, states of sensations, and *inhibitions* of perception, including spatiotemporally remote perception [*Fernperzeption*], inhibitions which are certainly "useful" and deeply rooted in the organism, are considered the *optimal possible* perceptions for us. Moreover, memory is regarded as merely an impoverishment of the contents of perception—rather than as necessary assistance to perception; memory works together and cooperatively with perception, finding its way into the depths of the image itself: this is a type of *penetration* of perception [*Perzeption*] into the consciousness-transcendent image *itself* and its *richness* which is impossible for perception [*Wahrnehmung*] to have on its *own accord*; and this holds true in a similar manner for expectation. A further misconception is that the objective meaning of the object, which is not contained in the image—and which would have an ideal condition, if there were no thinking human beings—rather is determined simply through the mediation of the *gestalt* of the image, and is considered to be our human "concept" "of" this objective meaning. What was not realized was that the objective *coincidence* of all objective meanings with the *whole* image presents the corporeal image itself (as "*verum in se*"), and that the coincidence of our possible image perceptions in general with our concepts *of* meanings articulates the possible *cognizing* of the corporeal image for us. The peculiarity here is that every partial error in this chain of errors challenges the *entire* chain—going all the way down to the understanding of sensation—and shows that you cannot refute a part without refuting all of it. Also, in the first of the three points already mentioned, it is *sensualism*—the prejudice that sensations have a primary givenness—which bears the responsibility for the deepest [315] errors. Sensualism utterly failed to recognize that what we mature and civilized human beings call vague and average "perception" is rooted in a historical and spiritual-historical *process* of continually and progressively *casting off* and uncovering *tradition*, a tradition that is social, collective, and historical, and which enmeshes itself in perception. This perception is certainly vague when compared to the "idea" of pure, material, being-thus determined perception. Already the natural "perception" of present-day human beings rests in a very gradually developed *inhibition* of the almost omnipotent, original force of fantasy (fantasy activity) of the human being as drive-being. At first, this inhibition was willful, and then it became automatic due to custom and habit. Only a "little" genuine perception has been surrendered in a fight over the course of a millennium—a millennium full of success and failure—to the predominance of memory-blind "*traditio*" and drive-conditioned "*fictum*"—to the latter as the self-creating object of thoroughly *originary* fantasy. Perception was originally only the concept of a *direction*, and more of a *negative-critical* direction than a positive activity; namely, the critique and negation of the "tradition" of forcefully *concretizing* memory, and furthermore, the critique and negation of the fictions of the drive and wish fantasy on the basis of the success and failure of practical behavior—with regard to the *fictive* objects given "initially" as having a perceptual character and having the character of a thing or of an image.

Perception is thus an end and a goal, but certainly never the beginning of soul-spiritual development. This is quite certainly the case, if we were to express this point in accord to rather vague laws such as the human being comes closer to "idea" image perception, compared to the animals; the adult compared to the child; the male compared to the female;[28] the individual compared to the mere "member" of the collectivity; the historically thinking and systematically *cognizing* human being compared to the human being who moves through tradition and is "caught up" in it, i.e., a human being who is "caught up" in tradition in such a way that he or she cannot see in the distance of the past memory that has been concretized and temporally localized.

2. The Relation between Sensation and Perception: The Drive-Motor Conditionality

What follows are fundamental new insights regarding the relationship between sensation and perception as well as for *philosophical epistemology*.

[316] (1) Sensation is not a phenomenon, but rather a never entirely pure emerging *condition factor* X for the realization of perception. (2) The so-called *constancy hypothesis* and the hypothesis of "unnoticed sensation," with regard to the relation between physicalistic stimuli and possible sensations, should be discarded. (3) All of the simplest perceptions are *drive- and motor-conditioned*. (4) Every perception [*Wahrnehmung*] is remote perception [*Fernperzeption*], and also the "simplest" perception [*Perzeption*] (5) Perception and representation originate in the *same manner* from the pre-form of "eidetic" images of intuition (Jaensch). (6) The originating syntheses follow the direction of the *intended perceptual* objects. (7) Moreover, the organ sensations are only the particular fulfillments of previously given, accompanying body [*Leib*] schemas.[29] (8) Specific sense energies [*Sinnesenergien*] are those of the function, not the qualitative contents, and of the stimulus selection through the mechanisms presented to the sense organs; they do not create the quality.[30]

From these insights, it is necessary to explore some further points for the sake of our problem.

Ad 1. In the progress of modern psychology, a general tendency has emerged more and more clearly to *return* fully to the *logical, ontical, and genetic relation* of the concepts of perception and sensation. Sensation is for modern psychology no longer valid as a proven component of the contents of our perception which can be defined through analysis and which can be created experimentally, for instance, as isolated "pure" sensation. Rather, sensation is only valid as a *relatively* simple and *relatively* constant and identical constituent part of different perceptual experiences, a component part that enables the approximate experience to be brought about through different methods, e.g., through a change in the conditions of drive attention, without which there are not the simplest perceptions or even the relatively "simple" parts of such perceptions. That is, if S (sensation) = f (St + A) [= function of stimulus and drive attention], then I can let the drive impulse change in comparison to more concrete perceptual acts and can see what is left as constitutive parts of the reduction to "S." Furthermore, I can let the possible residuals of memory (M) as fantasy content (F), which constitutively penetrate into every perception, change with every perception of posited intentions (I) in comparison to many perceptions, in order to discover in this way the simplest S, relatively speaking. I can also attempt to discover, through studies investigating the breakdown of normal perception in cases of a manifold pathological disturbance of the perceptual process and its appearances, [317] those constituent parts of perceptions which are the *closest stimulations* and the *relatively "simplest" stimulations, most proportionally.*[31] It is unlikely and rarely actually occurs that I always obtain the same constituent parts of perception through this method. Nonetheless, this would be the ideal. What is absolutely clear from this process is that the following holds true according to the directional law of my conceptual framework. (a) The sought-after X of "pure sensation" would be that which *has a clear, constant, and precise proportional relation* to the physical stimuli. (b) Everything that I discover factually is *not* this X, but rather tends only *relatively in the direction* of this X in an ordered, gradual series of reconciliation. (c) Everything that I so discover is not and cannot be something concrete (a concrete experience or phenomenon), but rather only an identical generality, and thus a *conceptual* object grounded in abstract partial contents, but not the "piece" of a whole. What has thus happened to sensation and sensations is very similar to what happened in modern physics and chemistry to the "components of extended material substance" (the molecule, atom, electron system, positive and negative electrons, etc.); their constants are no longer absolute, but rather are *relative* to certain functional connections of being-thus conditions [*Verhalten*] which should make them understandable to us. On this point, so far as I can see, everyone is presently almost in agreement. Koffka, Köhler, Jaensch, Poppelreuther, Pick, Schilder, and Grünbaum, to name just a few, absolutely reject a "simple" sensation as concrete experience or as a concrete constituent part of experience.[32]

If sensation is only regarded as an abstract constituent part of the *collective reaction* of an individual organism to its unique environmental surroundings,[33] and sensation is not the limit case of a "*perceptio*," but rather the limit case of a spontaneous "*reactio*," a limit case *assumed* for the analysis of the lawful relations between the "behavior of the organism and *changes* in its environment," then the idea that "sensation" [*Empfindung*] is a psychic *thing*, which has haunted philosophy and psychology since J. Locke, can no longer be part of the discussion. Sensation as the indication of an (abstract) partial content from the perceptual appearances (as image aspects) is then merely some X in the appearances which is given as the "closest stimulation" in the function of the senses, whereby the psychologically [318] indifferent *qualities* (as ideal content) could *just as well* constitute such appearance and image determinations *as* "contents of the senses."

Ad 2. Further implied in what has already been said is that the question of the fiercely contested "*constant hypothesis*" between stimulus and sensation, the hypothesis which has been so fundamental for the possibility of a psycho-physics and of a measurement of the sensations as extended things, for the possibility of a determination through observation (and experiment) of the named state of affairs, has in principle been overcome. What is absolutely certain is that not only is *there in general no* concrete, demonstrable experience (whether it is bodily or environmentally related) that would be a clearly constant function of the physicalist stimulus, but *there could not be in principle* such an experience by virtue of the essence of all life, by virtue of the idea of a thing that reacts [34] (and thus "stimulated") in a different manner *spontaneously* to environmental things of the same type. This *alone* is in fact for certain and has been confirmed (though not established) by all experimental observations. There are already many who have shown that the "constant hypothesis" is false (such as Bergson, Köhler, Koffka, Schilder, et al.) and others who have provided proof (such as Cornelius and Krüger) that in all analytic activities of noticing, attention, observation, and above all in any experimental research of such analysis there are not new perceptual and epistemic conditions for something already experienced—as the constancy hypothesis posits—but rather conditions for the *existence and coming into existence* of something that is *not* yet experienced. Given such proof one is absolutely correct in opposing the counter hypotheses (such as the ones posed by

C. Stumpf, W. Wundt, T. Fechner, C. von Sigwart, T. Lipps), and thus correct to insist that sensation ought to be described and defined (in some way) *phenomenologically*. From the entirety of the stimulus, which affects a normal organism, only a very small number of stimuli are bound to relative "elementary experience"—and this (when the stimuli are equal) in very different quantitative and qualitative ways. The number and kind of stimuli depend on the gestalt and preferred gestalt factors, which are ultimately a characteristic of the *kinds* of living beings, and on a great fulfillment of other factors which, before any ontogenetic experience, lie *in the* organism itself and its blueprint (central factors, fresh-fatigued and the mood of the organ, drive factors, maturing and practice factors, etc.). It must necessarily—what is often overlooked—be stressed that this *essential inconsistency of stimulus and concrete experience* proves valid for the consciously awakened as well as for the unconscious "experience," insofar as one believes for truly convincing reasons that we must accept different zones of consciousness for psychic experience. It must also be stressed that with regard to the concept of the [319] drive and voluntary "unremarked sensations," or we could better say, elementary experience, the concept of sub-waking conscious elementary experience is in no way rejected. It is only claimed that this sub-waking conscious experience (e.g., dream experience, the experience of anaesthetized, hypnotized, somnambulistic, or ecstatic consciousness) is at no time a stimulus function, but rather is likewise co-determined by the levels of subconsciousness and the increasing degree of sub-waking conscious drive impulses and other factors. The "unremarked sensations" have absolutely nothing to do with the distinction of relative "levels of overt and subconsciousness," a distinction suggested by *different* factual series. Yet, as certain as the statement is regarding the essentially lawful (and thus also valid for *all* levels of consciousness) *inconstancy* of concrete experience in contrast to physicalistic and other stimuli, it is still not logical to transfer the unremarked sensations, when the concept of sensation is grasped in the sense defined above, to the relation between stimulus and sensation. For, according to the above definition, sensation is simply *the direction* of possible variations of experience, a direction that moves out to a *constant* relation between stimulus and concrete experience. Accordingly, the proposition becomes: "S(St) is a constant function" to a definitive constituent part of the concept of sensation itself, as of the concept *of the* experiential difference [*Erlebnisandersheit*] whose direction this definition indicates. We are thus able to say that, first, the constant hypothesis for the relation between stimulus and experience is essentially wrong, and second, that it is a constituent part of the definition of "sensation" (in the nonphenomenological sense).

Before we say something important about the significance of abandoning the constancy hypothesis for the problems of the relation between perception and sensation (in a philosophical respect), we should recall the *history of the abandonment of this hypothesis,*[35] at least with regard to the theoretical theory of the threshold of stimulus and difference:

T. Fechner clarified the stimulus threshold as an absolute threshold (Weber) in the sense of the difference threshold, to which he gave his very famous *psychological interpretation.* For him, the sensation differences just mentioned are distinct unities of sensation, and he presupposes that they are strictly the same in every area of the stimulus range. The "soul" itself begins initially with a certain minimal amount of stimulus (which in its psychological consequences does not change with regard to its stimulus value on the soul), and responds to the stimulus [320] with a sensation as the soul gives an ever-similar distinctive sensation difference, which coincides exactly as sensation difference with its markings, with the strengthening of the stimulus and with the strengthening that is proportional to the size of the stimulus at the outset. The improbability of Fechner's theoretical interpretation of the absolute stimulus threshold is obvious. Because any vital reaction of the organism, as well as any reactive movements that have nothing to do with sensation or anything psychological, has an absolute threshold of accompanying stimuli (their minimum, maximum, optimal), and it is absolutely improbable that the physicalistic stimulus could be enough to reach the so-called soul without change in its stimulus value (and thus without being modified through the physiological intermediate process in this value), a *physiological interpretation* steps in for the stimulus threshold in the place of the psychophysical. Since Pfeffer has shown that the movements of the tendrils follow the stimulus adequate to them in Weber's formula, it is no longer feasible to grant the absolute threshold anything other than a physiological interpretation. If only a physicalistic measuring instrument impels a specific energy amount to tip the scales, then this impels the sense apparatus. Instead of trying to grasp and see the unity of the clarification of the stimulus and difference threshold, which was the virtue of Fechner's theory, if one were unable to explain physiologically the facts, which the investigations of the difference threshold established, then it was assumed that one had to give a totally different explanation for the difference threshold, namely a "*psychological*" interpretation.

The view that T. Lipps, W. Wundt, and C. von Sigwart follow has been critically developed in particular by C. Stumpf in his "tone psychology." According to this theory, the experience of a difference in a sensation does not, as for Fechner, coincide with its "being noticed," nor is the noticeability difference a condition of the becoming of the sensation.

Hereafter the sensation and the sensation change should be a *constant function* of the stimulus and the stimulus change, and only between these constant sensation changes and the independent *actions* that judge and notice the changes should any number relation take place that the experiment establishes as the "difference threshold." The constancy is given to us experientially through the sufficient speed of the stimulus increase or decrease (e.g., in a glissando); when it is given to us through slow, continual stimulus change where the *sensation* change follows erratically, this fact should be explained (without giving up the continual sensation change) through the erraticality of the remarking threshold. The arguments that Stumpf gives for this interpretation, which underlies the acceptance of the constancy hypothesis in its most critical form, are not investigated here. These arguments rest collectively on a *material* [321] view of sensation, in which sensation is regarded as a thing, about which we could "confuse" ourselves. Hence, the main argument runs as follows: if, with regard to three stimuli A, B, and C, the comparison between A and B and B and C gives rise to the judgment "same," but with regard to A and C, there is a judgment of difference regarding the corresponding sensations a, b, and c, then—insofar as for each of these, a single stimulus corresponds to a single sensation, and in addition their temporal place value in a *succession* is disregarded—a logical contradiction undoubtedly results:

$$\begin{array}{ccc} \mathrm{A\ \ B} & \mathrm{B\ \ C} & \mathrm{A\ \ C} \\ a = b & b = c & a > < c \end{array}$$

This contradiction obviously disappears when the sensations a, b, and c do not correspond to the stimuli A, B, and C, but rather are regarded as functions of the three stimulus relations in the three attempts A—B, B—C, A—C; since in this case the first a is not equated with the last and the first b is not equated with the second b, b must be given the indices of different *stimulus consequences* (written as a1 = b1, b2 = c2, a3 = c3), and the contradiction disappears. If we were to speak about how we deceive ourselves with regard to sensations, we could only speak of the *stimulus* difference and not of any of the "sensations." We could only say that the contradiction resulting from this "delusion" forces us epistemologically *to accept* continuous stimulus successions which, for the physicist, are not related (e.g., Natorp, Henri Poincaré, Bergson, et al.). In opposition to Stumpf, Ebbinghaus assumes for good reason that there is an erratic change of sensation in the case of a continual stimulus change (given the same stimulus at the outset), and he also holds the theory that the sensations construct a steady series and a steady function of the individual stimuli. Nevertheless, he is committed to the assumption that the places in which the advances take place are not fixed points on the stimulus scale, but are themselves a function of the selected stimulus at the outset.[36] The initial stimulus of the stimulus series can always be so chosen that every sensation of the continual series of sensations ascribed to an individual stimulus is experienced. G. E. Müller has demonstrated cases in which the Stumpfian notice-threshold breaks down. It breaks down in the case of the series of two stimuli A and B, in which A is somewhat smaller than B; in this case, not only do the correct judgments and judgments of equality exist, but the *false* judgment A>B also exists. This false judgment can, however, not depend on merely the failure to notice. Müller clarifies the divergence from the consistent relation between a single stimulus and a single sensation through different classes of the already mentioned "co-determination of the sensation," which could lie (1) in the stimulus, (2) in the sense organ, (3) in the oversensitivity of the entire nervous [322] system (e.g., the influence of alcohol), (4) or in the attention (with this word taken in the Herbartian sense).

H. Cornelius initially rendered the crucial service of resolving the above-mentioned "contradiction." He solved the problem through the fundamental *surrender of the principle* that a single sensation consistently corresponds to a single stimulus by suggesting that there are "unnoticeable sensations" and in general a steady series of sensations as a continual stimulus function (and also in the Ebbinghausian sense). He thus broke with the constancy hypothesis in a different manner rather than by just a different definition. The gestalt psychology based in particular on Wertheimer's[37] work regarding the "seeing of movements" has perfected the Corneliusian theory to such a degree that it has become fact. It sees in the stimulus constellations and spatiotemporal gestalt stimuli not only the primary cause of any weakening of the constancy of the relation between a single stimulus and a single sensation as far as the so-called sensation of difference is concerned, but also, as A. Gelb has recently demonstrated, the so-called absolute stimulus threshold of color stimuli. Whether, in the case of differently selected speeds of the exposition of two lines, a right-left movement from A to B is seen, or in the case of acceleration two parallel lines are seen simultaneously, each of these phenomena is fully dependent on the type of succession of the stimuli itself, and not on the psychic act of identification, the act of noticing, etc.

As the constancy hypothesis with regard to the proportionality of stimulus and sensation (and also the thought of a *measurability* of the sensation) for experienced phenomena has been proven to be false, but still defines sensation as a limit value, the further assumption that every single stimulus constitutes for itself a clearly defined "sensation" is also absolutely false, and false already for the stimulus threshold itself.

However, the consequences that the foregoing conclusions have for the philosophical theory of cognition appear to me up to this point to be riddled with misunderstandings. For first of all: What do "senses" and "sensation" in principle mean as we have thus defined them? (We saw that the purely qualitative content of a sensation has in every case an ideal, psychophysically indifferent existence which appears otherwise in each of its concretions either as objectively constituted or as state of affairs constituted, i.e., as the *content* of the senses.)[38] Does "sensation" still mean something that somehow has *existence*, or is it merely a fictional token that is further bracketed out in the final result? Furthermore, how then does a physicalistic cognition of nature become thinkable if the concept of "sensation" is completely broken from the assumption of a constant [323] or if the concept would be merely such a token? What measure of clarity and validity comes to the formal mechanisms of movement in which we somehow still "ground" observed phenomena, when truly, as Koffka expressed it, "very different stimuli can correspond to similar sensations, and under other conditions very similar stimuli to different sensations"?[39] We still depend on our possible observation in the case of the intellectual construction of these mechanisms! These questions were quite easy to solve under the old assumptions of strict constancy and proportionality. These assumptions have proven even for this reason to have a stubborn life span—even against the facts—because they were fully enclosed *within the old mechanistic view of nature* and because they enabled the cognition of physics (in this old manifestation) to occur too easily.

Our definition of sensation harbors a peculiar *paradox* that I want to express in crude form: sensation indicates an X-experience that we never have and never *can* have as long as we live, but which we would have in the limit case if we were "dead"; yet the experience is nevertheless peculiar since, if we were dead, we would certainly no longer have "experiences"! We could also say something which appears less paradoxical: an experience is something that we would have if we were nothing other than a purely corporeal mechanism and a perceiving [*perzipierenden*] spirit, as Descartes held. In this fundamental Cartesian view, which is the one Helmholtz fully holds and to which his theory of the "unconscious conclusions" ultimately owes its philosophical origin, sensory physiology and psychology are in principle only theories of the possible "physicalistic deceptions": a view which for centuries accepted, on the basis of logic alone, the theory dominant in Continental rationalism that all qualities are not only subjective but are also only "dark and muddled" representations of movements. Here the thinking demonstrates—what the *essence*, not merely the essential attributes, of the "soul" should be—not only, as with Helmholtz, the departure of appearances from stimulus-proportional sensations and from the sensations corresponding to a single stimulus (simultaneous color contrast, constancy of the visible thing in contrast to the angle of the face, etc.), but also something more, namely, that the *qualities themselves* in this interpretation, which committed Helmholtz to specific sensory energies—adopting a theory of Johannes Müller—assume that the "sensory energies" correspond not only to the specific seeing-hearing-tasting functions, but also "bring forth" mode and quality as *appearances.* This is undoubtedly false and is also, in a functional sense, only philosophically meaningful under Müller's strict vitalistic presuppositions.

[324] If the above-defined "sensation" (as *appearance*, not as function) should be *more* than a "counting token," then sensation defined in this way can mean only one thing: *the quality itself belonging to images* is a *physical-objective appearance determination* that is also *transcendent* to human consciousness. The sensation *itself* as concretized in a spatial-temporal point and not as a content of the sensation has a constant and proportional relation to the physicalistic processes that produce a particular stimulus for a living organism. Such a constant and proportional relation can *never* exist between the same processes "as" stimuli and experienced phenomena. This means that we have reached, almost unexpectedly, the theory of the *objectivity of the qualities,* which does not exclude their real-ontologically "founded" and "secondary" nature in contrast to, for example, the space-time gestalts, extensions, and movement; and we have also reached a *new* justification for the *trans-conscious existence of "images."* Not only does a gestalt befit these images, but it also befits the *qualities* as dependent things of the forms of the single stimulus and its relations. What is "subjectively" and biologically—and this in no way means the merely psychical—conditioned is only the *selection* that different organisms execute based on the specific energies of their modal sensory *functions* of the available, incomparably *richer* qualities of the images, which are among the exceedingly manifold reasons for the *inconstancy* and *disproportionality* of our or other animals' sensings of them themselves.[40]

Upon the realization that the qualities as determinations of physically *objective* appearances and images ("appearance relation" is a fortunate expression by Tschermak) are not functions of physicalistic single processes that behave according to laws of the formal-mechanistic structure and the principle of results, but are rather functions of the spatial-temporal formation of the single processes, we can now express the following *philosophically important principle*:

The being and non-being of specific qualities ("specific" according to ideal color and tone systems, etc., and their a priori relations) as determinations of the appearance are *absolutely relative* with respect to all being and happening, which in nature are able to be *explained* in a purely *formal-mechanistic manner.* The same formal-mechanistically comprehensible individual processes, which serve the preservation of this or any of the formed systems, can, in principle, underlie many different qualities, and, in the broad limits, different individual processes can underlie the same qualities. The *non-clarity* of this formal-mechanistic explanation of the qualities simply attests [325] to the fact that in order to obtain the desired clarity, a new force, the "soul," or specific sensory energies in Müller's sense, must be introduced (like the theory of the subjectivity of qualities), but only for the *same result* to *which the discussion of the validity of the formal-mechanistic theory of nature* led us: that this theory can *never decisively* determine the appearances of nature, and it continues to remain a playroom of *many conceivable mechanisms* which clarify the same appearances equally well (Maxwell).

The *identity* of this result of two fundamentally different considerations, one epistemological-physicalistic and one sense-physiological and psychological, is for us of extreme importance, since it indicates how, in the development of the physical sciences since Newton and in the entirely independent development taken since Helmholtz, Hering, von Kries, and others, our understanding of sensible appearances (in particular through Hering's penetrating research) has slowly *converged to form a new collective philosophical view.* This new collective view transforms our worldview to such a profound degree that it breaks with the strongest traditions of the newer philosophy. If we also consider that the principle of the "threshold" of the event, according to quantum theoretical physics, is most likely the basis for any physical event, and does not begin primarily at the organic level, as was held by the old mechanistic theory of nature; and if we consider further that, for instance, the extent of the mechanistic mass factor in a movement grows with the acceleration of the speed in a relation that corresponds peculiarly to Fechner's formula of stimulus and sensation log S = Se,[41] when we analogously posit S with the acceleration of speed and the dynamic factors determining it, and Se with the size of mass, then we are able to get a sense of how deeply the *most general structural laws* are *ontologically founded,* laws which we thought were only biologically, if not entirely psychologically, explainable.

Since the images are not merely contents of perception or even the ordering of "possible" contents of perception, the qualities, which equip the images, are not *merely* contents of sensation. Because the qualities as image determinations are *objective, a physics is possible despite* the inconstancy of the sensation of the qualities in relation to the stimuli. Every natural appearance, as it is given to immediate consciousness as the content of experience, must be *clarified* in its components, both *physicalistically and physiologically,* from the outset. It cannot just be clarified initially, an approach which would think and construe nature as merely stimulus combinations for the purpose of explaining our sensations. Such an approach has corresponded to the fundamentally flawed theory of "critical realism" since Descartes, who causally "inferred" the physicalistic object from [326] perception. Only the logical convergence and absence of contradiction of *both* explanations of the appearances are able to assure us of conclusive and philosophical truths.

The so-called "*simplicity*" of sensation, a notion which has completely and thoroughly lost its absolute character, was accepted by the old psychologists and sense-physiologists to such an extent that not only was the sensation as a constant and proportional function of the single stimulus thought to be the *simplest* constituent part of the content of perception, but it was also considered *genetically* to be the *earlier* constituent part. Both determinations of sensation's "simplicity," the analytic and genetic, are, in D. Hume's concept of "impression," for example, bound to form a logical unity.

Is this theory more tenable than the rejected theory? Not only is it *not* more tenable, but it flies so fundamentally and completely in the face of a rarely seen immensity of firmly established facts of comparative genetic sense theory that it is still much easier to reject than the theory of the "consciousness" character of sensation. The following statement can serve as a standard and unanimous result of the relevant inductions and experiments: every kind of *deviation* of the relatively simplest, immediate experiences from an *ideel*—intended to be a limit case, stimulus constant, and stimulus-proportional sensation—becomes ever more *considerable* (and where measurable, the greater) and ever more obtrusive the more it concerns the *earlier* stages of maturation, of development, and the genetic gradations of the life phases; and every kind of deviation decreases with the maturation and experience of the sensible psychophysical unities of life, noticeably in the direction of the *approximate* realization of the *idea* of sensation. Hence, the constancy of size and gestalt of the visibly appearing thing *diminishes* in the development of humans from childhood to adulthood so far as the visible thing varies from the seen angle and gestalt stimuli. This is no less the case for the constancy of color independent of the lighting, which E. Hering had initially demonstrated with greater precision. According to E. Jaensch, the same holds true for the transition from adolescent's optical images of intuition of the youth to the "adult's" images of perception, perceptual images that come closer to the stimulus proportionality. These transitions are not the relations—so far as they are experienced originally, and that means, they are not yet cognized as such. Rather, they are the opposite. They are the *foundations* of relations, which gain *independent* existence in the process of genetic development and become more easily recognized and identifiable (a presupposition for the understanding of all primitive conclusions), to such an extent that through this process the perceptual world assumes a *more richly organized* form. Yet, this "pattern" does not arise because greater or richer relations are placed between qualitative contents of experience given as relation-less or relation-poor,[327] but rather it arises because, as if in a type of construct of nets, the points of overlap become ever more distinct and precise, and somehow already form themselves. It is a *process of dissociation,* not a process of *association,* which is tied to the law of gradual development found in the progression of human-ape to human, of child to adult, and of primitive to civilized humans.[42] Or as E. Jaensch expresses it: "'Elements,' insofar as they are in general provable in the intended sense, develop far more from the *decomposition* of an original unity than the reverse case where the unity came to exist through the joining of originary elements."[43] With great exactitude and preciseness, Jaensch summarizes, in another article,[44] not only his own extensive research in the areas of perceptual and sensation theory, but also the results of many other researchers: "It happens in the exact opposite manner from the traditionally accepted view purported (a view held by Kant, Helmholtz, and the view Hering has held, which is already being disproved here). The clear arrangement of stimulus and sensation according to the schema Se = f (s, s′, s″) does not exist at the beginning of the development, but rather constructs its ideal, never to be obtained end point. The assumption of a 'pure sensation' at the beginning proves itself to be an untenable construction; and this is obviously the case for the further supplemental assumption that the visual perceptions of normal adults have come to exist in their present structure primarily through an additional processing of this 'pure sensation.'" Furthermore: "every appearance that this explanation attributes to 'additional processing' must have *increased* in the process of development.[45] However, *the appearances* actually *decrease* in the developmental process so far as we have traced them up to this point."

The importance of this cannot be overstated. Not only the entire sensualistic-positivistic epistemology of modernity, but also Kant's epistemology and all Kantian schools founded upon the ancient theories of perception and sensation, as well as the ancients' highest principles, have been utterly and undeniably refuted. E. Jaensch has made his claim, which I have never tired of repeating (without, unfortunately, any effect on the aforementioned schools), in the most valuable [328] and thoughtful manner as an object of specific investigation. This investigation has restored the almost completely forgotten relations between the early structural theory and the philosophical problems of epistemology.[46] I fully endorse these investigations.[47] Still dominant in every Kantian school is Kant's conviction that what is given as the material of cognition is a chaotic mass of unrelated elements, which are ordered after the fact by the functioning of the *subject of consciousness,* i.e., elements are united and connected, and necessarily only the "subject itself" is able to form all the unities and connections, since this activity is an act of its self-activity (Kant).[48] E. Jaensch correctly shows that this prejudice of Kantian philosophy is prevalent throughout every Kantian school, regardless of how differently the theory of givenness has been developed, as in the case of Liebmann, Cohen, Natorp, Cassirer, Fries, Nelson, Windelband, and Rickert. Moreover, Jaensch places Kant's philosophy in the correct philosophical light when he remarks that in this regard—which is also the case for Kant's philosophy of mathematics, physics, biology, and, as I have already indicated, his ethics—*Kant's philosophy is only an epistemological and philosophical justification of the old mechanistic theory of nature from the Newtonian time period,* a theory of nature which adopts the false idea concerning the relation among sensation, stimulus, perception, and image not by chance, but—from the perspective of a pure worldview theory—by *necessity.* What Jaensch calls the "titanic fundamental feature" of the Kantian philosophy, particularly for later Kantians, is primarily the view that all connections, orderings, relations, and gestalts of natural experience and of the experience of science are born out of an indeterminate mess of sensations. Regarding this type of thinking, Jaensch insightfully remarks: "This approach rests ultimately on the psychological underpinning of the philosophies historically preceding Kant, and on a theory of perception that adopted the mechanistic views of the natural science of the eighteenth century without any concern for the basic aspects of consciousness still unexamined at this time."[49]

Yet, the *simplest* experience of *relation* and experience of *gestalt* have not the least to do with a *thought* creation, with a "something" that is only accessible through thought or which can only be "grasped" by thought. Not only is [329] what the experience gives ontologically and genetically "more basic" than a relatively *independent* quality, it is also in addition to its essence *pre-given.* And insofar as it is an essential condition and fundament that is pre given to any other relational and gestalt givennesses. Finally, the nervous apparatus, whose being given is determined through its function (as a functional field)—is—in respect to what concerns its givenness in concrete cases and relates to a particular psycho-physical organism—in all cases the more primitive, relative sub-cortical, and this means (according to Monakow) most likely the older in respect to its developmental phylogenetic history.[50] All appearances, which approach the stimulus-proportional "pure" sensation and simultaneously approach the singular-content that is identifiable in different relations, are thus without doubt bound to the *very highest* cortical functions that are tied in general to perception. The pre-logical mentality of primitive peoples, as Lévy-Bruhl has so superbly and informatively described it,[51] is not only characterized by the *ecstatic* character of its perceptual world, by its directedness and dependence on tradition and the interest perspective of the *group*, by the predominance of its drive-emotional force and value givennesses regarding the imageness in the object, by the fixated eidetic level of the greater indifference of representation and perception (E. Jaensch), and by the dominance of identification [*Einsfühlung*] over empathy [*Einfühlung*], but also to a greater degree by a deficient independence of the series forms and series structures (spatial, temporal, quantity, number series) whose intuitive givenness makes discursive *thinking* and a broader use of its lawful functions (e.g., the principle of identity and contradiction) *possible*—a type of thinking which appears to be a specific accomplishment of the structure-building neural functions that are most pronounced in the cortex region of the nervous system.[52] The studies of child psychology by Binet, Bühler, Koffka, Stern, and others have already shown how much harder for a child than for an adult it is to grasp in different types of relational structures the similarities of their basic components and the constituent relations in their different gestalts; to grasp in different concrete gestalts the differences of [330] their metric characteristics and their directional meanings (e.g., mirror writing that the children can read); and to grasp in similar gestalts the differences of their basic components (e.g., the different absolute pitches in a melody).

There continues to be a great debate in particular over the *experience of relation.* Even a distinguished researcher like Lindworsky has joined in on the debate, maintaining the thesis that all "relation-grasping" is by virtue of a "spiritual" grasping, a capacity which is only possible for a human soul and is thus wholly *absent* from the entire animal kingdom.[53] We can distinguish six different types (or levels) of relation-grasping: (1) to have something experientially simple that is only physicalistically a stimulus *relation* and not a specific stimulus or a stimulus relation corresponding to a specific stimulus, thus a "sensation of differences"; (2) to have something experientially indivisibly simple which is the same with regard to environmental things, but which in the development of a maturing being becomes something divided into foundations and relations whereby the classification proceeds from the *foundational* construction; (3) to have a relation with an unfilled, blank space of foundations in an ecstatic, preconscious manner; (4) to have the very same as something "of consciousness," i.e., something that is related and ego-related; (5) to have the same with one or both determinate classifying relations; and (6) "to cognize" a conscious (in the sense of types 4 and 5) "having as" relation in general and as this or any relation—all cognizing is rudimentarily "to have consciously something as something"—which already presupposes the separation of a relational *meaning* (e.g., the meaning of "same," "similar") from the givenness and from the "*conscious*" givenness of the *intuited* relation.

For me, there is no doubt that the human being and *only* the human being has level 6. I have already remarked earlier that this type of relation-grasping lies not in the relational character of that which is given, but rather in the separability of *hic-et-nunc* existence from being-thus, and ultimately in the separability of *existence from essence in general*, a separability that only the "spirit" of the human being can carry out. However, this is valid particularly for the tone C or for a simple red of specific nuance. Whether animals can reach levels 4 or 5 has yet to be determined, since it touches upon the most fundamental questions of animal psychology which are not our concern here. But it seems certain to me that the higher vertebrates reach level 3, and that all animals which demonstrate more than [331] merely trained, associative, or instinctive "practical intelligent behavior" reach level 3. Level 1 is an entirely general vital characteristic of any sensation, of any apparatus and functions contributing to it, of any non-psychical reaction of a living being in general, which are joined continually to *changes* in the physical and chemical environment, but never to permanent conditions.

The problems which concern us here belong exclusively to level 2. At this level, the question certainly arises: are we still able to call the having of something experientially simple an experience of relation, if it is given "as such" in the reflexive retrospect from the level of higher maturity? Remarkably, the expression "transition experience," which is used quite often for certain well-known appearances, partly in order to describe the essence of the relation experience (G. E. Müller), and partly in order to describe an apparently lower level of the actual relation experience (lower than "grasping"), a level which Lindworsky concedes to exist for animals—is used only from the perspective of a higher maturity. The transition experiences (e.g., the thickening of a line on the right side at the end because of the stimulus successive presentation of two lines so that an entire line is seen, lightening or darkening, etc.) are only signs and criteria indicating that a particular successive stimulus relation took place. The transition experiences presuppose the *original* of the *experienced* relation as given, and thereby in no way the secondarily conceived relation-grasping of a relation *as* this or any relation. This original itself cannot be a "transition experience," nor can it be merely a conceived relation.

Ad. 3. Every one of the above facts: the preexistence of the image *prior* to the perception; the priority of the perception as distance-perception [*Fernperzeption*], and as an intentional functional *unity prior* to the variety of the contributing modal sensory functions; and the priority of the functional appearances and *their* laws *prior* to the sensations possibly close to the stimulus (as higher-consciously experienced and non-experienced "body stimulants")—all of these must be brought into sharp relief in order to assess the full meaning of any of the conditions of the events of higher functions, which we now indicate as *their drive-motor conditionality*. The great error of the pragmatism of perception, which indeed correctly recognized in principle the motor-drive conditionality of perception and all of its partial functions, but then also wanted to ground a *merely formal-mechanistic cognizability of nature*, whether upon apriori realistic grounds or upon idealistic grounds—was that the pragmatists *retained* the old—here dispersed and rejected—sensation concepts (constancy acceptance, stimulus proportionality, pre-givenness, [332] and the genetic, ontic, and logical priority of a sensation experience). It was through this process that our entire *environment* became *a function of our "work."* On the other hand, the Aristotelian-Scholastic theory of perception—to which these errors cannot be attributed and which, though it was so underdeveloped in the positive-scientific sense, came much closer to the philosophical truth as we understand it today—rests on the complete and total neglect of any "subjective" drive-motor *becoming* condition of *perception* and of any of its partial functions. The true and actual subjective conditionality of perception was not considered in any way in the Aristotelian-Scholastic theory. In the theories, logically complementing one another, of the (absolute) mechanistic view of nature and of sensualism, a "subjectivity" is in a vague sense indeed recognized, but it is sought in an entirely *wrong place*, namely in the apparent subjectivity of the image itself, of the gestalts, and of qualities—under the presupposition of the constancy and proportionality principles. Subjectivity was sought here rather than in something totally different, namely, in the drive-motor conditionality that is *selected* through perception and at the *level of the being-thus relativity* of the object of perception to the *living being* itself.

The true *meaning of the life of the drives*—of the affects and feelings bound closely to the drives' movements [*Regungen*]—on the one hand, and the drive excitement of *attention*—of the mediation of the drives and our representations—and of *motor impulses* on the other hand, for our entire perceiving life (perception, representation, memory, fantasy, thinking) is, in our opinion, still today with fewer and fewer exceptions totally underestimated. Certainly there are a handful of names to which we can give credit for the progress in our understanding of this matter. Among these, I count Schopenhauer's always readable, powerful, and stimulating treatise on the primacy of the will over the understanding; many works in E. von Hartmann's psychology; Nietzsche's great insight understood from his point of view, that the life of our representations and thoughts is only "a sign language of the drives and affects"; and much by Bergson and considerably less from H. Münsterberg ("motor condition of perception"). With regard to exact cognitions, it appears to me that the following thinkers ought to be included: N. Ach's investigations regarding the will and temperament and the introduction of the concept of a "determining tendency" in the theory of memory; E. Jaensch's insights regarding the role of attention (its "dynamic" side) for the facts of the Aubert-Försterin laws, the cultivation of our spatial intuitions, of the eidetic phenomena found in them, and of the consciousness of reality; some great insights by Dilthey and Frischeisen-Köhler are important, as well as some things in the works of Müller-Freienfels. By far, however, despite all its vagueness, uncertainty, consternation, and one-sidedness (sexuality), the best contribution is from Freud and his students. The one researcher, however, in whose [333] works genuine cognitions in this Freudian direction of a generous theory of the drives are combined with a critical knowledge of experimental psychology, psychopathology, and the relevant parts of physiology and morphology, as well as the developmental history of the nervous system, and also the phenomenology of drives and affects based upon important, clinical, and often ingenious and analytic experience in living human beings and important philosophical education, is—as far as I can see—Paul Schilder, whose *Medizinische Psychologie* combines all these strands into a peculiar and even beautiful unity and appears to me to contain by far the best work on the questions touched upon here that, as far as synthetic works are concerned, we have in the German language.

Let us bring to light, before we take up the drive-motor conditionality of perception itself, some of the *main reasons* for the contemporary situation which is scientifically so unsatisfactory. These reasons are partly methodological and partly objective [*sachlich*]; they lie partly in the divisions within the work of psychology (philosophers, medical doctors, experimental psychologists, physiologists, biologists), and partly in the handed-down worldview traditions which are so fundamentally different from one another (spiritualism, theism, the mechanistic worldview, rationalism, and intellectualism). And then there is the increasingly stricter *segregation of psychology* and *biology* as an independent fundamental science. In respect to biology, the segregation concerns the theory of the inner aspect of life that is completely and totally *identical* to the outer aspect in respect to manifoldness and their elementary forms of connection.

The *methodological* reasons are as follow: the perceptiveness, the imageness in our soul life is its most extreme, most graspable, and most determinable layer. Although these imageness elements (of any kind) are to the structures of the drive dynamic lying behind them exactly what the "images" in the objective space-time system are to the forces (centers and fields) which are the basis of them (according to a dynamic theory of matter), the *dynamic factors* (impulses, drives, forces) are in both cases the *furthest* from our cognition in a variety of ways and are only very indirectly rationally determinable.[54] If we are so systematically focused that we want to divide up every "inner-becoming" of the psychic into what we generally call "consciousness" as a perceptive form of knowledge and reflective act, [334] then the central, determinant "willing" of such an attitude remains *transcendent* overall, and we understand very well from this lawfulness that there are a number of psychologists who have rejected any dynamic factors in our soul life (Herbart, Ziehen, and Wilhelm Wundt despite his "event" voluntarism). This view, however, is mistaken. It is mistaken because the directions of the changes and movements of our representations can never be grasped from mere laws of association and reproduction, and similarly can never be grasped in the content and in the spatiotemporal relations of content—that would just be an exclusion procedure—and it is also mistaken because the "inner-becoming" of the unperceived parts of our soul life is a much more comprehensive form of having of the psychic than are "inner perception" and "observation." We become "aware" in an entirely *un*mediated manner that we hunger, thirst, and wish for what "I want" and what "I do not want"—without having to "represent" (perceive) something to ourselves. Moreover, we become "aware" of this in the psyche *as well* as in the *objectively* given vital phenomenon so that any place and quality change appearances which are directly perceivable, as well as so-called movements and changes, size increases and decreases, gestalt and relational changes and displacement, etc., are given as direct *consequences* of earlier changes of the originally directed, unperceivable tendencies, impulses, and drives. Thus, the basic "dynamic factors" are not derived from the initially noticed appearances, nor are they "founded" upon these appearances; and there is a fundamental difference between the givenness of these dynamic factors and what is undoubtedly the case with the founding of all appearances of the world that are given to us as dead, as *not*-living ones. These dynamic factors are pre-given in two respects. There is the *pre*-givenness of the psychic, dynamic factors, of which one can become "aware" *prior* to perceiving—regardless of whether these concern the impulse, drive, will, wish, inclination, need, interest or any act, function, etc.—and there is the pregivenness of the physical, dynamic factors prior to the place change and quality change of any kind in *the* type of movement that we call "spontaneous"[55] ("self-movement" according to Aristotle) and which is the originary phenomenon, according to which we ascribe "vitality" to a thing, body, or event (be it real or not, when the originary phenomenon appears in them). *Both* of these pre-givennesses are rooted in an *identical, common* pre-givenness that I call the *pre-givenness of the directed dynamic* which is *prior to the "appearance."* The word "appearance" refers to an immediate or inferred ego-related *subjective* appearance, [335] as well as an immediate or inferred object-related *objective* appearance. I refrain from making this distinction.

In this law of pre-givenness between *merely* becoming aware and imageness, we have now gained an *idea of life* which in no way rests on inductive experience and which—this is the important point—grasps the living thing as still fully *psychophysically indifferent*, that is, it grasps the living thing in a rudimentariness of becoming—for life is becoming and only becoming and unbecoming—wherein the living being *has yet* to be split into the two dimensions of the basic types of givenness that we call "psychic" and "physical."[56] Recently, A. von Tschermak[57] has demarcated the difference between the dead and living body in the exact same sense that we have. He writes: "Accordingly, the living substance has the essential characteristics of life, i.e., specific appearances and processes, and indeed by ambiguous changes and autonomy, and thus not specific physical, chemical, or morphological qualities. No characteristic, which is solely or predominantly based on such qualities, would be definitive or exhaustive. The mere physical, chemical, morphological makeup does not sufficiently demonstrate the difference between a living thing and a non-living thing. The same makeup could be just as likely understood as a difference of the appearance, i.e., of the process of change." As *body* [*Körper*], the organisms are thus "*images*" as any other images are with all their ultimate constituent parts and their laws. However, as the *highest centers of spontaneous movements* and changes, which are rhythmitized according to building up-breaking down, in inseparable essential relation to an "environment" whose structure is just as original to the hierarchical ordering of this purposive and relational form of happening (physiological function) and is located in strictly opposing parallel coordination of "changes," these living organisms are *not* in any way images of any kind. If one wants to place the continuous monarchical construction of ordered, purposive functions in a real causal relationship to death, then one needs ultimately to do that obviously not in the sense that one places them in relation to the (entirely non-effective) ideal images of the dead world, but exclusively in relation to the forces that bring about the body-images and their spatial-temporal ordering.

The psychic (psychical epitome of function) and physiological (physiological epitome of function) are thus in no way something dualistically different—either in the final elements of a qualitative and structural kind from which the appearances and their lawful forms come into existence, or in the dynamic [336] factors and their lawful forms, which are at the root of these appearances and which are called "life" in the distinctive sense. When P. Schilder once said, "In the motoristic, the physical and psychic appear to be bound to one another in a very intimate manner," we are convinced that it is the *same* in a concept, grasped only deeply, of the (spontaneous) "motor"—in its fundamental being. The organism as body is merely the form of the becoming image, and the organism as morphological compositional is the form of the becoming unity of its function and drive structure.

The characteristic feature of the attitude of being-conscious, the only attitude in which the drive factors can be given to us, is that these factors are very *difficult to obtain* in their specific respects and in their construction through the *experimental* method. It is hardly a coincidence that doctors, physicians, and perhaps more often biologists and sociologists have given us the primary building blocks for a psychology and developmental theory of the drives for animals and humans—but experimental psychologists have done so least of all.[58] The best of what there is—I include here all the works by N. Ach and E. Jaensch—reaches only up to each intermediate stage, through which the drives become determined according to the becoming, constructing, and gestalting of the perceptive life, i.e., determined by forms of oscillation of the so-called *drive* or passive *attention.* The distribution of attention, distributed according to size and direction, always leads back to the peculiar life and weaving of the *drives.* The drive attention can be described as the pulverization of the drives by their entrance into that consciousness, accessible to inner observation, which is perceptive consciousness, and it can simultaneously be called the manner of appearance of the life drive *closest* to the perceptual sphere. We should not forget that behind the drive attention—without which *no* kind of perception is given to us and which constitutes the *realization factor* of any perceptual content—stands the specific drive *constellation* of the psychophysical organism, and oscillations of the attention first become intelligible through this constellation. While the drive—and in particular the *feeling-urge,* which in its most primitive form has yet to be differentiated as a feeling or drive, and with regard to objectification has yet to have a specific type or pre-form—constitutes *the most fundamental root* of any psychic whole, the root into which the organism itself and whatever is objectively cognizable about it are sunk—it also *constitutes* [*constituiert*] the most fundamental root of a "psychic" being's existence (as Schopenhauer rightly saw). In contrast to the drive, sensation, representation, perception, or rather anything which [337] can be called *perception* [*Perzeption*] in the broadest sense, exist on a higher level of the soul-life, probably on the distinctive *animal* level—on the level of the reporting-back of a condition and resistance of the feeling urge to a center; thus, they in no way constitute the *being-for-itself* [*Fürsichsein*] of a being and the possible *being-conscious* of its existence and being-thus.[59]

If psychologists in their studies of the image-appearances of the soul do not even come close to the *drive-motor,* which is *continuous* and not merely occasional, *co-conditionality* of all having and living representation [Vorstellungen-haben und -leben], then this also holds true especially for *perception* and *sensation.* There are particular, non-mysterious reasons for this: perception (the "outer" above all), to the naive glance, appears to be any act of perception [*Perzeption*] grounded in what is most often *outside* of us, and at the very least *inside* us; perception and its objects appear to the vital-drives as absolutely "*in opposition*"—like a mechanistic natural event. In the existence and being-thus of its appearance, perception occurs in all cases where it is not *sought* either by the drives or willfully as a perception of this or that procured thing (seeking sustenance, hunting, etc.), and thus arises wholly independently of the vital-drives. The fact that this could be rooted in a temporally significant *constancy* and in the case of *balance* in the drive-motor status of the affected organism—so that in relation to individuals of a certain type, the constancy of a condition is confused with its *nonexistence*—appears to the naive glance at the thing to lie very far away and even more so when the concept of attention is formed only in respect to the willful and in this manner "secondary" attention and the chasm of difference between the willful attention and drive attention is not recognized.[60] If one is so inclined to regard the drive attention as a practice and habit phenomenon of the *willful* attention of the spirit—an attention which in fact temporally almost always comes after perception and presupposes an appearance—then one remains far removed from the path that can lead to the truth.

A fundamentally mistaken divorce comes to exist between a perceptual range [*Perzeptionsumfang*] and an apperceptive range of consciousness from the thought of a measurability of these ranges (W. Wundt). One specific error results from the acceptance of pure perceptions [*Perzeptionen*]: the error of focusing *merely* on [338] a microscopic investigative type of soul things while neglecting the macroscopic. The motor-drive conditionality of perception and all of its partial functions is, from a microscopic investigation of the process, the most difficult to cognize. The microscopic approach looks only at *how* something is perceived, when it is perceived, and not at *what* is perceived. Moreover, these investigations take place mostly only under artificial conditions, created initially by the specific "tasks"—without being directly dictated by the trial leader—and attitudes rooted in the drives. These conditions are falsely accepted as continuing to exist outside the laboratory. Just as the living being "senses" very little of everything that is taking place in its milieu sufficient for "stimulus"—this is the case for the entirely normal state of its nervous system—and this stimulus is only a fraction of what is taking place, a living being "perceives" very little of all that it *could* perceive with regard to the external and non-drive conditions of perception. Every living being thus reaches a particular *selection*, which is dependent on almost all the *drive-motor* factors which correspond to the various *group*-concepts of the being under which the being can be classified (kind, herd, function in herd, floor; by human "race," "occupation," "class," etc.). However, these differences elude both microscopic and artificial investigations, and only become entirely clear through the *comparative* investigation of these groups and further through *developmental-theoretical* considerations (e.g., perception in the primitives and the civilized, children and adults, this and that old man). The life drive, and certainly the entirely involuntary and indigenous life drive that is *not* subjugated to the principle of experience and practice, is not directly as artificially influenceable as are the representations; it is in a sense automatically influenced by our attention to the object, an influence that is not cognitively desired and which is bracketed out with much difficulty.

Obviously, it appears at first glance as generally improbable that there should be just as rich and inherently differentiated a manifold of *differently directed drive impulses* and the motor dispositions of the organism corresponding to them as there are different cases of perception. Are not the thousand different things that we perceive entirely indifferent to us, and don't they have no influence on our motor behavior and its modification?

We ought to dwell on this argument a bit longer. A question of strictly theoretical and philosophical import can be raised in opposition to this argument. If the content of perception is *not* considered, which is our position, to be an aspect and partial content of the "*images*" *themselves* which are transcendent to human consciousness, and not primary in the being-thus of the image, and if it is assumed [339] that this content itself (and not only the function of perception and the particular choice of this content from the many different contents possible, which are likewise partial contents of the image) is directly in the cortex region of the brain and in specific processes in it—processes that are only causally determined and not otherwise through the physicalistic stimuli—then it is nonsense to accept that there are as many drive impulses and motor impulses as there are different contents of perception. It is—obviously—impossible to assume that there are just as many different motor drive impulses as there are perceivable bodies in nature. Yet, if we avoid this error, which presupposes a production of gestalts and qualities through the organism, and if we recognize that locally no single content of perception could imply anything other than that the affected cortex field is the *physiological functional field of functions* which can have a clear dependency relation only with the *psychic function* of perception (and its partial functions), then every criticism of this thesis, the criticism that every perception is necessarily drive-motor co-conditioned, is absolutely nullified. Whether I perceive a cat or a tree—the mere *how* of the perception, its nerve-physiological and psychological automatism, is for the sake of this difference alone entirely the same perception. *What* I *can* perceive, i.e., the objective possible epitome of perceptions, alone determines the "*image*"—the nature of the cat and of the tree. What is *realized* through the undisturbed flowing of the perceptual automatism (by virtue of the specific sense organization) from this objective playroom of aspect possibilities, is what determines—while refraining from the spiritual acts brought into play that can be based on the functions of the vital soul of human beings—negatively and positively the *motor-drive behavior* that the stimulus triggers in the indivisible gestalt unity of the temporal course of the physiological sense-motor function with the centripetal processes.

In this basic view, nothing is in principle mysterious or muddled—as it is when perception is regarded as determined through end processes and brought about mythologically from the nerve-processes or from soul productions that should bring forth the perceptual content as an "immaterial image"; this is utter nonsense, since causality is possible only between the *real*, not between the real and the ideal. The immaterial image should stand with a body divested of any gestalt or quality in an entirely opaque causal connection ("critical realism"). If one should then still mean—when one shakes off this error—that there could not be as many different combinations of drive-motor functional processes as there are and there could not be different kinds of sensor- [340] centripetal, physiological functions (and on them clearly bound psychic partial functions), then this would be a completely unfounded prejudice with regard to the construction and the physiological meaning of those aspects of the nervous system that are still unknown to us. Is the activity, or is even the simplest component of work of any basic kind which the present, highly developed physiology of work breaks every act of work down into,[61] less complicated and, with regard to the most varied strata of the nervous system, less problematic than perception? And psychologically? When does one have the right to think of the "drive impulse" only as the unified, radical jolt of hunger, thirst, or sexual impulse and not also think of the drive impulse as its ramifications and refinements into inclinations, needs, and attitudes? In a more central and conscious direction, the developing life drive fans out *ever more richly* in its most extreme branching out and fluctuating to and fro (in the form of "oscillations" of the passive and drive attention impulse). If we speak of "indifferent" or interestless perception or a purely "passive" perception, then there is either self-delusion or imprecision in language. These words mean only that we turn to the perceiving with no *voluntary* attentiveness or *spiritual interest*; or that a majority of impulses which are always antagonistic like the drives corresponding to them (the accompanying feelings of ambivalence) are the counterbalances and thus bring about the positive condition of the "indifference." In reality, there are only nuanced gradations in the "passion" of perception, as P. Schilder one time curtly and insightfully remarked.

It is a great error to bind the drive impulses more to the sensations of the *lower* senses than with those of the higher senses. What is probably more correct is only that the drives to preserve and increase the species have a lasting connection with the organ sensations and the sensations of the so-called lower senses than with the drives that serve individual and collective preservation, like all nutrition and power drives. Schilder[62] remarks correctly: "In seeing and in hearing, there lies a drive affection [*Zuwendung*]. An object in the lateral field of vision awakens the instinctive affection for it; expressed differently: awakens the drive to look at it." Jaensch[63] has shown how dramatically this particular field of vision restriction varies. In the case of stricter restrictions of the lateral field, this drive impulse still remains (and thus through a greater number of eye movements the defect is able to be offset) [341], but in the case of very weak restrictions grounded in the sensing retinal elements, the simplest conditions of orientation are severely damaged. He has further shown which fundamental role befits the wanderings of the involuntary attention in the case of freeing of the optical content for the spatial place value—so that the objects remain in their "place" through eye movements, and the optical intuitive place-system is relieved of its content. The distinction particular to any perception between "figure" and "background," a distinction grasped through the sense modalities and, for the becoming of the subjective spatial intuition, one of the most secure points of departure, seems to me, despite Rubin's[64] objections, to have its ultimate roots likewise in the points of emphasis of both constituent parts through the drive attention (as the co-condition of experience itself).[65] The kinesthetic experience grasped through all sense modalities does not create an additional "ordering" of a tactile or visual space to the spatial schema, which vaguely exist without touch or vision, of one's own body and of the environment. This experience is the *common root* of the spatial intuition in general, as E. von Hartmann and H. Bergson correctly realized.[66]

Yet, even more certain is how the facts of *comparative physiology and psychology* speak in support of our investigation. Every sentient being has at its disposal the qualities and content of possible sensations which have an indicative function for environmental things, indicating what is beneficial and harmful to the being and its drive-motor behavior.[67] All qualities are *primarily* given as *value* qualities, for example, such things as mating and warning calls. As a consequence, they also become fixed signs and indications for the *being-thus* of the particular objects which lie in the value direction of the drives and their antagonists, and furthermore, they become objects of consciousness as qualities *without* this indicating function.[68] As is very much the case in the animal kingdom, the "lover" and the pioneer precede the "knowers," the fact conveyed by [342] von Frisch that there are "scout bees" and "collectors" within the bee species: for the former, the colors and aromas of the blossoms are a "mating call," while for the latter they are "indicators." The extent to which the felt value qualities and their power directly attracting the life drives *pre*cede the image qualities, and the extent to which those value qualities which are merely *biologically* beneficial or detrimental precede the *spiritual* meaning (striking, for example, in contrast to the beautiful), and no less precede the sensible meaning corresponding to the feeling sensations, are all problems I have addressed elsewhere.[69]

The elements of truth in the pragmatic theory of perception are confirmed ultimately through the objective sequence of events of *ontogenesis* and *phylogenesis* which exist among afferent neurons, efferent neurons, and effectoric organs (as the simplest elements of the nervous system). According to Sherrington's well-known works, the afferent neuron should come along initially, then the efferent neuron, and then the effectoric organ enters into the morphogenetic process. However, T. Graham Brown sought to show, in a penetrating critique of Sherrington's proposals, that the true morphogenesis unfolds differently: that "the simplest nervous mechanisms of the efferent neuron and the effectoric organ are constructed independently and that the effective stimulus has been originally a stimulus equivalent to the blood stimulus in breathing"—thus a vegetative stimulus.[70] First of all, the central stimulus image organ, which responds to inner stimuli like a food shortage or a drive impulse, as well as needs of all kinds, and the locomotive organ are morphologically separate—and then as the organization progresses and the efferent center and the outer world are distinguished from one another more distinctly, an afferent neuron (as the point of departure of *all outer* sense organs) comes along. It is thus the *primary* task of the structure-imaging vital function to confront swiftly and extensively the changed condition of the organism itself *through a motor reaction*, and not to construct organs which can be stimulated in the most diverse and sensitive ways by things in the environment. This also corresponds to the fact that the lowest layers in the central nervous systems of the higher animals are such a vital function for blood stimulus, e.g., vital functions such as the respiratory system that remains active in narcosis or also in the case of failure of the efferent parts of the reflex arc (Vagus). The sensible organs ascribed to the outer world [343] have, according to this view, already been constructed under the determination of an inner *stimulus system* (which manifests psychically in a specific structure as a *drive system*) and under the locomotive system directed outwardly—as systems of help and control for the active movements of the organism.

The motor-dynamic theory of perception is further strongly supported by the fact that, according to Pütter, the education of the optical apparatus follows the way in which the species has developed and the means of *mobility* of the organism. In general, where the utility of a quality and modality through the *movement* of the organism—in accordance with its inner intelligibility and drive stimulus—is not present, a function and an organ appear not to have been constructed for the effected quality. Thus, according to Edinger, a lizard does not hear a pistol fire, if it does not change its behavior—when by contrast it turns and flees at the slightest touch on its head. The bees possess, according to von Frisch's excellent experiment, a rich sense for colorful flowers, and particularly for the ultraviolet quality that is missing in humans—yet no sensation for scarlet red; this is the case because they dwell among the flowers that they visit for honey and nectar, and because they fertilize flowers that emit ultraviolet rays but not scarlet rays.

This validates the law: *an organism has only the sense qualities as the alphabet of its possible world-image which can be the luring and indicative signs for the objects* that are *meaningful for its drive-motor behavior.* Thus, the sensation appears ultimately only as a means of setting the indices for present or approaching *resistances* that oppose the active movements of the organism in order to control, with the help of these indices, the act of movement, to supervise, to mete out purposively the innervation of the movement *before* its success or failure.

Thus, this *justifies* what we have found above in relation to *the interpretation of the mechanistic view of nature absolutely through the theory of perception*—and moreover, what we will have to say about the givenness of reality is also prepared through these last comments.

Perception and Fantasy

And yet, there is still one final and quite difficult point to clarify: it concerns the *relation between perception* as well as sensation and any activity of the vital-psyche that we call *fantasy*. It is necessary to examine this problem—though we cannot do this to any great extent here—because the facts appear to impel us to distance ourselves from the sensualistic and empiricist views which are still so strongly disseminated with regard to this problem.

[344] What is still currently and widely dominant is the theory that all fantasy images derive from the *reproduction* of original stimulus-conditioned and stimulus-proportional perceptions insofar as parts or pieces of these perceptual contents and their memory residues, under the different and particular influences of a drive or emotional type, form a connection to some whole that does not exist in reality, whether through assimilation or in accord with the rules of association. What is rejected apriori, however, is the existence of an *originally productive* fantasy that is either close to or independent of this reproductive fantasy, which undeniably exists. The denial of such an originally productive fantasy rests not on some set of facts, but rather on the attempt to preserve a theory of the genesis of our representative world according to which there "can in no way be" something otherwise.

However this view is developed—whether one accepts only physiological or additional psychic residues, as F. E. Beneke and most recently E. Becher in his psychistic theory of memory have done—the totality of facts which we have gleaned from the soul life of the child, from the soul life of primitive peoples and the most ancient humanity in general, and from the disintegration of the higher soul functions in the case of mental illness, in particular schizophrenia, support, at least at an initial and vague glance, the greatest *opposition* to this empiricist-sensualist theory of fantasy as is possible. This theory of fantasy mistakenly assumes that this original type of productive phantasy is present in the *primitive* stages of psychic development. It is rather absolutely clear—when all deeper questions and all finer distinctions are laid aside—that this productive fantasy emerges as a very *late product of development*, namely at that stage when there is stimulus-proportionality between sensation and perception! Following this theory, we would expect that with increasing experience and development, fantasy images would interfere to an ever-increasing degree in perception and memory and would push us more and more away from genuine perception and memory. The glaring fact is that all psychic and historic development of the human being is a long process of *disillusion-*

ment and *disappointment* regarding primary fantasy images posited as real, and is a rising *resignative hesitation* of the original project of the *will* in the mere *wish* sphere; and this fact is completely incomprehensible for this theory. In the problems of the development of the will, the empiricist theory of the will—the "heterogenetic" theory, as W. Wundt calls it—has been proven without a doubt to be false, as C. von Sigwart and W. Wundt have already recognized. In no way do the experiences regarding the incidental success and failure of projects of the will stem from movements of a reflective character. Rather, there is in all kinds of living beings an inborn system of antagonistic *drives* [345] and instincts which are ordered according to their intensity, the urgency of satisfying the need, and above all according to originally given, dynamic directions: drives and instincts directed toward a particular *value* sphere and its accompanying course of feelings; drives and instincts that are originally goal-directed, holistic, lasting, and also effective in respect to rhythmic change of more intensive movement, and are genetically the point of departure for chosen and willful actions as well of for the so-called reflexes. Only if one accepts that the drives *themselves originally bring forth* the representational images relative to them, can one understand the fantasy world as a form of primitive, childish, and ailing emotional life—but never if one thinks of them as combined afterward from pieces of perceptions. If all *stimulus*-conditioned representing, perceiving, and sensing are considered in relation to this *original forming of impulses and drive fantasies*, then the relation is not one in which representing, perceiving, and sensing serve as the pre-given "materials" for fantasy, materials from which every construct would be constructed, but rather they serve as an increasing *restriction* and *correction* of fantasy. This means: the constructs of fantasy, which are not cognized in the early stages of spiritual development *as* such fantasized constructs, are cognized to the extent that our *behaving* toward objects and our movements toward them *disappoint* our expectations through continued failure. For since the phenomenal perceptual character can be strictly identical to image contents (genuine hallucinations, illusions, sleep phantasms in which states of affairs are suggested positively or negatively through hypnosis) determined entirely or to a great extent by our nervous system, what legitimates perception as *subjective*—objectively it defines the stimulus conditionality in the sense of approximating proportionality—is only the *success of our practical behavior* toward objects and indeed above all its *lawfully recurring success.*

If we accept this still very raw hypothesis—putting aside many pressing objections—then we must raise a very radical question which necessarily appears when we remember our earlier results: first, the intuitable content of perception never leads back to sensation complexes, and second, it is an identical *partial* content of the "*image*" *itself*, which is conscious- and knowledge-transcendent and is continually co-intended in the perception, and which constitutes the object of perception. Would it not be the likeliest of cases that the identical partial aspect, which is the same in both the perceptual content and image—seen from the perspective of the subject—*is always the content of fantasy*, namely every *part* of the construct of the spontaneous drive and impulse fantasy, which is indifferent with regard to the meaning of reality and references to reality, a construct that *proves itself* and prevails in the practical experiences of [346] success and failure of our behavior and our movement?

Psychology teaches us—insofar as it is sensualistically oriented—in a host of investigations (among which the works on the psychology of reading are most outstanding) that quite a large part of our perceptual content is owed to fantasy without us being in the least *conscious* of it as fantasy content (bracketing out the blind patches through fantasy; continual optical and tactile fields of discrete sensations, etc.). If we keep to our aforementioned strict division between sensation and perceptual content and maintain that sensations are only found where our intentional movements and the accompanying impulses run into resistance, and we maintain that sensations can never portray or "mean" something objective, but rather, they are actually only an organic condition which controls our activity, then the hypothesis appears to me to be fully justified that the *content of perception* as such is *entirely and utterly content of fantasy*—and is "*proven to be so*" in the above sense. Furthermore, such fantasy content stands—and indeed *must* stand—in lawful correlation to conscious and unconscious sense organ sensations, since the same drive and motor impulse-tensions [*Züge*], in which a fantasy unity is proven as perception, co-condition the simultaneous sensations that are originally brought forth by stimuli. The strict lawful connection between perception and sensation is proven in this hypothesis to no less degree than it is in the sensualistic hypothesis. Yet, the functional *unity* of perception, in spite of the many participating sense organs and functions; the leading pre-given rules that are certainly established and which are so fully paradoxical under the sensualistic presupposition; the uniform cooperation of sense functions of different modality in the case of genuine hallucination; and the fact of perception suggested in hypnosis—all of this and much more would become much easier to comprehend if we accept this presupposition.

Yet, it appears to me, this view of the activity of fantasy—not as the final genetic result of sensation or of reproductive and assimilative processes, but rather as the *most original*, spontaneous, perceptual activity which remains readily attentive by virtue of the drives, as an activity which would be *restricted*, *restrained*, and above all *constructed* by reproduction and sensation—would *physiologically* be very much in agreement (particularly given the great number of newly discovered facts) with the already mentioned psychical facts of development. If any *chrono-genetic* meaning in biological development—a meaning Monakow has shown it must have—is to be given to the different segments of the nervous system, which must pass through the physiologically parallel process of every simple experience in order to become level by level (as we could reasonably isolate them in the pathological breakdown of experience) what we discover as already finished in normal [347] consciousness, then it is to be expected from our hypothesis that the perception *nearing* the sensation and perceptual is the *result of the inhibition* and the breakdown of inhibitions, which exercise the *highest*-most localized cortex functions on the activity of the most deeply rooted centers. The sensualistic and empiricistic theory of fantasy would expect the exact opposite to take place! It would have to expect that the lower-lying centers and the processes taking place here would have psychic correlates that come fairly close to the stimulus-proportional sensation. This theory would also expect that, in accord with the old representation of the fibers of association, the countering roles have fallen to the highest cortex function to reshape the punctual sensations constructed in the lower-lying centers into *accompanying* constructs of perception, representation, and thoughts. Moreover, the fantasy activity that already presupposed, according to the sensualistic theory of fantasy, sensation, reproduction, association, assimilation as one of its becoming principles—and a rich work of the same principle—would have to belong to this fundamental conception of the cortex function. However, the fact that there is an *increase* in fantasy activity during sleep, i.e., the fact of dream fantasy, and the preponderance that spontaneous fantasy gains in many cases of mental illnesses, demonstrate the fact that there is a powerful stimulability of fantasy through the evident and partial *elimination* of the restraining activity of the highest centers in the hypnotic and somnambulant condition, and further through narcotics of all kinds (alcohol, hashish, opium, etc.). The fact that there is a tendency to the realization of the object, a tendency, according to G. F. Lipps's correct view, which comes to every drive-lead perception (but not every voluntarily caused perception, as Baudouin incorrectly maintains); the fact that there is a quite expansive influence of the gland activity and other physiological-vegetative processes (digestion, beginnings of movement in the case of fantasized walking, according to Plesch, and sexual processes) through representation processes, and indeed this to the extent that they are not voluntarily caused, but are led up *automatically* through drive impulse into consciousness—all of *these facts together demonstrate* the exact *opposite* which would be anticipated by the sensualistic theory. These facts also demonstrate that fantasy activity, in contrast to conscious sensation, perception, and memory, is bound to relatively *lower* segments of the nervous system; they demonstrate further—if we were to examine fully the impact of these facts, which cannot happen here—that for fantasy the *highest* cortex centers and the processes belonging to them (as they continue to be more precisely represented) mean something much more *isolated, restrictive,* and *selective* in the utilization for external tasks, further removed from consciousness than being a positive condition for emergence of fantasies. The established aspects of psychoanalytic research [348] demand the recognition of a spontaneous, continual, unconscious, effective drive and urge fantasy which, found generally only in a few pieces and buried by the "waking censor" or only interpreted symbolically, projects into consciousness and reaches *as far back* as drives and urges in general.

How intimately fantasy activity belongs to the life drive is demonstrated by a different fact, which is not always recognized to the fullest extent: the fact of the *value indifference of fantasy* with regard to *spiritual,* objective value that befits *jointly* the drive and fantasy. In this sense, Kant already calls fantasy the "force of imagination," a "blind" capacity of the soul. Since the drives are not bad or good in the ethical sense, but rather playful and demonic and thus indifferent to ethical values, fantasy is *indifferent* to what is true or false, reasonably realistic, or contrary to reality. This latter point calls attention to the tendency in the common vernacular *to equate* fantasy constructs with *unreasonable* perceptions of reality: the fantasized is already in itself untrue, contrary to reality, illusion, etc. That this is not so and cannot be so is, however, already demonstrated by the fact that *fantasy as spiritually directed activity* plays the greatest, most conceivable role in any realization of objectively spiritual actual values [*Sachwerte*]: that fantasy plays quantitatively as much a role in mathematical, natural scientific, and spiritual-historical research—as combining and constructive fantasies in the inventor, technician, statesman, and strategist—as it does in the soul-life of the paralytic and the schizophrenic. Just as a human being in the existential [*existentiell*] sense remains deficient without a strong and differentiated life drive, even when he or she lends an ear to any ethical demand, so too do cognition and research remain "deficient" without a strong fantasy activity even when all logical laws are sufficient.

Drives and fantasy are jointly the *fruitfulness of the vital-soul* without which "*spirit,*" which is fundamentally only *negative,* limiting, inhibiting, and disinhibiting (as thinking, willing, preferencing, etc.), would have no *substrate* for its effectiveness. It can easily be shown, generally, that when we cannot grasp the real through sensible perception (because of its limitations) and when we strive for an intuitive, general image of reality, we are instructed by nothing other than fantasy. The person who reconstructs animals and plants from fossils according to the known construction laws of an extinct species, who wishes to make an image of the surfaces of Mars, the Moon, or of the interiority of the Earth, etc., is instructed by fantasy.

For *metaphysics*, which is co-defined through the state of affairs and deals with objects that are real in themselves, objects which neither directly nor indirectly have an effect on [349] our empirical sensibility, fantasy is *eo ipso the single intuitable cognitive force*—a fact that is in no way grounds for an objection to the possible *real*-reasonableness of metaphysical cognition. The value of fantasy accomplishments of any kind wholly concerns whether the fantasy, which is the original effect of the drives and drive impulses, is or is not placed under the right *control,* i.e., the directing and channeling of it through acts of the spirit of any kind. Therein alone lies the difference between the fantasy images of error and the fantasy accomplishments of geniuses of every type.

"Fantasy" in the waking life of highly civilized human beings and human beings coming into maturity is for us not a highly complicated construction that is built from perception, reproduction, assimilation, etc. Rather, fantasy is for us the *remnant activity* of the perceiving [*perzipierenden*] activity of the *vital soul,* activity which has not yet been integrated into the useful accomplishments of *work,* or any other accomplishments in the real world; fantasy has therefore not yet been specified. Fantasy is the continual surplus of the perceiving [*perzipierenden*], still *undifferentiated* in memory and perception, *life* which has yet to be used in a task in reality. It is the original form of the perceiving [*perzipierenden*] life itself—and is thus not a late reorganization; fantasy is the original form of the yet unspecified, vivid, unused part of the vital-soul energy, *of the "fantasy-urge" itself.*[71]

In this respect, speculative and romantic philosophy's concepts of the "creative," the "productive" force of the imagination (Kant, Fichte, Schelling, Carus, etc.) become truly legitimated. We thus now understand the facts (1) that there is no *pure* reproduction—every representation is a *new* construct and so is the most precise, clearest, and most objective honest representation of memory; and (2) that the development and experience go in the direction where the productive fantasy constituent parts of the memory image—even in those cases, from the standpoint of its cognitive value, where the "forgery" of fantasy is recognized in the memories—*gradually decrease,* i.e., *more* and *more* is recognized as the "mere product of fantasy" in that which is in the intention of the remembrance grasping past reality. In the life of the community, *historical, critical science* thus takes the place of *myth,* legend, and fantasy-laden *tradition,* and *distinguishes* reality from the unreal.

Our view that there is an *original* drive fantasy, which must be distinguished from the reproductive fantasy that already works with the elements of perception and reproduction, appears to us to be strongly supported through the still new insight of psychology that *perception* and *representation become more and more distinct from one another* in the course of psychic development. [350] Since the psychophysical organism tends (through its drives, and appropriate to its drive structure) from the first moment to produce a fantasy image, and likewise the organism from the first moment of its existence is under the stimuli of the environment to which every drive fantasy, through the movement impulse, seeks to adapt to images of the outer world, then it cannot be otherwise than that the "intuitive constructs" resulting from these *antagonistic* tendencies *neither* bear the characteristic features of representation *nor* any of the features of perception in developed stages. The investigations by C. Stumpf[72] have convinced us—further abandoning the old assumption by Meynert, Jaspers, etc.—that there is a specific, clear, and gradual difference between representation and perception. Even before the "eidetic" investigation by E. Jaensch and his collaborators (who followed a suggestion by Urbantschitz), Lindworsky, in an impressive investigation of the clear and gradual emergence of the difference between representation and perception, has proposed the thesis that both of these construct types differentiate themselves in the course of development. Jaensch was able to thoroughly confirm this statement at the time for the optical area. It is important to note that these theses do not propose that the human being learns through an *experiential* process to *distinguish* what are in isolated cases representation and perception. It is not the remarking or the judgment regarding this perceptual content (*Perzeptionsinhalte*), but rather the *constructs themselves* that differentiate themselves from a perceptive pre-form.[73] The old fantasy theory is rejected in principle through this important insight. For this ancient theory presupposed that every representation stems from perception and from the stimulation of the residues posited from perception, and the theory was only able to grant a genesis of the *conscious* differentiation of both constructs. Something quite similar holds true for the differentiation between genuinely intentional *remembering* and any content related to *tradition*, and to sensible memories (e.g., memory of color), which masquerade (in contrast to genuine remembering) as present and real, as similar to the perceptual object, and yet stem from reproduction and practice. A *dissociation* (not an assimilation from what was previously divorced contents) breaks this construct into two objects: the genuine perceptual object and the genuine memory.[74]

[351] We are now clearly unable to refer to these contents of perception [*Perzeption*], contents still undifferentiated in both respects, without some additional reference to "fantasy contents," and we are particularly

unable if we understand by fantasy image the intentional fantasy image known already *as* such. Already in experience, the fantasy image is already distinguished in varying degrees from memory and perception and is moreover always already an admixture of both originally productive and reproductive (having constituent parts arising from perception and memory) fantasy. If we address the "original perceptions" [*Urperzeptionen*]—as we at one time wanted to say—as the content of an original drive fantasy, then we are able to do this in the sense that the original production of fantasy accessible to us is only theoretically and hypothetically co-active in the flow of constructs that is unstable, graphic, and which springs from and is the consequence of the drive impulses. The stream of constructs is what we call "fantasy" in the differentiated and developed emotional life.

At this point, we can anticipate some obvious questions: Should nothing whatsoever have been inferred from perception and reproduction in the constructs of original fantasy activity? Don't the boldest fantasy objects (*ficta*) presuppose experiences of reality that are subsequently newly combined, formed, broadened, narrowed, and set together like mosaic rocks arbitrarily and playfully as always? Does not the dragon presuppose the sighting of an empirical bird, the flying angel the sighting of a child and bird, etc.? And when everything about this is denied, must not, at the very least, the *qualities* themselves, which are used in the construction of the fantasy, and the ontological *forms* and the corresponding forms of thought in which they are imagined, be indebted to the sensation and objective experience of actual existing things? Doesn't this mean that we have to accept some things as "inborn representations" when we dare to say no to these questions? And finally, from where does the similarity between any type of fantasy construct—which include the fantasy constructs of group fantasy, the constructs of myths, of the sage, and of the popular poetry, as well as those fantasy constructs of the individual—and the milieu of reality, a similarity that any fantasy gestalt of the individual person or of the people demonstrates decisively? For the northerner and southerner, the collector, the farmhand, the hunter, the Negro, Yellow, and White, etc., have other fantasy gestalts—and isn't this otherness the difference relative to the actual world area in which these groups live? Where do the precise limits of the productions force of the vital spontaneous subject lie?

Up to this point, there has been no agreement regarding these questions. W. Dilthey himself, who had looked [352] so deeply into the inner workshop of fantasy creations in his essay on "The Force of Fantasy of the Poets,"[75] writes: "All constructs of the emotional life are made up of perceptions as their elements; also works of poetry." "And when Homer, Dante, and Milton exceed this earth and allow us to see Olympus and the underworld, heaven and hell, they must use colors and impressions, which delight us here, for their sensible images of the glory of heaven, and colors and impressions which frighten us here, for their images of gloom and fervor; they must piece together and intensify the inner states of desire and suffering, which they have themselves experienced, for depictions of the blessedness of the gods and the pure angels as well as for the powerlessness of the deceased or the agony of the damned. When Walter Scott and Conrad F. Meyer transport us back into historical situations that are entirely foreign to our own, no elementary feeling, no representation can be used that is not created from our present and the situations experienced in it. Locke and Hume already sought to formulate the psychological reason for this. We are able to invent not a single element of the emotional life, but rather must take every element from experience."

Paul Häberlin[76] takes an entirely different position: "One often believes that the fantasy representation is constructed from elements of object representation, a kind of combination of real elements. This holds true perhaps in the specific sense for the secondary, reflective fantasy, but certainly not for the primary fantasy about which we speak of here; the primary fantasy creates purely from the personal interest present in feeling form up to that point." M. Palagyi seeks to carry out a similar distinction between primary and purely productive and reproductive fantasy in his lectures on natural philosophy.[77]

A precise response to this question of the *limits* of fantasy activity and its dependence and non-dependence could yield precise phenomenological, developmental-psychological, and experimental research into the *levels* of fantasy activity that exist between the most primary and most reflective fantasy activities. This is an important task of the future, which we cannot undertake here. We must be content with just a few further remarks.

The fundamental errors of "Locke's and Hume's view"—errors curiously shared by W. Dilthey himself—lie in the fact that the tremendous variety of ways of givenness of our intuitable representation world are not clarified, that the developmental thinking is fully missed in the consideration, and that the entirely different theoretical clarification possibilities for meaning, gestalt, and structure analogies which undoubtedly exist between perceptual reality (in the phenomenal sense) and the fantasy world [353] are not thought. Consequently one listens far less to the facts than to the quite impoverished natural theory of "healthy human reason," if it "could" be nothing other than that all fantasy images and their *objects* (from which irreal *ficta* are to be distinguished) are made up of real pieces of experience.

Let us then question whether the acceptance of a primary, creative fantasy drive actually amounts to the acceptance of "innate" representations and ideas. This is certainly the case for those intellectualists who either reject drives in general or who assume that the differentiation of the drives in such different "directions to something" already presupposes an image or meaning *representation* of this "something." Then the representation of the nest would have to be "innate" in the nest-building bird, and the representation of womanhood and possibly of the different sexual genitals would be "innate" in the sex drive of a man. Yet, this conclusion does not arise when the *drive conditionality of any* representation is taken seriously and the directionality and goal-directivity *to objects* are conferred primordially upon the drives, and when we assign the gradual differentiation of the life drives to the *maturation* of the psychophysical organism in the rhythm of aging; when the becoming of the original fantasy images themselves, which is a psycho-vital, automatic process, is distinguished from the *reflection* on those images, i.e., from the *consciousness of* those images. If by experience one understands this "consciousness of," then we experience in it the images of these images, but we do not experience in any way these images in fantasizing, but rather *their objects*—hence, for example, the (non-real) golden mountain *itself*—but not, for instance, a fantasy image that thoroughly belongs in the sphere of the real and highest effects (e.g., on our salivary and digestive glands).

That the drives possess such *original* directions demonstrates most clearly the phenomenon of the experiences of *fulfillment* and non-fulfillment (and experience of conflict), when real objects, according to which our drives are originally ordered, oppose or stop them in perception. However, if the drives possess original directional determinacy, then it is not possible to see why the drives are not also able to give to our representational activity—which is certainly not acquired through experience, since this activity is the vehicle of *all* experiencing—under the determination of automatic stimulus processes the specific impetus to create original objects for the *kind* of being and value that—were they to be real—would be suitable to satisfy these drives. Nothing is entirely "unthinkable" here. On the contrary, the innate instincts of animals, in particular the insects, compel us at the very least to genuinely posit this as a possible thought. Nonetheless, the *partial identity* of the elements of the fantasy images and the contents of perception do not need [354] to arise from the idea that the fantasy images are only "combinations" of parts of the contents of perception. This is shown by the fact that not only the fantasy images but *also* the contents of *perception are co-determined by the drive impulse in its becoming*, and that the milieu structure and drive structure of the organism stand in strict *reciprocal correlation* from the beginning. This is the case because the existential level, from whose area the objects and parts of the fantasy images, as well as its imaginary objects, should not be constructed and combined according to empiricist theories, is neither the level of physical reality nor of the metaphysical world "in itself," but rather solely that of the *environmental sphere,* which is different from species to species, though of identical physical reality.

The drive structure, and also the dynamic modification of the drive structure in the aging process, are for the fantasy world *and* the perceptual world a *dynamic constant.* The acts of movement and tendencies of movement which lead to new perceptions are always *already directed* through the drive fantasy in the form of a vague sketch of something "of the type" like that which corresponds to the satisfaction of the drive and, on the other hand, like that which the sensible organ material created by the stimuli "motivates" the drive impulse to the formation of perception, which is nothing other than the act of perception.

Yet, along with this factor, which explains every partial coincidence—*without* the empiricist theory—an entire host of other factors arise that convey still further analogies and partial similarities of both worlds of objects. The productive force of the imagination has—so to speak—everything in the givenness at the disposal of the productive force of the imagination—so to speak—for the construction of its constructs, which in the developed consciousness is to be found in the *non-sensible apriori content* of our knowledge, will, and feeling: the a priori of intuition as well as thinking, loving, preferencing of values, and also the will as action and construction. It places at its disposal the purely objectively valid, formal, and material being apriori as every psychical functional lawfulness that we have earlier pointed out and distinguished from the thing-apriori. This is the case because this gigantic knowledge area of apriori object determinativeness, like the apriori function forms corresponding to them and originally acquired in every determination through "functionalization," can be gained in reflective cognition of the fantasy object just as in perceptual experience. Everything which, after the phenomenological reduction, either remains or newly reveals in knowable objectivity a something—and everything that is also something of possible fantasy activity—must in no way be born from the "experience of reality."

There, available to fantasy, are the purely logical forms and laws and all forms of being and relation which determine the structure of reason, [355] forms according to which the fantasy worlds of art and poetry, the pantheon and pandemonium of the world of the masses, are originally constructed in no less a manner than the natural and scientific experiences. They are not all taken from the experience of reality—as "Locke and Hume" thought—but rather all prescribe to this experience no other laws than fantasy experience. In the fantasy world, there are things and effects, forces and relational forms of all kinds, etc. like those in the experience of reality. There is movement, time, and space in which fantasy plays out its symmetries and rhythms—the preferential forms of the type in question, in accord with race—without a model from the experience of reality. The entire objectivity of "pure" mathematics is a pure fantasy objectivity of "pure" imaginative force, usable for the order of experience of natural reality, since the "fantasy space of the geometer"—as O. Liebmann remarks—can be used extensively for approaching congruence with the space of nature of the physicist; and this is the case because—as E. Jaensch has shown[78]—the representational space develops from the genetic, aging spatial relations of the *intuitive images* with the perceptual space together with the distinction between perception and representation.

The "spheres" of the "outer-world," the "body schema," life center, person center, environment, ego and environment, holy-divine, and the "inner-world" are *pre-given* to fantasy activity as the playrooms of its creation in no less a fashion than they are pre-given to perceivable reality.

The same holds true for all "*original phenomena*" and for all genuine "*ideas*," as well as for the *values of beings* and their structural relations insofar as they are functionalized. They lead the movement of fantasy into the spiritual fantasy activity. The measure of "truth" which belongs to artificial fantasy creations exists in order to produce intuitive, concrete constructs that are as clear and pure, rich and meaningful, and expressive-laden and meaning-depth as possible, constructs that correspond to the material apriori of *any possible world content*; and where possible they even surpass actual nature—as Schopenhauer says, calling out to nature: "That you had 'meant' nature, but you did not entirely succeed."

Yet, not only perception fantasy but also *feeling fantasy* blends real feelings with never-felt feelings, and it accomplishes this all the more so the more it is not the real process laws, but rather the sense laws of the life of feeling come into their own.[79] It is truly *not the richness* of actual life and experience [356]—it is its *poverty* compared to the real existential conditions possible for *an* individual and *a* life, a poverty that is the most powerful impetus for all artistic creation and all enjoyment of art; and it is no less the impetus to exceed in the historical humanities the "small" life of every historical moment with its blinders and to view and feel the world through the unrealistic structures of spirit.

When we descend still further into the *concrete* of fantasy content, the empiricist theory does not hold true. It cannot hold true even in the slightest for the sense qualities. The answer to the question as to whether we would not be able to imagine a color nuance that would never be able to be sensed as a real, adequate stimulus, when the so-called basic colors and the apriori order structure, which there are certainly the world of color and tone and most likely for the remaining qualities, are given to us and when we change them in fantasy through blending—is at the very least not as certain as D. Hume had thought in his famous questions. It is just as unclear to us that we ourselves are unable to produce sensed appearing colors (and analogous to other sense areas) by virtue of possession of the most elementary color sensations; whether we must have sensed actual splendor in order to radiate "splendor" over an artistic construct. What we can say with confidence regarding the (above-stated) dependency of all—as well as the most elementary, but still experienced—sensations of attention, language, and of the temporal, spatial, and other formations of objects to which a perception intends (and to such an object belongs any sensation), is that all of the inner factors, which co-determine the *appearing* of qualities, can certainly have an effect on the *primary* fantasy activity, since they are not dependent on the function of outer sense organs as more or less central factors. The tremendous educatability of all meaning—through practice, artistic activity, occupation with an area of sensible appearances—beyond the givenness of the natural worldview alone proves the far-reaching meaning of these inner factors.

However, if we leave this question open here—the question of how simple experiences must be that "the soul" cannot discover them—then the no longer entirely original, but already in some respects "reproductive" fantasy must not presuppose the experience of actual things and events through perception and memory, as the empiricists maintain, but rather must only presuppose a level of givenness of the object world—of the outer and the inner world—that far renounces an experience-relative knowledge of the actual world of things. *The* givennesses of the outer and inner world, [357] which can be described as the *intuitable* state of affairs of appearances as they stand according to the mean between the state of affairs graspable only in judgment and the concrete thing perceptions of the order of givenness, are sufficient as empirical stuff for the fantasy activity. The peculiar character of this level of givenness is that the solely real, concrete thing and effect centers (which manifest themselves in the "images" and real experience unities), and with them all specific spatial and temporal localizations of these centers, remain *undetermined*, and only the intuited being-thus of something (X) is incorporated in the experience. It is the enormous realm of the non-genuine, not strictly apriori *essences* and *essential state of affairs* that I have in mind. Hence I can know, for instance, through the memory of states of affairs of an intuitable sort, that I have already perceived at one time "such a thing," or that I have perceived something the same, similar, or equivalent to the present facts in this or any basis; or that someone has informed me of this (=X) or any one of them (a sense unity)—or perhaps I have only read something of the kind. Thus I can perceptually grasp the being blue of something or the being spherical of something in the distance; but I am also able to grasp slenderness, coarseness, rawness, fineness, softness, vitality, and even felineness, masculinity and femininity in things, remaining undetermined as things, of factually the most different kinds and species as material, so to speak free-floating phenomena. In this sense, it is absolutely the case that there are, for example, non-lionly lions and lionly men, feminine men and masculine women, etc. These floating appearances to which these examples are drawing our attention certainly are not conscious analogies and definitely not abstract, conceptual meanings universal in nature, i.e., *as* thought to be universal in nature—at the very least not at the development level where such appearances first come to experience. Analogy as empirical universal meaning already presupposes a material differentiation and grasping of the concrete *bearer* of these appearances that is *not* originally present. As abstract, these appearances are given when the experience progresses up to the experience of material concretion. The appearances are absolutely meant as single objects and are found as "the same" in every possible, concrete situation and any possibly remaining, entirely diverse kinds of things. They do not have a trace of material pieces in them—and are not, on the other hand, abstract contents that would have come into existence through negative or positive abstraction. They are simultaneously truly the genetic point of departure of our material experiences *and* our abstractions, for which ultimately they must share the identical "respects" and "aspects," which abstraction and generalization presuppose. Spatial and temporal in no way [358] classify the one space or the one time, and they have likewise formed spatiality and temporality within the limits of their intuited unities. They construct, so to speak, a freely suspended realm—in contrast to the material ordered reality and the succession of real experiences in time—a realm of ghostly content that is truly unrelated to intuition, and which is unspeakably *vivid* for the drive, wish, and need, easily dissolved, easily joined under the determination of a genuine idea.

The *first* level of reflective fantasy has its original material in this appearance. Is one able to say that these appearances are taken from the objective world of images and appearance, the world intended to give us *perception*? I answer: the *well-being of the image world*, insofar as it contains traits that *contingently cover* themselves with the intention goals of our drives, wishes, and needs—*but not of the perception* insofar as it is related to real unities. That is already a pleonasm. For it is the reality relatedness that makes perception perception. The education of the perceptual world must itself, where it is developed, pass through *the* levels in which fantasy activity sets up in order to cultivate the material. The same holds true for the world of appearance.

Only those fantasies that work with the givenness of these levels richly and diversely developing in psychic life—but do *not* work with already hewed stones and pieces of reality that fantasy sometimes omits, or sometimes adds, combines, enlarges, shrinks, or that work with mere abstraction—are the creatively valuable fantasies that provide organic unity in the work of art. W. Dilthey feels this despite his theory of fantasy, which rather closely follows "Locke and Hume," when he remarks: "A fantasy that only dissolves, strengthens, and lessens, enlarges or shrinks is weak and reaches only false ideality or caricature of reality. In general, where a true world of art comes into being, a central unfolding of images through positive filling-in takes place. This process is very hard to grasp."[80] Yet, it is clear: the "central filling-in" does not lead from the "caricature and flat ideality." If each part of an artificial construction is created according to the leadership of the idea in entirety, then "filling-in" cannot go further. Through his empiricist theory, Dilthey ruined his chances of acquiring the most genuine understanding of artistic imaginative force, despite the many profound insights found in his essay. [359]

6

The Metaphysics of Perception and the Problem of Reality

The Work and the Cognitive Possibilities of Human Beings

Having concluded our philosophical discussion of the problem of perception and fantasy, let us review a few of the theses we proposed. Regarding our first thesis, the images of objective appearances do indeed have trans-conscious, ideal objectivity, but *reality* is given only to the three kinds of dynamic centers: the *force centers*, *vital centers*, and *person centers*. Meta-scientifically, we must relate all finite appearances given to us to these centers as their manifestations. Let us recall the second of our theses, namely that perception possesses a content (the purer the perception is) which is neither an immaterial depiction (in consciousness) of extra-mental body-images [*Körperbilder*] nor an effect of some object or body movements—which themselves belong to the spheres of irreal and powerless *images*. Rather, perception is a relevant *partial content and aspect of the image itself*. Furthermore, the *qualities*, the building material of the images, which are just as original, can become the content of the sense functions (like a part of these objective qualities). If we combine these theses concerning a philosophy of perception with our thesis regarding the *originality* of fantasy activity at all levels as the most original form of spontaneous representation activity, then the question necessarily arises regarding how it is possible that such a purely subjective content of intuition, i.e., a content of intuition determined exclusively in the psycho-physically united living being and vital center, which is the case in our opinion for the content of perception—and that means for us only in so far as that part of the drive latent fantasy-content that can be utilized as symbols and signs for the resistance centers of the world, as these resistance centers are solely given to the practical intentional experience as a result of the *activity* and *work* in the world and have proved to be successful in the practical juxtaposition between the human being and the world—is not only able to be similar but also partially *identical* (even if always inadequately and commensurate to the existential relative level of the objects) to the "image."

This question regarding the identity between the contents of intuition and the images resolves itself for us nowhere other than in the *metaphysics of perception* and is entirely analogous to the question concerning the possibility that the forms and laws of thought, as well as the pure forms of intuition of our *spirit,* are able to correspond strictly with one another at least partially to the forms of *being* (which as spheres are far more incomparable than our forms of thought). It is thus ultimately the *same spirit*—as the one attribute of absolute being—that determines [360] the structure of the "possible world," of the essential world in its *ideas* and *original phenomena* (and in both corresponding in their *essences* and their structures); the same spirit in which human beings participate, in part, in different individuated act centers; and the same spirit slowly growing in contrast to the abundance of the divine spirit to the extent that it enables its essential insights to *functionalize* and *learn to synthesize* with one another the different, subjective spiritual *structures,* which are developed through the history of spirit in us and through us: gaining greater and greater participation in its acts, in an essentially infinite, never-ending progression. No parallelism and pre-formation system, as was thought in the old theism, no adaptation to the being forms in the sense of contingent forms of reality, as it is held by sensualism and empiricism (Spencer), but also no "Copernican turn," a theory which holds that human understanding prescribes its laws by virtue of absolutely constant functional laws of mere objective appearance immanent to understanding—a theory that already precludes the undoubted inconstancy of the structure of reason in history—can solve this old and famous problem. *Only the acceptance of identity allows to resolve this problem*—but only an *reciprocal* identity in which the human being not only "learns" *in Deo,* but also *Deus in homine et per hominem;* and this identity is *not* a substantive, i.e., more than functional and act constant identity, but only a *functional* constant and with regard to the most universal *being* of spirit this identity is only substantive and structural in terms of a *becoming* identity.

However, spirit alone and its ideas, original phenomena, values, etc., whether it is infinite or finite, makes intelligible to us neither the *existence* [*Dasein*] nor the contingent *being-thus* of *some* object; and spiritual will cannot be effective, a will that is in every respect only negative, inhibiting, or allowing—a notion of the will standing in direct opposition to Aristotle's understanding of it. *Reality is* in its subjective givenness *an experience of a non-spiritual drive principle in us:* an experience of a united, always specializing itself *life-urge in us.* Moreover, reality is, as something objective and transcendent to our experiencing, necessarily *lawful through* the originally spiritually-blind, *dynamic principle* of *urge*—of the principle, still cognizable differently by us, of the primordial ground [*Urgrund*] itself. The contingent being-thus of the "image" is for us the product of each original *urge fantasy of all-life*—which is idea blind in its activity, but yet effective in determining the *negative* scope of certain essential *im*possibilities, essential impossibilities that spirit constitutes.

How the unity of urge and its being-thus-positing fantasy relates to the three main centers of the dynamic centers: *persons, vital-centers,* and *energy-centers,* and how unity here relates to variety in general, are matters beyond the scope of this investigation.[1] Here, it concerns only one point: the *metaphysical understanding of perception in relation to the images.*

[361] We only have a right to accept trans-conscious images and objective appearances if we not only accept—as Fechner thought—a more than individual "consciousness," but also a *more than singular life* for which the essential laws that we discover in our sensible, intuiting functions and their qualities and other content (without thereby creating these essential laws) still hold true—*a* life that differentiates itself in functional bundles as *teleoclinal*-ordered process determinants and which, breaking into the dynamic *fundementum in re* of inorganic nature, *not only* develops the corporeal-images of the organisms *but also* the images of the dead corporeal-world. Since all psychophysical, unified functions of our and every animal organism and their vital centers are only parts and members of this one-creating life, the contents of perception of any psychophysical organism must *correspond* to the corporeal images in the same way as the *drive impulses* and psychophysiological functions effective in the organism, which construct the perceptions of the effected organism, have the *same direction,* the same ordering of effectivity, and the same rhythm as the drives and functions of *all-life.* It is thus also the *partial identity of our life with the image world* of *that which grounds life* that ultimately clarifies our possible *partial participation* in the images through our "*perception.*"

Just as the supra-individual spirit, which makes the partial identity and correspondence between the forms of thought and being and the principles, etc., understandable to us, is not a *finished,* all-life is also not finished. We understand the all-life as the higher level of the functionally uniform *urge,* effective according to laws concerning all inorganic *and* organic special lawfulness—the urge as the second principle of the attribute of the world ground knowable to us, namely the principle positing existence and contingent being-thus. Moreover, all-life is *becoming and growing self*-functionalization—becoming and growing *in the course* of its experiences of success and failure which came about in the conflict with the force-factors of the inorganic world. What all-life thus "learns" (having only images at its disposal)—always transmitting new functional bundles that ground the ideal system of the organism's world according to its manifoldness and unity, up until the transitory, aging, and dying *individuum*—allows *all-life to use it newly again and again.* This is the case because between all-life and every living being there exists a mutual *dependency in solidarity.*

If we shift our gaze away from this metaphysical digression and back to our *problem of work and cognition,* we notice the following:

Pragmatism is certainly not incorrect when it assigns the greatest significance for perceptual cognition and its education to the impetus of *activity,* to the practical juxtaposition of the human being with the world. [362] What has been taken from the original preponderance of the fantasy world of the human being and made into an essence that *lives* in the preponderance of its entire perceptual world [*Perzeptionswelt*] *in the sphere of perceptual reality*—this does *not* relate to any contemplative behavior, but rather originally to *the work of the human being* in *the world,* the effective power and the dogged defiance in the fight with nature and in the new conquering of the world's *resistance.*

Primarily in the course of work in the world, the human being is acquainted with the *contingent,* objective image world and its laws; primarily as these images in perception become for human beings symbols for the *point of attack for the human activity* and mastery, human beings seek with the symbols themselves to have active contact with the world and learn to forget slowly the content of their dreams related to their drives and desires. In this sense, work—and not contemplation—is in fact the *essential root of all positive science,* all induction, and all experiment.

However, the human being also possesses an entirely *different* cognitive possibility than those types of cognition whose vehicle is the sensible perception always related to reality and is of any practical understanding that seeks the laws of the contingent image world in order to discover the point of attack for the mastery over the appearance and non-appearance of the image world. The *philosophical cognitive disposition* is any cognition that through conscious *annulment* of the *practical* disposition *tears itself loose* from the contingent images and the being attracted and repelled by the images. The purpose of this disposition, the conscious making *non-real* of this world of images, is to keep an eye out for two different movements: the movement to the kingdom of essences, i.e., to the original phenomena and ideas for which these images are only "examples" and more or less good "copies"; and a movement toward the stream of the drives, urges, and forces that manifest themselves in these "images."

It is not "work" on the world that leads to such cognition possibilities:

Only *wonder, humility, and spiritual love lead to the essential,* gained through a *phenomenological reduction of the existent*; secondly, *Dionysian devo-*

tion leads into emotional identification [*Einsfühlung*] and becoming one with the urge that is part of all of *our* urges, wishes, and drives.

It is only in the greatest *tension* between both these dispositions and primarily through the *overcoming* of this tension in the unity of the person, that genuine philosophical cognition is born.

This is not the place to provide a detailed analysis of the essence, technique, and method of the "*phenomenological reduction*"—E. Husserl's expression—which is fundamental *for all philosophical cognition.*[2] Yet, a primary *presupposition*, in order to gain clarity about the technique [363] and method of the phenomenological reduction, a presupposition that exists in an occasional *annulment* of the *reality* modes given as a matter of course and naively to us in any natural worldview and scientific research, is without doubt the insight into *what the reality moment in the objects is and how it is given to us.*

For this reason, we would like to conclude this essay with a brief discussion of this important point regarding a philosophy of perception, which obviously only returns to our *fundamental* thoughts without either stating the fulfillment of the types of evidence that there are for its justification or stating the facts that correspond to these types of evidence.

Pre-given to *everything* else that is given in the natural worldview—as well as to all sensible qualities, relations, time, space, being-thus determined things, events, the differentiated spheres themselves of the outer-worldliness, inner-worldliness, bodily sphere, psychic and spiritual with-world, and forms of existence (categories)—is the still unqualified *reality of the world in general*, and the general thesis corresponding to it: "There is in reality a world." If you could imagine the entire content of the natural world being dismantled piece by piece, allowing all colors to fade, all sounds to die away, all spheres of body consciousness and their content to disappear, all spatial and temporal forms and all forms of being (categories) of the things being leveled down to an indeterminate being-thus, there remains as the not-able-to-be-dismantled a basic, fundamentally simple *impression of reality in general*: the impression of an absolute "resistance" opposing the spontaneous—regardless of whether it is characterized as voluntary, involuntary, or as willing or only as drive impulse—activity that supports our conscious having and being in continued execution. *Being real is not objective being*, i.e., it is not the identical being-thus correlate of any intellectual act; rather, it is being resistant to the original arising spontaneity that is one and the same in willing, in attending of any kind. If any resisting, indeterminate being-thus X which I experience and which I experience in willing *itself* comes to be the object of an intellectual act, then this object as with any object is given "transcendently" to all content of *consciousness*—where this *being given*, being known, and being conscious of that which is truly transcendent itself can be given in reflective acts. This vague, undifferentiated, indeterminate being-thus reality—this being real of "something"—cannot or need not be "imagined" or "disclosed" in some sphere of being that is likewise "pre-given" to any empirical content of experience, as idealism and all forms of the so-called "critical realism" falsely maintain. It *is there*—*before* any thinking and perceiving in their intentional *meaning* of "receptive" acts; it is as unreachable to everything that we call our intellectual, representing, thinking behavior and to all its possible contents and givennesses [364] as color is to hearing, as the number 3 is to tasting and smelling. The being real *can* be pre-given to all intellectual acts—whose only being correlate is the "being-thus" and never the "existence" of a thing—since spontaneous activity, which experiences in its striving the standing-against and the counter-effect as "*being real*" and simultaneously as something different from the activity of the subject, already has as *pre*supposition of its taking place a spontaneous act of passive *attention* (in changing, original "direction") and is initially *founded* through such an act. If the simplest sensation S is not only a function of the stimulus and of the nerve process, etc., but is also a function of the quantum of at least the *drive-related attention* directed to the object, $S = f(St + A)$, then the impression of *resistance* can and must surface in a position where only the first stirrings of the act of this spontaneous being-active take place and the stirrings have not yet posited the entire and completely necessary co-condition for the realization of sensation made possible only through the stimulus process.

Recently, W. Dilthey[3] has defended quite well the in-principle correct foundational idea that the being-given of the being-real is attached to the experienced dynamic relation between "impulse and resistance." With great clarity, he has realized that the experience of resistance is a genuine experience of the will, and should be sharply *distinguished* as experience from those *sensations*, e.g., tactile and articulation sensations, accompanying it. If, for example, the experience of resistance is brought about through a stick that I press against a wall, then the different places of both appearances show the difference between the tactile sensation and the resistance: the resistance is experienced at the end of the stick, the tactile sensation in the hand. Dilthey quite correctly judges: "The assumption is unsatisfactory that this objectifying is caused through the sensations (i.e., tactile and articulation sensations), in particular through the pressing sensation, which is localized in the finger, setting off as constituent part of the experience of resistance. This would only result in a dead spatial sensation, nothing from the experience of the living force in the resistance to consequence" (p. 102). Unfortunately, Dilthey speaks in his essay still further of "*sensations* of resistance," which clouds over the state of affairs of the inhibition of the will, which is experienced as accomplished through a force (from the side of the object) directed oppositionally, because obviously an experienced stoppage of one's own activity has absolutely nothing to do with some "sensation," call it what you will. The best proof for this is that the experience of resistance and [365] stoppage (namely, the inhibition as a result of the object exerting the resistance, and not the other way around) is bound to *no* (particular) sense modality, since "resistance can surface in any sense modality." The proof is that the *what*, i.e., the content of what is resisting my activity, can be given to me both optically and acoustically (by virtue of the inhibition of dynamic attention through what is forcing itself upon me in the optical, acoustic, and other sense appearances) and in *non*-sensible acts of perception and self, such as the non-intuitive thinking of something (in memory, expectation). Resistance is thus an absolutely *central* experience [*Erlebnis*], an experience [*Erfahrung*] of the *active self*, and has nothing to do with the peripheral *sense* experiences in which the *being-thus* of what resists can at the very most (but must not) present itself. Yet, the intention of this central experiencing of resistance, as far as it is concerned, goes *beyond and through* the sense content (where such intention conveys it). Sensations do not resist, but rather the things themselves resist ("thing" = force center), things which only manifest themselves with regard to sensation in their qualitative attributes.

Dilthey, who in his treatise had insightfully shifted the question over onto the right track, unfortunately attached to his important discovery a host of *errors*, errors that the polemics from H. Rickert, J. Rehmke, O. Külpe, et al. appear in part to justify.

1. Although Dilthey aptly remarks that "the human being, seen from the inside, is originally a bundle of drives, which in all respects, in connection to the feelings of reluctance and need, emits the most diverse strivings and volitions" (p. 102), the present-day, fully established view is still foreign to him, the view that every sensation, perception, representation, i.e., every perception in the widest sense of the term, is *conditioned* through a *drive*-striving and an accompanying *motor* nerve process. For this reason, he cannot see how it is possible that the impression of reality is not *given* only through the resistance experience of the will and other dynamic activity, but is also necessarily *pre*-given to all perceptions. "The primary and thus constitutive process is this: an impulse to move with a specific intention continues and is even strengthened, and instead of the

intended outward movement, the *sensation* of pressure occurs. This link between the consciousness of impulse and the stoppage of the intention that lies in the aggregate of the sensations of pressure is there every time. We come to be conscious of the outer world only through mediations. The grounding of this belief cannot be resolved through some kind of exaggeration, or through the acceptance of a direct experience of the will of resistance, or through the psychological fiction of direct being given [366] of some kind." (ibid., p. 103). Dilthey even calls an aggregate of the sensation of pressure the "precondition" for the experience of resistance.[4] It is exactly the *pivotal* experience of resistance that is rejected here.

In these statements and in everything that Dilthey concludes from them, there is, on the one hand, a *fundamental error* regarding the relationship between drive and perception and, on the other hand, an error about the relationship between the experience of resistance and the emergence of image contents of the intuitive attribute of the object. This "immediate experience of the will," which Dilthey explicitly denies—for example, in the statement: "in the sensation of resistance an experience, an independent thing from me is not given in an immediate experience of the will"—indeed *exists.* It can also be shown phenomenally in the special case where the resistance in conjunction with pressure, tactile, and articular sensations is experienced as preceding them and "independent of them." The experience of weight and pulling, e.g., what I have while picking up a material body, is not only *different* from the simultaneous sensations of pressure and touch in the joints, hand, and arm, but also the sensations themselves clearly *follow temporally* the hardly noticed experiences of weight and pulling. If Dilthey is correct that the experience of the resistance of drive is continually mediated through some kind of "sensations," then the central vein of his entire theory would be destroyed and one cannot see why he is against the theory of critical realism, according to which reality is *derived* from an experience of consciousness of sensations. For this reason, Rickert is, according to this presentation, fundamentally correct when he criticizes the volitional theory of reality held by Dilthey.[5]

Throughout his entire essay, one also notices how Dilthey allows himself to be directed and led, despite his better fundamental insight, by the now fully contradicted theory of Helmholtz regarding "unconscious conclusions." Dilthey thus states: "We have seen that the acceptance of the Scot [Reid], by Jacobi and a few French researchers of our century [he probably means here Maine de Biran], of an immediate certainty of the reality of the outer world is false. We could also expose the origin of this appearance; the experience of resistance arises namely in a compounded process, but subsequently emerges in our consciousness as something simple. Mediated thought processes are always necessary to bring about the thinking experience of reality. The contention of the immediacy of this experience springs only from the shortcomings of fundamental psychological analysis. This contention is definitively refuted by the analysis of the perceptions of the face [367] and tone in the works of Helmholtz, and the so-called theory of the intellectuality of sensual perception is conclusively demonstrated by it" (p. 127). Yet, in direct opposition to Dilthey on this point is the fact that Helmholtz's theory concerning the unconscious inferences is *refuted* in every way—since Helmholtz makes use of this theory (constants of sizes, constants of colors, gestalt constants of the object seen, etc.)—by the works of E. Hering, E. Jaensch. D. Katz, and others to such an extent that the theory cannot serve as support for these questions. The meaning of mediated thought acts inserts where either the *X already given as real* should be *more precisely* determined in its actual *being-thus*, i.e., what the already pre-given reality is should be determined in a specific spatial and temporal position, or where the question arises as to whether de facto reality comes to a content that has already been determined in its being-thus through a perception.

Gyula Pikler, one of our most imaginative sense-physiologists, developed a theory of the strength of sensation and in particular of the Weberian laws according to which the "strength of sensation" must be understood "as the expression of the size of the drive fulfillment."[6] "For the weakling, the same resistance of weight is felt in the act of lifting to be heavier than for the strong person, for a child to be heavier than for an adult. And in the reverse case, in order to feel the same heaviness, the stronger person needs greater stimuli than the weaker person." "We can be convinced of this when we lift one and the same weight in different conditions of force; the difference between the sensations is entirely the same as when we have in the same conditions of force at the one time a lighter and at the other a heavier weight. The same holds true for resistances of any kind and for any movement. The strength and intensity of sensation, which a stimulus provokes, is not determined through the absolute strength of stimulus on the area of the sense of force, but through the relation of the stimulus strength to the force of the person sensing."[7] There is, according to Pikler, for every individual an "appropriate greatest stimulus strength," which is also the optimal stimulus for *its* organism; and the relation of a stimulus to this greatest stimulus strength is what determines any of its sensation intensities. "Two human beings, for whom the greatest weight appropriate to them with regard to a certain manner of lifting is 100 and 200 kilograms respectively, not only sense in their lifting the same weight, but also the same for the weights 90 and 180, 80 and 160, 10 and 20." "Intensity of sensation proves objectively, organically, and somatically to be a practical, biological, teleological concept, and not a physicalistic or, as one calls the intended application of physics on the manifestations of life, a physiological concept."[8] It is not the greater or lesser stimulation [368] of the sensible nerves and their central processes and final positions or the measure of the decomposition of stuff (dissimilation) in these constructs that corresponds to the experienced strength of sensation. A. Goldscheider's theory, which Dilthey quotes in his essays,[9] that the tendons construct the substrate of the sensations of weight, is called into question by Pikler, who also criticizes the view by Frey. According to Frey's view, "the physiological presuppositions for the perception of the movement resistances are given through sensations of tension, through the perception of tensions, in which the active muscles and their tendons come up against something. These tensions are the consequences of development of force when the muscles are excited through the movement resistance. The perception of the tensions is transmitted through certain endings of afferent nerves present in the muscles and tendons." Frey writes: "Out of these sensations of tension or perceptions [!] the resistances of movement are *derived*." Pikler is quite correct when he finds that both researchers' assumptions are in flagrant contradiction with the facts cited by him. The "sensations" of tendon and muscle tension only hypothetically accepted and "derived" here (should their origin lie "in" them as intentional content, or as these researchers say, entirely as "perception"?) would have to be much more proportional to the stimulus as it corresponds to the factual weight phenomena and could in no way contain in themselves any "adequation" regarding the greatest and optimal stimulus strength in the sense of an individual constant condition. Correctly, Pikler draws attention to the fact that "straining" and the "experience of straining," upon which the "father of the theory of the sense of force," E. H. Weber, and Maine de Biran *founded* the experience of weight, are entirely different than the sensation of tension in the muscles and tendons, since the magnitude of the development of force on the stimulus not only manifest themselves in this experience of weight, but also in the relationship to this development of force has to the force "the individual" already possesses. These facts would appear to demonstrate definitively that the experience of resistance arising out of the relation between the spontaneous impulse of movement and some existing force must concern something much more central (and likewise as something primordially founding the sensation of "strength" rather than as something founded through the sensation) than some kind of sensation in general. If this is indeed the case, we are led along the same lines of thought that Pikler charted regarding his law of "adequation" holding true for the intensity of sensation of all other senses (p. 150). even though he has not provided sufficient evidence for the *central* nature of the experience of resistance. This *independence* of the law of adequation from the peripheral and central sense organs and their special facilities *proves* that the law of adequation concerns something *foundational* to the senses in general and their function [369] *universally*. This law further concerns a *drive* factor of a *unified* type, *against* whose drive-impulse, an impulse necessary for all sense sensations and their possible coming into being, the experienced resistance first *grows* as phenomenon, a phenomenon according to which the experienced intensities of sensation subsequently adjust themselves. Yet, this corresponds exactly, only with different words, to the objections leveled against W. Dilthey. Obviously, the "inference" or "unconscious" inference is omitted from sensation—which would be "given" proportionally to the stimulus and the nerve stimulation as well as to the muscle and nerve work originally and prior to the experienced resistance—about which Dilthey and Frey both speak.

Pikler's basic position that sensation is the result of *spontaneous* activity of adaptation between the psychophysical organism as a whole and the environmental stimulus is of great significance and is an additional constituent aspect of the philosophy of perception that we have already developed. Correctly, he draws from all of his works on the theory of sensation the following: "All sensing always already presupposes the activity of the *waking-drive* in contrast to the *sleeping-drive*, and presupposes a *drive longing* for sensation and perception. The attentive character of the sense functions for the preservation of the organism is anchored in these drives." Schilder has also, in his work on hypnosis,[10] drawn attention to the fact that there is a normal rhythmically alternating (which can be disturbed by different pathological conditions in myriad fashions) sleeping and waking drive upon which the sense sensations are dependent. When Pikler remarks: "If we sense, we always also have the wish (better to call it "drive") to sense, and we sense as a result of this wish; the sensing is the activity of a drive for the adaptation to stimulus, for the balancing of stimuli, for the preservation of our being by means of self-reorganization in response to changing conditions, and for increasing self-preservation, and not the consequence of a stimulation through a stimulus independent of our drives; these figure, in contrast to sensing, only as the means of satisfaction of spontaneous, independently existing drives"—then this part of his basic position[11] corresponds precisely to what we have shown in the sections of this essay regarding the "philosophy of perception" and already earlier in our *Formalism in Ethics*. When Pikler reduces the unfilledness of this hunger for sensation to the phenomenon of approximate empty time and empty space (which is why, e.g., boredom allows the phenomenal duration to grow so much), we must agree with him. Here is not the place to address these questions.[12]

[370] 2. A second fundamental error of the above-cited essay by Dilthey resides in the way he poses the questions: How is the *reality of the outer world* given to us, and how is *consciousness* (instead of the *having* of this being-real) given to us? Dilthey begins his essay with the false statement of phenomenality, i.e., the primary immanent consciousness of everything given (entirely like Descartes, Schopenhauer, and others). He knows nothing about the fact that *ecstatic knowledge* (and also, in the case of non-intellectual givennesses, ecstatic "having") *precedes* all consciousness and that the having of being and the relations of being itself *precede* all knowledge. Thus, it can no longer be understood how the experience of resistance should come *about* from consciousness. For this reason, Dilthey does not see that what makes the experience of resistance *primary* in us, namely the *activity* of our psychophysical *vital and drive centers* reaching out from all sides in the impulses of attention and movement, is *prior* to the experienced resistance and *without* any relation to the ego and "consciousness"—that a drive-consciousness does not therefore lead to experienced resistance, but rather the experienced resistance *gives rise to the act of reflection* through which the drive impulse can reach consciousness and motivate it. *Becoming* conscious, or the coming into relation of the ego, is at all levels and degrees in which it takes place always originally the *consequence of our suffering due to the world's resistance.* It is the *drive impulses,* in contrast to the central, spiritual "I want," externally approaching our conscious ego, *not*-directly, but by virtue of the *vital* center (and in respect to spatiality by virtue of the sphere of the lived body). These drive impulses originally constitute the unconscious and preconscious parts of our real soul-life.[13]

3. Yet, not only does Dilthey (in a mistaken solution) mix this "problem of consciousness" up with the problem of the having of reality, he also fails to clearly distinguish the *problem of the "spheres"*—as I tend to call it—from the problem of reality and therein mixes the problem of reality into the sphere of the *outer world.* Instead of asking how we come to hold as real an X *given* in the sphere of the outside world, Dilthey questions the reasons and motives for our "belief in the reality of the outer world"—as if the origins of "having of the outer world" and "having-something-real-in-the-outer world" (and also the reality "of the" outer world) would have to come from the *same* process. If Rehmke therefore asks in a critique of Dilthey's essay cited by the latter himself: "How could the willing will movement *without* presupposing the outer world?" then he

has on this point correctly criticized Dilthey, and the latter is unable to refute his critique. Dilthey also overlooks the fact [371] that the spheres problem, which is fundamentally different from the problem of the having of reality, stands in relation to the problem of reality only insofar as the problem of reality comes back into *every* "sphere" (with the exception of the sphere of the idea and of consciously fictive objects where there is no reality). As there are on the one hand many irreal things in the outer world, e.g., shadows, mirror images, virtual images, rainbows, etc., so on the other hand the question, "What is real, and what is irreal?" is just as justified in the sphere of the "inner world" as it is in the sphere of the lived body, in the sphere of the alien-psychic subject, and in the intentional religious sphere of the "divine." What Dilthey pays for, in general as well as here, is not only presupposing the claim of the immanence of consciousness (in the sense of the consciousness "of" something), but also in presupposing the claim, already overcome by Kant, of the preferencing of psychic givenness over the physical, and of the inner-worldly over the outer-worldly—as well as denying the psychic the difference between reality and conscious appearance (Wundt). The question thus arises, how many spheres of being (and correlate spheres of possible consciousness of something) are there which are *not* reducible to one another; this question is a mistaken connection to the problem of the givenness of *reality in general,* which is one and the same for all contents of spheres, and which must be resolved like the problem of spheres. However, being in the "outer world" sphere is determined formally through everything that is in a homogeneous spatiotemporal "from one another" (in contrast to the "in one another" and the original inwardness of the psychic), and it is a mistake to accept that this *sphere* is *itself* a result of *mediated* experience (in contrast to the being-thus determinateness and order of the thing within this sphere). The sphere of outer-worldliness is not given only and originally to each subject, it is also *pre*-given to the sphere of the inner-worldliness—as Kant rightly saw.[14]

4. Finally, Dilthey still does not see the necessary connection which the problem of the givenness of reality has to the metaphysical problem of the (ontic) *becoming* of reality: that the *urge* and "thirst" *for* reality *precede the being-real*—the urge itself has indeed existence [*Existenz*], but yet *no* reality.

Aside from these errors, Dilthey's most recent essay—particularly when we disregard Maine de Biran's deep insights upon which Dilthey repeatedly bases himself—is still the best that we have on these questions, particularly in their phenomenological parts.[15] [372] We hope to present our own phenomenological proof for the voluntative theory of reality in a different place.[16]

We grasp the being-*real* of an undetermined something in the sequential order of givennesses before we sensibly perceive and think its *being-thus*. The being-real of a corporeal thing, for example, is not a group of constant perceptual or sensation possibilities (J. S. Mill, E. Mach), but is rather the pre-given fundament of sensation possibilities and intuition possibilities. It is thus the sensation which is only a "possible" sensation *before* a being-real is experienced as *resistance* in the process of spontaneous attention, whose still empty "being-thus" is *filled out* by sensation in essentially prescribed positions (which primarily supply the existential forms of the real). Sensualistic positivism totally reverses this matter, however.

The claim concerning the reality of things, which Maine de Biran, Bouterwek (Schopenhauer's teacher), Schopenhauer himself, Schelling and E. von Hartmann in metaphysical form ("being real is through the world ground being wanted, not being thought"), and more recently—as we saw—W. Dilthey and Frischeisen-Köhler have correctly grounded in an orientation toward the experience of resistance *in* the volitional act, is thus *neither* a possible result of *think*ing, *nor* is it perception and its processing, nor is it thinking plus perception (as O. Külpe sought to demonstrate in his "Realization"), which could lead to it. If *only intellectual* acts and their laws are drawn upon for the claim's supposed justification, then we necessarily arrive at *idealism*. The bearer of pure intellect would be an absolute idealist. The correlate of all possible intellectual acts is exclusively the being-*thus* and *never* the existence [*Dasein*]—and in the case of the determination of the being-thus or a *pre*-given reality, or in the case of the whether or whether-not decision of the belongingness of a *specific* being regarding *pre*-given reality, the intellectual processes, and above all the thought of particular lawfulness which is grounded in the essential nature of the affected regions, play *the* role that any "critical realism" would like to award them in the case of the positing of reality.

It is one of the greatest services that E. Jaensch has given to philosophy and epistemology to have demonstrated quite precisely the meaning of resistance with regard to the dynamic sides of the change of attention for the phases of the education of the experience of reality and its degrees. If he had more deeply and in greater detail substantiated in the instructive supplement to his book *Concerning the Perception of Space* the recent thoughts advanced by Dilthey and Frischeisen-Köhler on the voluntative theory of reality [373], then his new investigations regarding the "layering structure of consciousness" and in particular his proof that the *primary* stimulus result is not the sensations and perceptions of adults, but rather the "optical intuitive images" of the *youth* lying between images and perceptions (perceptual images and reproductions), as well as the voluntative theory of reality, would have been deepened considerably. The old wisdom of the language which sees in the "*practical person*" the genuine "*realist*"—the person who is concerned only with the real *singular being*—is meaningfully deepened by what Jaensch demonstrates; namely, that the consciousness of reality is developed less sharply at the eidetic level of intuitive images than at the level where perception and representation have distinguished themselves sharply and where perception comes somewhat closer to a proportionality of stimulus. At the eidetic level, the images possess a flexible, more relaxed aggregate condition than they do at the level of perception, and they follow from this lower autonomy and resisting of its objects still more easily to the drive wish, from which they detach themselves more distinctly at the perceptual level. It also becomes understandable why the *theoretical human type* on the one hand and the *eidetic* type—i.e., the type who, like the artistic and in particular the romantic genius, retains intuitive images in the time of maturity—have the least sharply developed "consciousness of reality" compared to the average, everyday person. The strongly impoverished, more caustic consciousness of reality of the primitive peoples, with whom "wish" and "will" are as undifferentiated as "image" and "perception," and whose *magical power-consciousness* over nature knows almost no limits, is understood far more deeply.

The experience of reality as *pre*-known and *pre*-conscious (and in comparison with the individual *regions* of being, of nature, of the inner world, of the foreign world, of the divine, as well as with the aggregate conditions of the body and the parts of nature, e.g., the heavens and the earth, the categorial forms of being, etc., and the preconscious) experience follows from the type and distribution regarding the being [*Seiende*] and to a greater degree the *experiences of resistance, experiences of resistance* that the human being makes use of in its aggressive *work* on things and in the attempt at the strategic channeling and *mastery* of the thing.

There are, though, specific types of lawfulness that remain constant in the development of the human spirit. Only some, which appear to us to be unambiguous, are named here.

In contrast to the "spheres" of being, which "pre-give" everything that occurs *in* them and which are not reducible to one another, the following laws are valid:

[374] (1) The reality of an *absolutely real Being*, a wholly "all-powerful" Being (and the reality of the total dependence on this Being) is *pre*-given to *all* other spheres of reality; and the being-thus, which in all other spheres is considered to be searchable, knowable, and cognizable and is

expected to be possible (as if it were an object of intentional inquisitiveness and intellectual curiosity)—a being-thus that is also merely a potential "problema" ("*questionable*")—is grasped and judged *according to* the changing contents of this "divinity."

(2) The reality of the *with-world* and community is *pre*-given as *you-sphere* and *we-sphere* to collective *nature*, such as organic and dead nature (after this separation is already grasped). It continues to exist as a "sphere" and as *a* kind of real X in the sphere for the experience, even when every single being-thus were thought to be eradicated or were left undetermined, everything of nature that is other than human. And it is real not just for "my ego," but rather for the "*we*" (according to its changing organization for "leadership" and "following," ultimately for the "leader") in the spheres of the outer and inner world or for what is regarded within the scope of the experience of a "we" in the pre-given spheres between the *singularity* of the "we" as identifiably being-thus—what is "regarded" as "real" in these spheres. Moreover, the reality of the "*you*" and of a community is in general pre-given to the real being of the "ego" in the sense of its *mineness* and its singular and individual "experienced-self," which proves to be always the same only insofar as it adapts to the *dominant structural forms* of the initially overpowering we-experience and we-consciousness. Self-observation is continually observation of its self—"as if" one were "another self"; it is in its intention, as a form of "alien observation," where it is directed to its own self.

(3) The real being of something (=X) in the sphere of the "*outer world*" is without doubt *pre*-given to the real being of something in the sphere of the "*inner world*" (as the correlate spheres of extroverted and introverted behavior) in such a way that resistance, inhibition, and suffering in the extroverted behavior (in operating or cognizing as conflict and contradiction) *throw back* the look of the human being on the inner world (*first* the we-world, and then the ego-inner-world), i.e., they provoke increasing implementation and practice of the *re-flective* act in which the *being* of the "inner world" is come upon.

(4) The real being in the sphere of the "*being of the lived body*" and in the structure of the original phenomenon "being alive" is *pre*-given to the being-real in the sphere of "being dead" in such a manner that primary and *ceteris paribus* everything given generally in the sphere of the "outer world" is given as embodied and alive—and given as such so long as a specifically disappointing *positive* experiential content of some outer-worldly being-thus is not brought to some special demonstration

as *not*-embodied and not-living, but as [375] a physical body and dead (= *without* a for-itself-being and inner-being being).

These *four laws of the pre-givenness*[17] *of the spheres* in relation to the *experience of reality* hold good in the three developmental tendencies of the human spirit: (1) from child to adult, (2) from primitive to civilized, and (3) in the genuine enlightenment history of spirit, e.g., of the West, in the strictest manner. The material which can be stated in defense of these developments—psychologically and historically—is hardly summarizable.

That (statement 2) the you-sphere and the realization of spiritual subjects in it precede the sphere of the outer world *and* inner world is proof for me that all types of "consciousness idealism" up to this point have stopped short of the "other ego": that there were no philosophical "solipsists." Doesn't this easily show that our conviction about the reality of a you is *original* and has an evidence that is independent from the evidence of conviction with respect to the dead and the organic world? Furthermore, this thesis casts an illuminating light upon the particular change of worldview, upon the change of the dead and organic world, as well as upon the change of the fundamental forms of social organization described by the ethnologists and sociologists.[18]

Statement (3) has already been correctly shown by W. Wundt in his critique of Descartes and immanent philosophy. O. Külpe has even experimentally substantiated it in his work on the "objectification and subjectification of sense impressions." The entire history of spirit—most clearly the transition of Greek natural philosophy to the psychologism of Protagoras and the Sophists, as well as to the self-knowledge of Socrates—testifies clearly to its truth. Inhibition and suffering (e.g., the "contradictions" of dogmatic natural speculations) lead to the execution and the practice of reflective acts. The "naive behavior" of present human beings is predominately outer-worldly directed, and is accompanied by a "natural reflection" which grants the human being the knowledge of the act in which he or she turns to the outer world. It is just as possible to discern the historically developmental *older* disposition of *ecstatic* devotion in perception, memory, expectation (child, primitive, animal), where this *natural* reflection is absent (and in the waking from narcotics, there is a place where it still is absent), and it is also possible to discern the [376] disposition of *artistic* reflection in which there is the attempt to grasp the inner world itself while refraining from the outer world and its existential forms and structures. H. Bergson correctly emphasized that our forms of thinking and our language are thoroughly "made" for the outer world and that we continuously allow ourselves to be duped by every psychology to look for space, the additive relations, and the forms of being of the physical world in the givennesses of the soul.

Finally, statement (4) remains, in its fundamental meaning, the least known. Everything "given" in the outer world—all formations and combinations of qualities—are preserved *primarily as spontaneous actions and as a field of expression by the living being*: the physical body given as an active thing is the kind of original phenomenon of the "living body"; and this not by virtue of a process of the experience of "empathy," the so-called "personification apperception"—or as it has been otherwise called, a fictive process—but rather by virtue of an, understood strictly *nativistically*, fixture of our organization. The structural form of the being of the lived body and the living, which we first discover in exemplary fashion in our self, in our "living body" and its spontaneous actions and experiences of expression, is the *original form pre*-given to the possible "sense sensations," in which they are assimilated into the outer layer. For this reason, an organicalistic, vitalistic view of the world, i.e., a view which intuits as "living" and seeks to grasp in the specific "biological" essential categories what the advanced view calls "dead," precedes a *dualistic* view and a more or less *mechanistic* view. This has been shown by child psychology and by research on the mentality of primitive peoples, as well as by the spiritual history of the Western view of nature, which was under the grip, up to the beginning of the modern era (in its socially predominant "life-communal" periods), of the Aristotelian theory of the organism.[19]

This is also why it was not a mere coincidence that the entire period of the organistic thinking of the world was epistemologically oriented *realistically*, and that the philosophical *idealism of consciousness* set in with the overcoming of this period and with the formal-mechanistic approach to nature. With the being-for-itself and also with the *spontaneous* movement that is not governable and controllable by us, with the indivisible individuality, the dead thing and thing given to us *as* "dead" lose extensively their character of reality—and this must consequently mean that their being would be assimilated into the mere being object for understanding. A strictly formal [377] mathematicization of theoretical physics, for which the physics of relativity has now paved the way, must for this reason necessarily imply the "idealism" of the dead world (with the accompanying presupposition of mechanistic in biology as well as in nature in its entirety), since this world-image is indeed "universal" and intersubjective, but can add no more "reality" to the object. Mere equations of transformation and absolute constants (e.g., the speed of light) befit no "reality," but only "validity"; if all that remains in intuitable being is relative to the "standpoint of the observer," and if finally the ether ultimately falls away and assumptions regarding absolute force centers as supposed organically conditioned insertions are given up, then absolute idealism is inescapable. The strictly formal mathematicism and idealism of the mechanistic theory of nature, as P. Duhem has already seen, not only permits an organically directed metaphysics of nature as a whole, but also—if its pragmatic conditionality is correctly conceived—imperiously demands a *new* way for an organistic metaphysics of nature, as we have shown above.

Our observations can be broadened still further. The four laws of the realization of the spheres follow *deductively* from the general voluntative theory of reality, when we make it clear to ourselves in which spheres and in which ordering that which resists or the real thing does not become contingent in them, but rather, in the case of similar contingent conditions *becomes more essential*, or said better, has a new *order* of magnitude. This is obviously the case where our and any possible *mastery* regarding the things and their determinability and conceivability through our "understanding" for the purpose of this mastery is the relatively *smaller* order—and from the nature of the thing itself is the smaller order. This order is the smallest in comparison to *absolute being* insofar as it is with regard to sovereign power posited as real, i.e., "all-powerful"; the order is the greatest wherever the world is similar to an ideal mechanism of strictly calculable movements. It is smaller in order of magnitude with regard to human *persons*—because we can either *cognize* it as "free" spiritual being without its consent, or *master* and force its acts, since free, spontaneously self-executed becoming belongs to the being of "spiritual" acts—in contrast to the non-spiritual organic life in human beings, animals, and plants. The order is also incomparably smaller with regard to life than with regard to the dead since the organic, despite its autonomy, pursues its own goals in phase-ordered unique development (never returning to the same phase, and for that reason nothing is predetermined) and as individual and whole is inseparable through us; because the factors of its becoming are never strictly isolatable from one another through experimental intervention, and because every intervention co-varies the entire thing, and this changes the process to be observed.

[378] The order of the realization of the spheres from this ground cannot be other than it is. Kant's transcendental understanding would like to "prescribe" its laws to a purely formal-mechanistically thought world of appearance: the world insofar as it truly contains the organic—and not only the apparently organic, i.e., the organic as concealed mechanism in which only our soul carries into the "appearance" of life—is able to prescribe to the understanding absolutely nothing: the understanding must *wait* for what takes place. The determination of the being-thus of every

vital appearance through the entirety of its arrangement and history (and not only through the content of preceding temporal differentials), the "historical basis of reaction" of every action (Driesch), the "meme" of any organic being (E. Hering), the "difference" of every condition of the living substance for the sake of the temporal position that alone possesses the condition in the qualitative phase-ordering of the affected life cycle—it is the same fact that expresses all of these formulations—does not make a strict prediction, and thus the full channeling of the appearances of life for the sake of our mistaken insight into the causal relations, but makes this *impossible by its very nature.* Only phase rules and rules of temporal ordering of the appearances are possible to find here in the highest cases—no longer metrically determined laws of *sequential* laws. Furthermore, this disappears where the willing and acting of the *free person center* is an option, and every self-determination of the being-thus of the action becomes possible through the (absolute) individuality of the person and its being-*there* [*Da*sein] through the fiat of the will (or its neglect). Since the person, who is able to stand above the vital-organic basis of existence and the effects of a temporal or spatial manifoldness, much is able to be objectively and correctly "foreseen," and by virtue of the *emulated* "*understanding*" of the sensibly united motivational process of the person's behavior is often factually easier and better than in the objective world the organic and dead nature where the "understanding" gets closer and closer to the zero limit—the motivations, from the nature of the thing itself, are never "forced" and never "necessarily effective" on the person's behavior. A strict "determinism" of what is real is therefore only possible under the fictive, "as-if" presupposition: as if there would be in reality *neither* genuine vitality *nor* genuine personal spirit. Yet, that is the presupposition which any formal-mechanistic worldview in fact makes and rarely conscious of its mere *practical motives*: A presupposition that entails the inherently and fully irrational axiom, the world "must" be in principle fully controllable.

Appendix

[447] Manuscripts regarding *Cognition and Work*

The "Spirit" of Pragmatism and the Philosophical Concept of the Human Being

I.

The problems of pragmatism have been forced upon modern philosophy by the fundamental changes that our entire conditions of living have experienced through the triumphant surging forth of industrialism and through the transformation of our *cultural ideals* tied to this change. Everyone knows and feels, day after day, the booming steps of the worker battalions, who daily oil and service the huge mechanism, a mechanism in whose tentacles our lives are played out, and which has also carried a new tone into our *spiritual* life, into our politics, literature, art, science, and religion; and, quite apart from the hundred thousand new problems coming into existence because of this, the movement of the 4th class has reshaped our *ideas,* and our scientific and artistic posing of problems. If we discover traces of a private law, for example, in a period of history so foreign to us as Greek antiquity, when we see Athens, a place in which our ancestors of the German classical epoch saw how isolated great gestalts transformed poets and thinkers, artists and generals and statesmen, filled with social and economic strife, or—an example from an entirely different area—when we see the attempt undertaken by a famous physical chemist, Wilhelm Ostwald, to ground our entire worldview of nature *and* the humanities in the concept of *energy* or *work* and their conservation—who would not see in this and similar examples how the *prevailing interests* not only steer our actions, but also press themselves into the cultivation of our views and concepts of things which [448] appear at first to be miles away from the scope of those interests. Adam Smith has already remarked that the type of activity of the human being fundamentally co-determines his direction of thought; and this holds true not only for the education of the worldview of different social groups, but also for the different time periods.

However well anyone is able to know this, it will still be new to some that this immense reality of *modern work* claims to have reformulated the *philosophical concept of the human being,* a concept which has remained unchallenged for several millennia, and as a consequence claims to have gained all of the highest forms of activity for the human being in the cognition of truth and in the cognition and realization of the good, and in its striving to have gained pious interest in the divine, to have allowed the glimmer of a higher world to shine upon the human being's life, and to have conferred a brand-new meaning upon the human being. One of the most insightful and outstanding philosophical researchers of the present, Henri Bergson, who is also one of the representatives of typical Anglo-American pragmatism, summarizes an entire series of his own theoretical results in this statement: it would be the greatest error of any philosophy previously and up to the present that is still dependent on the thinking of the contemplative Greeks to define (a definition thinkers such as Aristotle, Descartes, Leibniz, and Kant have, for example, conferred upon the human being) the human being as "*homo sapiens*" (= rational being), i.e., as a being that possesses a "pure" understanding of the cognition of reality [*Wirklichkeit*], an understanding independent from the particular abilities of sensations, perceptions, representations, and drives and distinct from the animals. A definition that would correspond much better to the human being's true gift which distinguishes the human being from the animals is rather "*homo faber*"—not the rational being, but rather the "being of work," or more precisely formulated, that being who constructs tools and discovers a system of moving and freely combinable signs in order to cultivate his environment with those tools and in order to communicate with others like him about this work. In this new definition of the "human being," there is to an extent the culmination of *the movement and the spirit of pragmatism* . . .

By "work," we understand any activity related to the mind or body in which a given material is in some way *reconfigured*. We refrain provisionally from a particular goal of such activity (use, satisfying of a need). What is understood by "*cognition*" in any language has in any case nothing to do with such a "reconfiguration of material." Whoever wants to cognize a thing does *not* want to *change* its actual existence; rather, that person wants to be intellectually united in some way with its existence—it is united rationally through concepts or intuitively through perception and representation—and indeed so united with it as it exists independently [449] from acts of cognition and genuinely independently from any further processes of any possible reconfiguration. Whether this is possible or not is for the time being irrelevant; but it does correspond to the meaning of the word "cognition." The solution of a task of cognition indirectly calls for much inner and outer, psychic and physical activities, as well as—in the case of experiment—practical assault in the relevant actual course of events: then these activities, e.g., all inner and outer armaments for the act of cognition such as *wanting* to know, activities of attention, the "remarking," "attending," "observing," the possible seeking of the thing by going into it, the support of our meaning through instruments of all kinds—our thoughts through lectures—and every experimental assault into the course of events is itself not an act of cognition, but rather serves the getting-hold of the thing, at the end of which the genuine act of *cognition* exists and is executed. The experiment is as such different from any technical assault upon nature, an assault in which we seek to steer the event toward particular purposes—insofar as nature is able to support both.

As far the relation between both of these so-determined things "*work*" and "*cognition*," there is a threefold problem: (1) the problem of *coming into existence*, (2) the problem of *origination*, and (3) the problem of *purpose and value.*

The last of these problems is easily differentiated from the other two. The great, and recently deceased French mathematician and physicist Henri Poincaré, at one time stated the problem in the form of an engaging question: Do we study the laws of movement of the stars (in astronomy) for the sake of being able to construct, with the help of these mechanistic laws, better machines—or do we construct better and better machines so that more and more human beings are further and further removed from the burdens of daily chores so that they can lift the gaze of their free spirit to the heavens in order to study the laws of the stars without practical concern or need? This question is—when broadened—a question concerning the *meaning of spiritual culture* in general. Does spiritual culture only exist for the purposes of practically directing our working grasp of the thing and symbolizing the respective forms of work—or does it have a brilliant self-value and stands above all mere civilization of work and use in the service of the goal to gain more and more leisure and freedom from the pressure of the needs of life for the cultivation of spiritual culture? The opposing answers to this question represent a "cultural conflict" in a serious and deep sense, as it is so termed in our political jargon.

The first two of the above-named problems are more easily confused and thereby need a much finer distinction.

[450] The problem of "*emergence*" concerns the temporal sequence that the development of work and cognition in an individual and the development of the forms and methods of cognition and work take in the course of the development of people and humanity. Do we discover that the human being must have *first*, in a temporal regard, cognized *theoretically* the area in question in which the human being then intervenes to work—or does the relevant cognitive growth for an area show itself to be a temporal consequence of the more and more intense *working* of

this area? Are we allowed, for example, to say that the modern technique of the production and transportation of goods has been a mere supplementary practical use of purely speculative natural cognition—or did a newly awakened work-will, e.g., a zeal unknown to the Middle Ages, to turn nature into an efficient human place of residence come before the discovery of the "laws of nature" so that the new cognition of nature since Galileo and Leonardo—as, for example, E. Mach means in his history of mechanics—was born from the beginning from the spirit of technique and from technical problems? This important problem is what underlies the presently highly contested pedagogic debate that revolves around the key terms "school of work" or school of learning and education. The problem must be posed both psychologically and historically. If our concepts emerge *after* or simultaneously from working on an area, then it would have, for example, no sense as it is customary to teach the specific weight of lead or gold to a boy in physics instruction in order to give him at some later time the task of determining the specific weight in a piece of lead. On the contrary, it would have to mean; here you have lead; you proceed thus and so—and now determine the X which I "call" specific weight. Out of the knowledge of the technical process of determination, the concept emerged. The completed accomplishment led to the concept of the specific weight.

Yet, the deepest aspect of this genuinely *philosophical* question has not been touched upon. This is, however, the question that I called the question of the *origin* of cognition, and which is entirely different from any genetic or emergence question. It goes: From and in which *spiritual acts* does cognition emerge—regardless of where or when and with whom there is cognition, i.e., apart from real individuals and reality? What is cognition for the nature and the *essence* of acts in which it happens? Or a more specialized form of our question: Are the necessary, in this respect, acts of our spirit able to lead back somehow genetically to those spiritual facts which play a particular role in the outer and inner activity of *work*—or are they "*original*" in contrast to this activity and *non*-derivable from each? Is there, for example, "pure thinking" (and a lawfulness inherent to it and its objects) [451], a type of thinking that can in no way be traced back to some consequence of images, images that animals, for instance, also experience—or is there no such activity as this pure thinking? Is this "thinking" further *dependent*, in its acts and lawfulness, on the relevant *consequences* of the activities that we execute by virtue of its judgments and the statements entailed in them so that it changes along with the changing consequences of these activities and the organs and functions serving them—or is it *in*dependent of them so that it, its results, and likewise its laws would hold true for beings who had entirely no real effect on the world, such as we humans do? This is one and the same question not only for thinking and the existence of a pure logic, but also for acts of pure intuition and perception and the partial functions and contents contained in them. Is there an unmediated experience of *reality* in *perception*—or does its entire content only express the relation of reality to our human nervous constitution? Reality posits itself ultimately for the emotional acts of spirit and the acts of spirit belonging to the sphere of striving, such as feeling, loving, hating, willing, etc.

The exceptional import of this question is readily obvious. Only *insofar as* we human beings are able in general to perform spiritual acts that are *principally independent* of the collectivity of our drive-related needs, of our particular human type of organization, as well as of our particular practical manners of activity, only insofar as we human beings are able to follow our own laws and harbor our own independent ends, will we be able to expect that it is, in principle, possible for us to take hold cognitively of the essence of the thing, and to partake in the world as ethical and artistically cultivated beings—activities which far *outstrip* any aspect that would enclose the human being in a corner that our *animal milieu type* constitutes, and which would make possible something like a *metaphysics*. If, on the other hand, this is not the case, and all cognition and all understanding in every sense have only the meaning of a lantern for our need for practical orientation in our environment, and the acts of our spirit exist only in combination with such activity that is directed to the useful reconfiguration of material—i.e., in the activity of work—then any kind of end-positing would be ephemeral. Being locked up into the core of our spiritual existence in the rigid web of the milieu in which our species has transferred the great development of life, means then to forever give up validity and such high goals and let it be enough to us to arrange ourselves cozily and practically *within* this milieu.

This question of origin regarding our cognition is—as I have said—fully different from the temporal question of the emergence of our cognition. It could be, for example, quite likely [452] that the answer to the former would validate the latter, that any awakening of cognition in the individual and in present-day history is a consequence of increased work in a worldly area. But this fact would still be no proof that work is more than a *trigger* for the execution of any existing, purely original act of spirit; it would be no proof that work is be *more* than something which would have to get the automatic function of our spirit rolling, so to speak. The question of origin would thereby not have been decided, and not decided in the sense of the pragmatic theory which rejects such an autonomy of spirit! If our concepts and intuitions of the things themselves emerge only in and during the process of work or after it, then this is not synonymous with the idea that concepts and intuitions arise *totally from it* and present only effective directing means for the process of work. It could be that a greater and richer world, a world in which the *sense* and purpose of this *work* has been to gain partially in *cognition*, begins to disclose itself to us in and during the work on a part of the world.

Yet, our response to the question regarding the value and purpose of work and cognition is dependent on our response to the question of origin. Only insofar as there are spiritual acts that possess an origin and independence and in which we can gain a direct share in the *being* and life of the thing, does it make sense to strive for a spiritual culture as its own self-value, and to grasp the civilization of work as a means that serves to emancipate in us this originating spirit. If there is no such spirit, then it would have to be valid that the practical demands of our civilization are in fact the ultimate goals and the alpha and omega of our existence—and anyone who claims that spiritual culture has a superior value is only making idle threats against human society, threats which have invented a beautifully justified name for their own laziness! (How this question is fundamental for the existence of a religion constructed upon sincerity [*Ehrlichkeit*] is addressed later.)

Let us turn then to *pragmatism*. By this term (also "humanism," F. C. S. Schiller), let us understand any significant movement of thought originating in North America as well as in England, Italy, and France that responds to each of the three questions posed earlier: that all cognition *emerges* from work, *arises* from work, and has only the singular *meaning* of directing work effectively. The concurrent most popular and suggestive presentation of this theory is found in William James.[20] I [453] would like to call this the *"spirit" of pragmatism* in contrast to particular theories, for the sake of clarity. Let me now say a few words regarding this particular "spirit."

The fundamental error of all philosophy up to this point, whether it has been naturalism or idealism, empiricism or rationalism, was—so say the pragmatists—to want to define or cognitively grasp the "world" in some way as it is *in*dependent of what we make from it and what it should become in our hands. The traditional concept of cognition goes back to the Greeks. It was only an expression of their well-known *disdain for work* and of their aristocratic intellectualism founded upon a slave economy. According to this concept, the contemplative human being is the most noble form of humanity, and the deity is—according to Aristotle—in its nature "thought thinking itself," an absolutized Greek "wise person." According to this concept of cognition, there should be a world of stable objects: ideal objects such as numbers and geometric figures, and real, ultimately corporeal elements and objective forms, as well as the extant and fixed absolute ordering between these objects—which are somehow possibly and valuably *mirrored* through the understanding and intuition. Yet, such a fixed world of objects and their steadfast order is—so say the pragmatists—pure imagination, and is thereby also a cognitive ideal. The "world" is rather always only that *which we make* and form *of it.* It is the certain X of our certain practical reaction to it! What is "given" to us of this so-called world without any help and without work on our part is absolutely nothing that would still be in some way positively determinable. It is rather only a pure chaos of ungraspable impressions that flow in an eternally fluctuating flux, a μή ὄν, an ungraspable and indeterminable *limit* of our possible *activity* on the world. All unities of things, events, bodies, egos, all distinctions between nature and mind, etc., all distinctions between reality and non-reality, numerical separation, space, and time do not belong to what is "purely given"—they are our additions. Yet, they are also not—as Kant assumed—the image [*Gegenbild*] of an eternal structure of a law-giving understanding which functions in every one of us according to the same forms and laws and which necessarily impresses these on what is given—independently of our needs and our will. (A transcendental understanding, there is not.) Rather, they are types born from human *needs,* which cobble together the "given" spiritually for us in such a way that we are able to construct purposeful points of attack for our *work* and for our will in order to *reconfigure* the world. The so-called categories of the understanding (substance, causality, unity, variety, space, time, activity, identity, and object), which appear to us today so fixed and unchangeable, were at one time in the flux of the [454] becoming and development; only the tremendous pressure of tradition developed over a millennium of adaptation and linguistic transmission is responsible for any apparent absolute fixity, and allows these categories to ossify into idols that the rationalistic philosophers mistakenly hold for gods of "pure understanding" and transfer to a transcendental heaven! In fact, the only rules for the grasping of the given are those which have been proven to be true and fixed for their *most effective working* and formation to a particular extent. There is nothing to suggest that these rules have an eternal duration or a timeless meaning that is the same outside of our goals of earthly work!

Those who fail to grasp this fact—say the pragmatists—those who desire to cognize a world that would exist utterly independently of our practical engagement with it and its effectiveness, make, through this type of will, only a *particular historical state* of the world and of the human spirit into the *only possible state*—and would thereby inhibit by definition any further practical reconfiguration of the world. They are simply *metaphysical reactionaries!* For this reason, all existential claims about things and all statements about what the things are would have to have the proviso: "insofar as the things will no longer be changed." "Absolute" existence, "absolute truth," "absolutely existing material," "energy," "absolute spirit," "understanding," and "absolute consciousness" are all nonsense. All philosophers up to this point, who have sought to grasp the world and reality as they exist prior to any possible action and as grounded in themselves, have only turned the old accomplishments of work into some false eternity and absoluteness; they have, instead of throwing themselves and human force boldly into the great stream of work on the world, instead of vitally taking part in the living drama of the world process, and instead of cultivating the world, merely *observed* and *looked* at the work of the ancestors, i.e., they have, out of laziness or the inability to do any work themselves, out of their status and the class to which they belong, made a particular virtue out of, and for this purpose, without knowing it, have constructed certain concepts such as "pure cognition" and "absolute truth." According to James, any so-called absolute being, any absolute truth—whether this being poses as the world of ideas in Plato, as a kingdom of creating "forms" at work in everything in Aristotle, or as atoms moving in an absolute space and in an absolute time for the materialists, or as "absolute energy," or as an eternal world reason or a so-called "universal consciousness"—every single concept of the world ending the further world work is actually only a *rash* conclusion about a world that *always becomes something new* through our work; and thereby creates a bed of laziness—a mythological expression for the simple sober fact that there would have to be "breaks of work." Or, as F. C. S. Schiller [455] expresses it in his book *Humanism*;[21] "We must endlessly think the world creatively and imaginatively, if we are to encourage the necessary enthusiasm for its transformation and amelioration." We are in no way allowed to determine anything as absolute before we have made through action the attempt and the experiment to determine it differently and to reconfigure it in some other wished-for manner.

This viewpoint should, however, hold true not only for any assumption regarding materials, forces, and souls, but also for any so-called natural law, for mathematical propositions, mathematical axioms, and logical axioms. A "natural law" is not the expression of a sacrosanct order of a universal universe, an order independent of our will and our needs, but only a certain reduction of our expectations regarding the course of appearances insofar as we artificially abstract from our unrestricted interventions into nature; its singular "sense" is to appropriately direct our technical interventions into nature: it is a "rule of work"! Not only the Greeks, but also the heroes of modern natural science, e.g., Galileo and Kepler, have wandered off onto mistaken paths. The Greeks believed in a cosmos (a harmonious order) that is objectively steeped in forms of reason, and is governed and controlled by eternal "ideas" that we are able to grasp through the power of thinking. Every modern thinker rejects such objective forms and ideas (forms, values, and purposes only equal the subjective reactions of human beings), but in their place, these thinkers place "natural laws," i.e., quantitatively determined, constant relations of appearances in which we are able to ascertain (normally concealed for the natural view, but graspable to rational-mathematical thinking) strict mechanisms of movement behind the colorful world.

Pragmatism rejects *both.* The Greeks—say the pragmatists—do not have the *spirit of work* of the modern human being. Their universe of stable, objective ideas and forms in its vivid, artificial harmony presents the content of a worldview that excludes from its essence an active, technical reconfiguration and amelioration of the universe. A world that is already rational and harmonious in itself does not *need* any rational reconfiguration! To look and gaze upon this world in reverence would have to be the final aim of life. Yet, every stable world construct of the Greeks has been tossed out of the history of science and civilization. In reality, this has thereby only transferred the life forms of the Greeks' *leisured* class, of the free citizens, into everything! The universe is thus not a rationally inspired cosmos, controlled by ideas and eternal forms, which is "given" independently of any possible work, but is [456] a "chaos" (the opposite of a "cosmos")—a chaos which awaits a continuously new determination and formation through our work. It is also not the case that any mathematically determined mechanism of the new physics, chemistry, and biology (and the picture which the English association psychology paints of our soul) is able to contemplate a so-called "true being" lying behind immediate appearances. This picture touches upon no definite reality, but has only the sense to direct our technical interventions in nature to demonstrate to us the point of attack at which we can handily move and channel nature according to our purposes. It is actually only a plan for our possible action upon nature: a universal plan of construction for possible machines and tools. But this construction plan has no relation to real things existing for us; this universal construction plan for a possible technology has no bearing upon an absolute reality lying behind appearances.

What we are to gather from all that has been said is this: the *spirit* which pragmatism breathes is the same spirit which hearkens out of Chicago's eleven storied buildings, which sounds like something from the verse of Walt Whitman, which must have been left from the unrestricted Puritan spirit of work when its original Christian-Calvinistic superstructure was broken, a spirit of work that created, first of all, modern America and—as Max Weber says—brought forth the "heroic time period of early capitalism" in Geneva and Holland. It is also the spirit of a people whose "world," whose basis and culture are still more malleable than the densely populated, very traditional old Europe.

There are still two further consequences to which I have already alluded.

First, pragmatism speaks on behalf of an unrestricted *freedom of human will and action*. According to pragmatism, for this reason, our will can be subjected to no laws of nature, since the causal principles according to which we construct and determine all so-called laws of nature are indebted to a free act of our will (which is motivated through our practical interests in the regulated and thereby able-to-be-directed appearances) for their dignity. According to this idea, the causal law is only a "postulate" of our free will! Pragmatism is thus strictly indeterministic and criticizes any philosophy which claims that there is any world development independent of our will, a world development in which we insert ourselves and which we would have to encourage. For this reason, the ethical, practical problems of life gain for themselves the most central position in philosophy. The truth is only a variation of the "good," which is in their opinion reduced to the "*useful*"—in the broad current.

Secondly, it lies within the consequences of pragmatism that pragmatism must reject any *ultimate unity* of the universe. If the world is only the milieu of work of the human being, and is a strict counter-picture of the human being's directions of need and work, [457] then there must be just as many worlds as there are directions of need and work. That these worlds are different for human beings than they are for other animal species and kinds of beings which do not reach into the milieu of human beings (James, e.g., was also a spiritist) is obvious. If the forms of thinking are only the result of the vital activity and adaptation to the environment of a particular organization, then the forms of thinking must change with that organization. James explicitly teaches the "*multiversal*," as he says, i.e., an infinite variety of worlds which are, according to the directions of work of the organization and the species, cut out of and constructed from the chaos of the originally given.

So much, at least for the time being, for the spirit of pragmatism.

2.

Pragmatism has proven itself, as (1) a general epistemology and as (2) a relational determination of life and cognition, to have fully gone astray.

Nonetheless, we must acknowledge pragmatism to have shown that both the universal ideal of all science (the clear determination of facts) and the specific forms of intuition and thought of science arise with the aim of a certain tendency of life; namely, to make the given *controllable through movement,* in contrast to those tendencies of philosophy originating out of the interaction of the pure acts and laws of intuition and thought.

We called this aim the "*positing of goals.*" It was not for us the subsequent use of scientific results, but "scientific reason" itself, and its collective system of forms and categories that co-originated from this goal-positing, which are active in the formation of the *natural worldview.*

Science is therefore, in contrast to philosophy, not presuppositionless. Since the presuppositions of any type of cognition are, in addition to the pure laws of logic, the pure forms of intuition, and the pure facts (and even those who would not deny that cognition has these presuppositions are those who still speak of a presuppositionless science), science still presupposes a principle of the selection of any pure form and choice of facts in accordance with an image of the world that living beings possess that will enable them to *master* and direct its environment. This characteristic state of affairs requires that the value of science and the image that science has of the universe depend on the values of any purpose to which any scientific reflection is relative: (1) of the *value of life in general,* and (2) of the value of the *technical purpose of the establishment.*

It is clear that science as such can in no way determine its own value. Both the *truth* that science contains and the [458] *level of relativity* of its objects are matters of *philosophical epistemology,* as I have sought to examine here. Since it is an initial, involuntary life tendency (in the natural worldview) and the deliberate positing of a goal by our conscious will in science (the technical positing of a goal) which determine the relativity of the scientific object—and any willing and any goal-positing is subject to *ethics* and to the *rank order of value* assumed by it—the value of science can thus be fully cognized when the value of the content of the goal is established whose positing proves to be a presupposition of science. Where this value is not posited, science loses its validity.

If we call any activity that takes place in the direction of the technical positing of purpose "*work,*" then we can formulate the problem as such:

What is the ranking of the value of "work" in the rank order of value?

And what is the *value of any human type* which the pragmatists regard as the human being in general, as the ideal of the human being—and what type do they counter to the "*homo sapiens*" of the Greek philosophers and to the "child of God" of the Christians: the "*homo faber*"?

For the pragmatists, the answer to our question is self-evident: the value of work is the fundamental value; or, work is the creator of all value. All ethical maxims are rules of work, and truth itself is only a subtype of ethical values. Everything that can be called the world picture, from the sensations of the world up to present-day philosophical and scientific cognition, is only an interplay between a condition of beginning that is a will and a condition of the end that is a suitable reaction to stimuli in the environment; and "*true* is this image" means that it is bound to a reaction that is *suitable* for the tendency of the being.

Pragmatism and More Recent Natural Science

Pragmatism bears a close affinity to the advance of Kantian philosophy, as Fichte had also done. For pragmatism, the world is only the material for a free activity of the ego, and, under pragmatism, the task of theoretical cognition loses its independence from the practical, moral consciousness. Additionally, for pragmatism and its modern successors such as C. von Sigwart, W. Windelband, H. Rickert, and H. Münsterberg, the concept of being is reduced to the concept of value, and the concept of "object" is reduced to the experience or recognition of a content through a judgment which should be a type of "assessment." We will describe in the future the above-mentioned theses of pragmatism understood in the broader sense to which we contrast pragmatism *in the stricter sense*, the pragmatism of James, Schiller, and Dewey. The closest [459] connection between the pragmatic theory of perception and these Fichtean presuppositions has been made in H. Münsterberg's work *The Essential Features of Psychology* [*Grundzüge der Psychologie*], particularly in his theory of action. What fully and internally distinguishes this thinker from *American* pragmatism is the latter's utilitarian character, i.e., the attempt to determine the good as a kind of utility and usefulness, the good to which they reduce the idea of truth.

In addition to these historical starting points in the history of philosophy, there are two other important points in the history of recent science from which pragmatism (in the strict sense) draws. The first is *modern biology*, and here primarily the theory of *evolutionary descent* advanced by Darwin; the second is that theory of cognition which since Maxwell has gained prominence in *theoretical physics* (I name for the time being only Maxwell, Mach, Boltzmann, Kirchhoff, Duhem, Le Roy, Poincaré, and Ostwald)—and which is supported by a group of *mathematicians*.

From any biological standpoint which is dominated by Darwin (and which historically was adopted by traditional English utilitarian philosophy), it must appear as an incomprehensible fact that in a particular line of vertebrates in the course of the development of life, activities and forces have been cultivated and have been fixed through natural selection that would serve only to supply a purely disinterested cognition of the world. All the organs and functions of animals are cultivated and fixed only to the degree that they accomplish, in some way, the preservation of life of the individual and the species. The pure cognition of reality—without it having a changing effect on the animal's practical reaction to the environment—is in no way able to accomplish the said preservation of life. Thus—one concludes—it is extremely improbable that the human being should possess an ability of such a kind ("pure understanding"). Since the sensory functions certainly do not serve in their gradual development in the plant and animal world as a mere speculative illustration of reality, but have only come into existence because the sensations conveyed through them serve as signals for practical reactions that are beneficial to life—signals to flee, or seek food, or capture the spoils—then the development of "understanding" in the human being should have the same sense of being a weapon in the "struggle for survival." The thoughts that underlie an understanding of this kind will have their ultimate criterion in their utility, and not in the fact that they depict a reality. There is a common expression: it is useful to construct reality according to representations, and harmful to live in illusions, [460] and thus the pragmatists answer: if thoughts are created in such a manner that they determine useful reactions, then the further assumption that they depict besides that a reality is entirely unnecessary. For this reason, the statement should be reversed: we call "reality" that which the being of our kind has with regard to its actions, and "truth" means nothing other than the force of thought to resolve useful actions.

Nietzsche diverges from this view. He is incorrectly considered to be among the pragmatists, but he does share with them the idea that the value of values is whatever benefits life—but in the sense of the increase of *power*, not the increase of utility. He still holds to the old concept of truth and does not try to reduce truth to the concept of whatever benefits life. He concludes the reverse: if the striving for truth is increasingly detrimental to life while illusion and lies are beneficial to life, then the striving for truth is an ascetic ideal inimical to life, an ideal that has its roots in the thought of the Christian ascetics. In this sense, he calls Kant's synthetic judgments "fictions," "a priori lies," and seeks to reduce all forms of thought to ways of taking hold of the world. More recently, H. Vaihinger has attempted to develop Nietzsche's idea further, particularly with regard to the concept of "fiction."[22]

Pragmatic epistemology obtained a very strong impetus from the methods that have been developed in *theoretical physics* since Maxwell.[23] Above all, the concept of "*hypothesis*" provided the point of departure. A hypothesis was originally understood to be an acceptance of a presupposed reality which could not be observed, and the consequences of this hypothesis were confirmed through the facts of experience or were not contradicted by a single fact of experience, and its probability, on the one hand, increased with the number of observable facts derivable from it and, on the other hand, increased with its independence. A hypothesis is, in this sense, the existence of atoms, of ether, etc. Often, not only observed facts have been "explained" with the help of such hypotheses, but also appearances have been predicted which are proven after being accessible to observation. In these cases, it is said that the hypothesis has proven itself as fruitful. Yet, the claim was always bound to the ability of the hypothesis to depict a *real reality*. In one of his famous writings regarding the electromagnetic appearances discovered by Faraday, Maxwell made use of certain image models (e.g., the model of a system of elastic, moving rollers) for the purposes of lucid summary of these appearances, [461] and he explicitly explains that these assumptions do not have to be understood as hypotheses, but rather only as image models that would be capable of supporting the theory of electricity. Zöllner, the well-known author of the book on comets,[24] misunderstood these image models as "hypotheses" and subjected them to a harsh critique. Later on (Oliver Lodge et al.), what Maxwell had done took place more often: such models and images were beginning to be introduced more and more in the theories. There is no longer any *claim* related to a *reality* being made about these models or images. These models and images derive their justification more and more from their power to prompt new problems, and to predict particular phenomena.

The *pragmatic epistemology* constructed from this process is an odd practice. While Maxwell modestly remarked that his models were not hypotheses, pragmatism made the claim about the essence of all hypotheses that their meaning lies in stimulating the action of the experimenter in order to obtain as the purpose of the experiment the sensations and observations desired by virtue of the hypothesis; and it claims that the essence of hypothesis would alone be in its power to lead, in its fruitfulness, and this would have no meaning whatsoever to relate the hypothesis to something real. This was certainly not what Maxwell meant by distinguishing a hypothesis from an image model—that there is neither true nor false, and there certainly also cannot be "probable."

Pragmatism goes still one step further. After pragmatism had so muddled the concept of hypotheses, it attempted to grasp and present every element of our judgment, statements, concepts, and theories, which somehow reach beyond direct sensation, in accord with this new concept of hypothesis. If everything which is truly valid to us goes beyond the sensation complex and is now (mistakenly) called a "hypothesis," then the following must also be called hypotheses: (1) the existence of the astronomical Sun; the Moon has a different half that is never turned to us; the flowing fiery core of the Earth; and still more; (2) a thing with qualities (e.g., a red ball), the causal chain, the actual and non-actual, material, and the soul; (3) the laws of nature and theories; and (4) all axioms of mathematics and the principles of logic like the axiom of identity. Everything possible: existing singular things, categories, laws of nature and theories, axioms—things that were earlier differentiated—would be "hypotheses" or would be differentiated from hypotheses only gradually (Le Vrai, Milhaud). Since hypotheses are to be measured only according to their fruitfulness and power to lead to new facts, [462] this criterion would be valid for any other element of our worldview as well. Moreover, logical and mathematical axioms, for example, are in themselves *conventions* which are arbitrary and without evidence, and their value rests solely on what can possibly be derived most simply from them. Connected to this idea is so-called *symbolic logic*, which poses the task of creating a practical system of signs whose laws of connections are chosen so that with their help actual orderings can be most simply ordered (Peirce).

It is very interesting to see how little by little the methods of modern physics came nearer to the thinking to which pragmatism gave expression. H. Hertz stated in the preface to his *Principles of Mechanics* three demands for a fully realized *theory*: (1) that it is logically right, i.e., all logical principles are observed in it; (2) that it is true, i.e., it accords with the facts; and (3) that it is the most *simple* one, i.e., the appearances are derived from a minimum of final assumptions. Very soon afterward, the attempt was made to reduce the first of these demands to the third demand. Logical correctness—as Avenarius, Ernst Mach, and Boltzmann sought to show—exists only in the greatest simplicity and spareness of thought in the grasping and description of a group of facts (the principle of the economy of thought); all grounding therein, for example, seeks to reduce an appearance A to a better-known appearance B, i.e., one that we, since we are already familiar with it and are used to it, is more easily grasped than a different one that is similar to it. (Hence, all logical principles.) As soon as this happens, it is taken a step further. Boltzmann wants to reduce the second demand to the first. In a series of essays,[25] he sought to show that the production of something desired beforehand through the practical reaction prompted by a theory is the final guarantee of security for that theory, and for this reason, moreover, the *technique* constructs the final and single guarantee for the value of *natural science.* In an essay concerning the methods of physics, he distinguishes three main methods. The first is the empirical-inductive method, in which one proceeds from the facts of experience and, for example, determines the concept of mass in such a manner that one leaves out and does not consider the successive qualities of a given body, such as a rock, qualities that with regard to the relation to be studied, e.g., its weight in changing altitudes above the Earth, do not come into question. The second is the Euclidean method, which is deduced from evident principles. Boltzmann shows that both methods have their disagreeable aspects. The third method, which he himself makes use of in his work regarding mechanics, is one wherein one makes arbitrary presuppositions that do not need to be evident, and presupposition that one cleverly chooses so that the known theorems and facts [463] find the best and simplest correlation. This method coincides exactly with what the *pragmatist* recommends.[26]

Finally, the view of mathematics—that refuge of rationalistic philosophy—as Henri Poincaré developed it, contributes to the support of pragmatism. According to this view, mathematics is neither provable nor refutable through the facts of experience. On this point Poincaré agrees, for example, with the Kantian a prioris [*Aprioristen*]. Yet, in opposition to Kant, this view argues that truth and falsity befit a mathematical axiom; it exists solely in a convention or in a concealed definition that is measured according to its effectiveness and convenience alone.

Simultaneous Grounding of the Theory of Perception and the Theory of Formal-Mechanistic Natural Science

Let us state a demand which has been fulfilled only very infrequently up to this point: the demand that the *philosophical theory of the limits of cognition, the categories of formal-mechanistic natural science,* and the theory of the types of any other cognition of nature should be treated with the most precise correspondence with all the facts and laws of the perceptual process (experimental psychology, sense physiology) known to us up to this point—in short, the *philosophy of perception.* (In which order do these factors follow in the perception of mature adults: [1] reality, [2] thingliness, [3] extension and duration, [4] gestalt, [5] value, [6] rational meaning, and [7] sense qualities? And which different types and levels of the so-called stimulus concept correspond to these constituent parts of perception?) It does not work, as has been attempted, to separate the ontological and epistemological investigations of the limits of cognition by the positive natural sciences, and in particular by mathematical physics, from the "philosophy of perception." This has led to the most grievous contradictions and circles (and in particular to the system of the mutual pushing-aside of the burden of proof). Both investigations must be so undertaken that their results collaborate uniformly and result in a thoroughly theoretical *total view*; that is, a *simultaneous grounding* of the theory of perception and the theory of physics.

In this lecture, I will first submit the philosophical interpretation of the formal-mechanistic lawfulness of nature to a critique and present the correct view; secondly, I will see which other kinds of the cognition of nature with regard to the correct view and interpretation of this theory of nature still remain "free"—the kinds that remain irreplaceable and justified with regard to the ideal, complete, formal-mechanistic [464] view of nature; and thirdly, I will develop some fundamental principles of the philosophy of perception and show that a correct view of the perceptual process corresponds exactly with the epistemologically discovered view.

Since my thesis contains the claim that the formal-mechanistic theory of nature only elaborates the factual lawful relations of points and elements of inorganic nature which are direct points of attack for our directing and guiding of the processes of nature for a spontaneous vital movement in general—and thus also for our human will to dominate nature and by reason of the ethical, non-conditioned value estimate of such mastery, I express a claim reminiscent of the thought-world of *pragmatism.*

I reject *philosophical* pragmatism in each of its forms. Philosophical cognition is *a*practical. Positive science must (on the other hand) be *true.* Yet, I claimed a *methodological* pragmatism as the principle of *selection* for the *formal-mechanistic view of nature* and sought to prove it.

"The Pragmatist, the Idealist—and the Wise"

Pragmatists will be inclined to change not only their ideas of causes and effects and their intentions in response to failures in action—as any pragmatist should—but also—what is troublesome—their *mentality*. The pragmatist does not want to say with Storm: "Whereas one asks what comes next, the other one asks what is right; this is what distinguishes the free from the servile"; the pragmatist will transform freedom into some degree of servitude. The pragmatist will not say: there is "eternal" evidence and truth (*verités éternelles*, as Leibniz said) which persists through any contingent sense experience and through any mediated conclusions because it constructs its own ultimate standard. The pragmatist will sacrifice reason [*raison*]—the *raisonnement* that becomes the appearing original phenomenon of the pure, sense-free intuition of the world's structure—to any observation of contingent realities. The pragmatist is a human being who—living in a world where two things and two other things have resulted in a fifth thing—happily cries out: 2 + 2 = 5, instead of saying 2 + 2 = 4, but I live in a world whose contingent reality requires me to accept a force that brings about five things by virtue of the real connection between the number two two things.

Yet, is it not accidental that pragmatism is in part right about the contingent sphere of reality (the *faits fortuits*), but is absolutely incorrect about the sphere of eternal essences and their interrelations? It is necessary. The reason for this "necessity" is that what distinguishes essence from existence is only the resistance to an activity—and indeed "activity" which is the same in the will and action on the one hand, in cognizing (as a [465] "way to knowledge") on the other hand, and also in the case of remarking, attending, and observing, as in mediated thinking

The pragmatist is lost in the contingent world of reality. The pragmatist does not see the essences or the ideas of things.

The idealist is one-sidedly enraptured with the world of ideas. The idealist does not feel and sense the "resistance of the world."

The wise sees and senses both—and the wise does not rashly seek to harmonize them in the being itself.

From what has been said, it becomes possible to insinuate what is meant by the statement, the "meaning" of a statement is the epitome of the consequences that it has for this world or a different "world," i.e., a somehow "changed" world; and the statement that the meaning of two statements a and b is precisely the same "meaning" when the consequences of these two statements change entirely nothing about the contingent perceptual content of the world. William James genuinely claims, for example, that there is no meaningful difference between the statement "God is" and "God is not" when for the empirical content of the world entirely nothing different "results" from them; even when the belief in one of these two statements does not encourage us to different actions. To give a different example, Einstein says the meaning of the words "simultaneous" and "non-simultaneous" is the same meaning when we, under the assumption that the speed of light is constant through light measures of the time that has necessarily a reversible movement between points A and B on earth, reach the same number of time unities.

Author's Notes

Chapter 1

1. For a good study of this problem, see Moritz Schlick, *Allgemeine Erkenntnis*, 2nd ed. (Berlin: Julius Springer, 1925), 89ff.

2. See my criticisms of Spencer's theory in my book *Der Formalismus in der Ethik und die Materiale Wertethik: Neuer Versuch der Grundlegung eines Ethischen Personalismus,* vol. II of *Gesammelte Werke,* ed. Maria Scheler (Bern: Francke Verlag, 1966), V, chapter 4; translated by Manfred S. Frings and Roger L. Funk as *Formalism in Ethics and Non-Formal Ethics of Value: A New Attempt toward the Foundation of an Ethical Personalism* (Evanston, Ill.: Northwestern University Press, 1973), section V, chapter 4.

3. See the essay *Probleme einer Soziologie des Wissens,* in *Die Wissenformen und die Gesellschaft,* vol. VIII of *Gesammelte Werke,* ed. Maria Scheler (Bern: Francke Verlag, 1980); translated by Manfred S. Frings as *Problems of a Sociology of Knowledge* (London: Routledge and Kegan Paul, 1980).

4. See also Ernst Mach, *Die Mechanik, in ihrer Entwicklung historisch-kritisch darstellt* (Leipzig: Brockhaus, 1883), where this thought experiment is critically presented as Newton's "most ingenious" accomplishment.

5. [Translator: Scheler places emphasis on the *Wahr* in *Wahr*nehmung in the original German. Literally translated, *Wahrnehmung* means "taking as true (*Wahr*)."]

6. [Editor's note: For Scheler's description of the "functionalization" of essential insights, see Max Scheler, *On the Eternal in Man,* trans. Bernard Noble (New York: Routledge, 2017).]

Chapter 2

1. For more on the Marburg school, see the excellent critique of the Cohen-Natorp teachings by N. Hartmann in his book *Grundzüge einer Metaphysik der Erkenntnis* (Berlin: Walter de Gruyter, 1925).

2. See E. Cassirer on Goethe's color theory and Newton in *Idee und Gestalt* (Berlin: Bruno Cassirer, 1921), see also the preface on the philosophy of language in part I of Cassirer's *Philosophie der symbolischen Formen* (Berlin-Leipzig: Bruno Cassirer, 1923).

3. See Schlick, *Allgemeine Erkenntnislehre.*

4. A thorough grounding and explication of what has only briefly been alluded to here as the "theory of the standards of knowledge" shall be found in the first volume of our metaphysics.

5. Furthermore, the pure designation of a sign in a clear manner to an object is still a subclass of such participation, even if only symbolically.

6. "Of this" essence within and as a member of the world's essential structure, for it is the structure of entirety that conditions the *singular* essence.

7. See the first volume of my metaphysics, to be published in about a year's time, where a precise theory and technique of this "bracketing" are given.

8. Bracketed under its "presuppositions," and this means likewise that it turns itself into the *object* of its exposition.

9. See also my later explications regarding the kinds of natural cognition in Section IV of the present volume.

Chapter 3

1. William James's work has been translated into German by W. Jerusalem under the title *Der Pragmatismus: Ein neuer Name für alte Denkmethoden* (Leipzig: Klinkhardt, 1908). Jerusalem is sympathetic to pragmatism; see his *Einleitung in die Philosophie* (Vienna: Wilhelm Braumüller, 1913). Regarding the history of the pragmatist movement, a history that has yet to be written in a deep sense, see Emile Boutroux's *William James,* translated into German by Bruno Jordan (Leipzig: Veit, 1912); and translated into English by Archibald and Barbara Henderson as *William James* (London: Longmans, Green, 1912). See also Julius Goldstein, *Wandlungen in der Philosophie der Gegenwart* (Leipzig: Klinkhardt, 1911). A more fully worked-out system of pragmatic philosophy is given by F. C. S. Schiller in his *Humanismus: Beiträge zu einer pragmatischen Philosophie,* translated into German by R. Eisler (Leipzig: Klinkhart, 1911); originally published in English as *Humanism: Philosophical Essays* (New York: Macmillan, 1903).

2. William James, *Pragmatism: A New Name for Some Old Ways of Thinking* (Cambridge, Mass.: Harvard University Press, 1979; originally published in 1907), 29.

3. For these different kinds of axiomatics, see the book by M. Geiger, *Systematische Axiomatik der euklidischen Geometrie* (Augsburg: Benno Filser, 1924), in which he has tried to posit an essential axiomatics of Euclidian geometry in place of the merely fruitful axiomatics that the strict nominalism and formalism of our present-day mathematics mostly recognize. The penetrating differences of both kinds of axiomatics have probably never been so deeply examined as in this book.

4. See F. C. S. Schiller, *Humanism,* ibid.

5. *Voir pour prévoir, prévoir pour prévenir!* (See to foresee, foresee to forestall!), Auguste Comte (1789–1857).

6. Regarding Bergson's strong effect on W. James, see Boutroux's book *William James,* 97ff.

7. See Dilthey's essay "Erfahrung und Denken: Eine Studie zur erkenntnis-

theoretischen Logik des 19. Jahrhunderts" (1892), in *Die geistige Welt: Einleitung in die Philosophie des Lebens,* vol. VI of *Gesammelte Schriften* (Leipzig-Berlin: B. G. Teubner Verlag, 1924).

8. [Translator: This is in English in the original.]

9. See Hertz's essay *Die Prinzipien der Mechanic in neuem Zusammanhange dargestellt* (1895), in vol. 3 of his *Gesammelte Werke* (Leipzig: Barth, 1910).

10. [Translator: *Proton pseudos* means fundamental or original error, i.e., an error in the premises.]

11. See W. James, *Pragmatismus*; and also F. C. S. Schiller, *Humanismus.*

12. Insofar as they are "*res nobiliores in mente quam in se ipsis*" (Thomas Aquinas).

13. See H. Bergson, *Matiére et mémoire: Essai sur la relation du corps a l'esprit* (Paris: Libraire Félix Alcan, 1896).

14. See Münsterberg's so-called "Aktionstheorie" in *Grundzüge der Psychologie* (Leipzig: Johann Ambrosius Barth, 1918).

15. See my *Formalism in Ethics,* Section V, Subsection 8.

16. See A. Gelb and K. Goldstein, "Über Farbenamnesie," *Psychologie Forschung* 6, no. 1, 127–86.

17. Ibid., 159.

18. See the previously cited investigation by Gelb and Goldstein, "Über Farbenamnesie," 178.

19. See the recent critique of logical pragmatism by E. Strauss, "Wesen und Vorgang der Suggestion," in *Abhundlungenaus der Neurologie, Psychiatrie, Psychologie, und ihre Grenzbieten,* no. 28 (Berlin: S. Karger), 1925. Strauss correctly shows that pragmatism does not take judgments in the social context in order to interpret them according to their function and state of affairs, but takes them in their original suggestive function to influence and convince others.

20. This has been worked out in the previous material.

21. See W. Wundt, *Die Prinzipien der mechanischen Naturansicht* (Stuttgart, 1910).

22. See M. Schlick, *Allgemeine Erkenntnis.*

23. See H. Driesch, *Ordnungslehre* (Jena: E. Diederichs, 1912).

24. See the deep and penetrating critique of Bergson by Roman Ingarden in his essay "Intuition und Intellekt bei Henri Bergson," *Jahrbuch für Philosophie und phänomenologische Forschung,* vol. 5 (1922).

25. See E. Husserl, *Logischen Untersuchungen,* vol. 1 (Halle: Niemeyer, 1900).

26. Also, temporal and spatial sizes would have to enter into this functional law as material determinations of their positions.

27. See in particular E. Mach's wonderful example in his book *Erkenntnis und Irrtum* (Leipzig: J. A. Barth, 1905).

28. See K. Gerhard's book *Machs Erkenntnistheorie und der Realismus* (Stuttgart: W. Spemann, 1914). See also my critique of Mach's theory in *Formalism in Ethics,* Section VI, Subsection 3.

29. See Carl Stumpf's well-thought-out exposition in his treatise, *Zur Einteilung der Wissenschaft* (Berlin: Königliche Akademie der Wissenschaften, 1907).

30. I will have to show in the first volume of my metaphysics that the former

is the case and the latter is not the case. Critical realism (E. Becher, O. Külpe) errs when it claims that trans-conscious reality is a presupposition of natural lawfulness.

31. [Translator: "Teleoclinal" is a direct translation of "*teleoklin*." These are words used almost exclusively for a biological concept referring to the purposiveness of a living organism. I have chosen to retain the direct translation since Scheler himself made use of a rare word, but one that was used in the study of biology in the early twentieth century.]

32. See Max Planck, "Das Prinzip der kleinsten Wirkung," in *Physikalische Rundblicke* (Leipzig: S. Hirzel, 1922).

33. See the explication of this idea in the preceding essay, *Problems of a Sociology of Knowledge.*

34. See the insightful exposition by J. von Uexküll in his book *Umwelt and Innenwelt der Tiere* (Berlin: Julius Springer, 1909).

Chapter 4

1. See Henri Poincaré, *Wissenschaft und Hypothese* (Leipzig: Teubner, 1906).

2. See L. Boltzmann, *Populäre Schriften* (Leipzig, 1905).

3. Since we can perceive nothing that (1) does not induce movements in us, and (2) that we do not "want" to move in some sense, the content of our possible perceptions must always be clearly determinable through a schema of movement.

4. See also what follows.

5. Since the discovery of the difference between the sense of vibration and the sense of touch by D. Katz (*Der Aufbau der Tastwelt* [Leipzig: Johann Ambrosius Barth, 1925]) and since the threshold difference in both respects—the thresholds of the sense of vibration lie so much higher than those of the sense of touch that Katz correctly calls the sense of vibration, in contrast to the sense of touch, a "sense at a distance" we also know that the experience of movement of the vibration (already in its simplest data "smooth" or "rough") is more *primordial* than the sense of touch ("something above the touch qualities 'hard' or 'soft'").

6. "And since, on the other hand, only what is perceptible for us is sufficient for the condition to be *controllable,* so too must everything that is perceived be mechanically explainable."

7. See Eduard von Hartmann, *Kategorienlehre* (Leipzig: H. Haacke, 1896); and his *Die Weltanschauung der modernen Physik* (Leipzig: H. Haacke, 1902); see also the philosophically insightful exposition by H. Weyl in his essay "Was ist Materie?" *Die Naturwissenschaften* 12, no. 28–30 (1924).

8. See the independent psychological reasons that led me to the acceptance of a unified super-individual life in my book *Wesen und Formen der Sympathie* [vol. VII of *Gesammelte Werke,* ed. Manfred S. Frings (Bonn: Bouvier, 1973), part A, IV; translated by Peter Heath as *The Nature of Sympathy* (London: Taylor and Francis, 2008)]. See also E. Becher's book *Die fremddienliche Zweckmässigkeit der Pflanzengallen* (Leipzig: Veit, 1917); and H. Driesch, *Philosophie des Organischen,* 2nd ed.

(Leipzig: W. Engelmann, 1921), especially chapter B IV, "Das Problem der Zahl der Entelechien."

9. See W. Nernst, "Zum Gültigkeitsbereich der Naturgesetze," *Die Naturwissenschaften* 10, no. 21 (1922): 489–95; and also Max Planck, "Dynamische und statistische Gesetzmässigkeit," in *Physikalische Rundblicke* (Leipzig: Hirzel, 1922).

10. A dynamic gestalt law, i.e., a law of the rhythm of the event, demands as its highest presupposition the quantum theory that A. Sommerfeld makes a judgment about: "Quite remarkable, with regard to these rules of intensity, is the exchangeability of the beginning and end condition. It appears as if the event were not given through a probability for the beginning condition of the atoms and some probability for the transition in the end condition, but rather as if the beginning and end conditions *equally* determined the event through their related quantum weight. This would contradict to some extent our traditional feeling of causality according to which we think that the course of the process is already established through the beginning data. It does not appear to me to be ruled out that the quantum experiences in this respect could reconstruct our conceptions. It is frequently brought up that, according to the Bohrian condition of radiation, the atom must know in advance which condition it is ultimately to be transferred to before it can radiate. Also, in the principle of the least effect, we accept a teleological and not a causal standpoint. One such teleological reconstruction of causality appears to me to contradict not so much quantum theory as the classical theory.

"What we must certainly demand, as long as there is a natural science, is the indisputable specificity of the observable event, the mathematical certainty of the natural law. *How* this indisputability is achieved, whether it materializes solely through the beginning condition or jointly through the beginning and end conditions, is not something we can know in advance, but we must learn it from nature." See A. Sommerfeld, "Grundlagen der Quantentheorie und das Bohrschen Atommodelles," *Die Naturwissenschaften* 12, no. 47 (1924).

11. In this sense, the Dionysian ecstasies in the life of feeling and drive are still today, as in all times, the singular way and key to nature itself, the singular form of partaking in nature. See my book *The Nature of Sympathy*, particularly the section regarding a general physiognomic and character theory of nature expressed as a universal grammar and hermeneutic of understanding.

12. I must refer here to my metaphysics which, I hope, will appear soon.

13. See the related exposition by Emanuel Rádl, *Geschichte der biologischen Theorien in der Neuzeit* (Leipzig: Wilhelm Englemann, 1909); and more recently, A. Müller, *Das Individualitätsproblem und die Subordination der Organe: Ein Beitrag zur Descensus der Keindrüsen der Säugetiere* (Leipzig: Akademische Verlag Gesellschaft, 1924).

14. For it is an irrefutable and fundamental principle of epistemology that the one to which an object is relative cannot underlie the same explanation (according to the same principle) as any object. If the object of a formal-mechanical explanation of nature is existentially relative to the living being, then a formal-mechanistic explanation of the living being must itself be impossible.

15. See the thoroughgoing critique of this most empty of all imaginations

by E. Becher, *Geisteswissenschaften und Naturwissenschaften: Untersuchungen zur Theorie und Einleitung der Realwissenschaften* (Munich: Dunker und Humblot, 1922); and see also W. Dilthey's "[Über vergleichende Psychologie] Beiträge zum Studium der Individualität" (1895/96), in *Die Geistige Welt: Einleitung in die Philosophie des Lebens: Erste Hälfte, Abhandlung zur Grundlegung der Geisteswissenschaften,* vol. V of *Gesammelte Schriften* (Göttingen: Vandenhoeck & Ruprecht, 1990), 241–316.

16. Regarding the objective character of the aesthetic laws of construction and values in nature, see the excellent exposition by Emanuel Rádl in his *Geschichte der biologischen Theorien in der Neuzeit* (vol. II) regarding the attempts to grasp these values as sensations and feelings that may arise from time to time in sexual selection. See also T. K. Österreich's *Das Weltbild der Gegenwart,* 2nd ed. (Berlin: Mittler, 1925); quite good also is E. Bleuler's *Naturgeschichte der Seele und ihres Bewusstwerdens* (Berlin: J. Springer, 1921).

17. See the thorough investigation of the process of understanding in my book *The Nature of Sympathy.*

18. To confuse a *metaphysics* of nature with the *understanding* of nature as the face [*Antlitz*] and field of expression of the eternal nature-generating urge [*Drang*] (as the second attribute of the world-ground) was Bergson's fundamental mistake. Ludwig Klages, who has done much valuable work, also shares in this error.

19. See the chapter regarding the relative levels of value in section V of my *Formalism in Ethics and Non-Formal Ethics of Value.*

20. See the related explication in part 1 of the preceding essay, *Probleme einer Soziologie des Wissens.*

Chapter 5

1. An exceptional critique of this theory of the possibilities of perception is given by Hedwig Conrad-Martius in her work *Zur Ontologie und Erscheinungslehre der realen Aussenwelt,* in *Jahrbüch für Philosophie und phänomenologische Forschung,* vol. 3 (1916).

2. See Armin von Tschermak-Seysenegg, *Der exakte Subjektivismus in der neueren Sinnesphysiologie* (Berlin: Springer, 1921).

3. See the very good and penetrating critical exposition against such a position by M. Frischeisen-Köhler, *Wissenschaft und Wirklichkeit* (Leipzig: Druck B. G. Teubner, 1912), 416ff.

4. See the work of Ewald Hering.

5. In the case of laterally blacked-out aspects of "sensations" of a real surface in a particular visual position by virtue of the increasing insensitivity of the retina, the visual *appearance* is nonetheless uniformly red.

6. See the example from K. Goldstein, "Die Topik der Grosshirnrinde in ihrer klinischen Bedeutung," *Deutsche Zeitschrift für Nervenheilkunde* 77, no. 1 (1923): 7–124; see also A. Gelb and K. Goldstein, *Psychologische Analysen hirn-*

pathologischer Fälle, vol. 1 (Leipzig: J. A. Barth, 1921). Moreover, see the essay by K. Goldstein that touches upon the examples mentioned above, "Zur Theorie der Funktion des Nervensystems," *Archive für Psychiatrie des Nervensystem* 74, no. 1 (1925): 370–405.

7. See Rudolf Ehrenberg, *Theoretische Biologie* (Berlin: Springer, 1923).

8. Altough, as C. Stumpf in *Erscheinungen und psychische Funktionen* (Berlin: Akademie der Wissenschaft, 1907) had insightfully articulated, the distinction between appearances and functions is fully grounded in the fact that both determinations can "vary independently of one another," this statement still holds true only for the most elementary partial functions from which any concrete psychic function exists. We have begun to call upon this for different psychic functions without being able to say that we already possess them. For complex functional unities that obey the accompanying laws of over and under functions, i.e., are hierarchical, the converse holds true that the appearances corresponding to them clearly "belong" to this complex and to nothing else. Every act of remarking, for example, is a different remarking, and is remarked according to differences (as appearance). There is not only a seeing function, but a function of seeing red, seeing yellow, etc. The functions circumscribe, "select," "beatify" the subjective, psychic "appearances" from the being-thus of the "image" or the objective appearance. The functions form these appearances initially in the form a subjective appearances (with ego-relatedness). Only in the case of fantasy functions do they create new appearances from the same original material of the quality circles which are tied to an individual and a kind, and construct their perceptual image contents. See the following exposition regarding fantasy.

9. That images cannot be caused, we have already seen; it is just as absurd to allow formal-mechanistic processes to start from image 1 and allow them to meet, for example, the eye.

10. It thus corresponds to the following factors: (1) The light-sense is the finest sense for spatial and temporal differences. (2) Light is the fastest movement and the absolute constant movement that we know of. (3) A brightening circle of two spatial points is still remarked (as place change) where no spatial change (either through dormant elements or their place change of other qualities given as "movement) is grasped more. (4) Light is the highest condition of remaining "*Kommerzium*" (Kant) between any parts of the corporeal world.

11. As did M. Wertheimer in his excellent work on the "Sehen von Bewegungen," *Zeitschrift für Psychologie*, 1912.

12. See W. Köhler's essay "Gestaltprobleme und Anfänge einer Gestalttheorie," in *Sonderabdruck aus Jahresbericht über die gesamte Physiologie und experimentelle Pharmakologie*, vol. 3 (1924): 512–39. See also Kohler's reply to G. E. Müller's criticisms of gestalt theory, in *Komplextheorie und Gestalttheorie* (Berlin: Springer, 1925).

13. See Köhler, "Gestaltprobleme und Anfänge einer Gestalttheorie," 520. See also there the other relevant literature.

14. Max Wertheimer has recently attempted to find and present the simplest laws of gestalt apprehension in a very significant series of essays in the journal *Psychologische Forschung*, 1924 and 1925.

15. See Hans Petersen, "Über die Bedeutung der aufrechten Körperhaltung für die Eigenart des menschlichen Umweltbildes," in *Die Naturwissenschaften* 12, no. 10 (1924): 186–91.

16. In this case, the firmness is in no way to be taken as only tactile content, because there is to a greater extent an original optical character of firmness.

17. See Roman Ingarden's essay "Intuition und Intellekt bei Henri Bergson."

18. See E. Rubin, *Visuell wahrgenommene Figuren* (Copenhagen: Boghandel, 1921).

19. See H. Driesch, *Relativitätstheorie und Philosophie* (Karlsruhe: B. Braun, 1924).

20. See W. Köhler, *Die physischen Gestalten in Ruhe und im stationäre Zustand: Eine naturphilosophische Untersuchung* (Erlangen: Philosophische Akademie, 1924).

21. In his book *Über die materiellen Grundlagen der Bewusstseinserscheinungen* (Freiberg: Lehmann, 1898), Johannes von Kries has shown in impressive fashion how little this direct identification of the seen and touched gestalts, and moreover, the recognition, for example, of melody gestalts with different tone heights and strengths, is thinkable. See also E. Becher's book *Gehirn und Seele* (Heidelberg: Carl Winters Universitätsbuchhandlung, 1911).

22. Köhler, "Gestaltprobleme und Anfänge einer Gestalttheorie," 521.

23. See the relevant literature cited in Köhler's essay "Gestaltprobleme und Anfänge einer Gestalttheorie."

24. See E. R. Jaensch, "Der Umbau der Wahrnehmunglehre und die kantische Weltanschauungen," in *Über den Aufbau der Wahrnehmungswelt und ihre Struktur im Jugendalter* (Leipzig: Barth, 1923).

25. See P. Schilder, *Entwurf zu einer Psychiatrie auf psychoanalytischer Basis* (Leipzig: Internationaler Psychoanalytischer Verlag, 1925).

26. Quite clearly, this lawfulness demonstrates the genuine things of hallucination which act completely like real and concrete things of perception.

27. Chimpanzees, for examples, were able to determine the differences between superficial colors and surface colors, as well as grasp color constant, gestalt constant, apparent size constant. This is, incidentally undeniable proof that this ability does not concern higher spiritual activities (like "unconscious conclusions," according to Helmholtz and others).

28. According to W. Stern, a girl's memory images contain more objective and appropriate characteristics than those of a boy of the same age, but they also contain greatly extended falsifications.

29. See P. Schilder, *Das Körperschema: Ein Beitrag zur Lehre vom Bewusstsein des eigenen Körper* (Berlin: Springer, 1923).

30. For the further elaboration of these concepts of specific energy, memory, etc., with regard to the entire physiology, see von Tschermak-Seysenegg, *Der exakte Subjektivismus in der neueren Sinnesphysiologie.*

31. Thus, for example, in an instructive work, Poppelreuthers's "Zur Psychologie und Pathologie der optischen Wahrnehmung," *Zeitschrift für die gesamte Neurologie und Psychiatrie* 83 (1923): 86–152.

32. Accordingly, I do not want to say that psychologists have achieved any great clarity and exactness regarding the concept of sensation. A phenomenal

concept and the genetic concept mediate through the stimulus concept, and furthermore, the attempts to treat both of these concepts as identical often run erringly through one another.

33. I have already worked this out in my book *Formalism in Ethics and Non-Formal Ethics of Value.*

34. See von Tschermak-Seysenegg, *Der exakte Subjektivismus in der neueren Sinnesphysiologie.*

35. This has been developed very precisely, historically accurately, and insightfully in an instructive essay by Koffka, "Probleme der experimentellen Psychologie," in *Die Naturwissenschaften,* vol. 5 (1917): 1–5, 23–28; see also the bibliography listed therein.

36. See H. Ebbinghaus, *Grundzüge der Psychologie* (Leipzig: Veit, 1911).

37. See Max Wertheimer, "Experimentelle Studien über das Sehen von Bewegung," *Zeitschrift für Psychologie,* vol. 61 (1912): 161–265.

38. In the natural worldview, the different sensation classes behave very differently in relation to original object relatedness.

39. See K. Koffka, "Probleme der experimentellen Psychologie," 27.

40. The ultraviolet color sensations of bees have only recently been grasped with certainty by K. von Frisch; also, the blossoms that they tear and those from which they take their honey send out ultraviolet rays.

41. [Translator: S is stimulus and Se is sensation.]

42. In W. Köhler's attempts to train the chimpanzee Sultan to choose a color from the black-white spectrum, the training of the choice "brighter"–"darker" is easier and needs fewer practice exercises than choosing an absolute shade of gray.

43. See Jaensch, "Der Umbau der Wahrnehmungslehre und die kantischen Weltanschauungen," 394.

44. See E. R. Jaensch, "Wahrnehmungslehre and Biologie," in *Über den Aufbau der Wahrnehmungswelt und ihre Struktur im Jugendalter* (Leipzig: Barth, 1923), 442.

45. See above.

46. For this, see my *Formalism in Ethics and Non-Formal Ethics of Values*; and also "Die Idole der Selbsterkenntnis," in *Vom Umsturz der Werte: Abhandlngen und Aufsätze* [Vol. III of *Gesammelte Werke,* ed. Maria Scheler and Manfred S. Frings (Bern: Francke Verlag, 1955), 213–48; English trans. "The Idols of Self-Knowledge," in *Selected Philosophical Papers,* trans. David R. Lachterman (Evanston, Ill.: Northwestern University Press, 1973), 3–97].

47. See Jaensch, "Der Umbau der Wahrnehmungslehre und die kantischen Weltanschauungen."

48. In a manner similar to my critique, Oswald Külpe points out that this is a prejudice Kant has taken from English sensualism and is an error underlying his entire philosophical theory; see Külpe's short book on Kant, *Immanuel Kant: Darstellung und Würdigung* (Leipzig: Teubner, 1907)

49. Jaensch, "Der Umbau der Wahrnehmungslehre und die kantischen Weltanschauungen," 381.

50. The research of the English psychologist Henry Head has produced quite meaningful results for this problem. He thinks that every sensation pro-

cess takes place on different levels, so that in each of the great centers that the stimulus passes through, a rearranging takes place at new levels. Regarding the use of this principle for tactile sensibility, and also for temperature and pain sensations, see P. Schilder's critical report in his book, quite valuable for our questions, *Medizinische Psychologie* (Berlin: Springer, 1924), 69ff.; translated by David Rapaport as *Medical Psychology* (New York: International Universities Press, 1953).

51. See Lucien Lévy-Bruhl, *Das Denken der Naturvölker*, trans. W. Jerusalem (Vienna: Braumüller, 1921); and his most recent book, *La Mentalité primitive* (Paris: Felix Alcan, 1922) [translated by Lilian A. Claire as *Primitive Mentality* (Abingdon, Eng.: Routledge, 2018)].

52. See also Wertheimer's beautiful work, "Über das denken der Naturvölker, Zahlen und Zahlengebilde," *Zeitschrift für Psychologie*, vol. 60 (1912).

53. Because, according to Lindworsky, gestalts are only relational structures, and because conceptual and inferential thinking should be possible where "relation grasping" is there, this condition is sufficient for its unfolding. This is Lindworsky's position in his textbook, *Experimentellen Psychologie*, where he was able to outline a very unified and simple theory of the human spirit, a theory he retracts fully in a more recent work. Johannes Lindworsky, *Experimentellen Psychologie* (Kempten: Jos. Kösel & Friedr. Pustet, 1921) [translated by Harry R. DeSilva as *Experimental Psychology* (New York: Psychology, 2015)].

54. Every dynamic, intensive magnitude of nature can only be measured through extensive magnitudes, e.g., speed through distance/time, magnitude of movement through m · v, vital force through mass-acceleration–distance. The *unity* of a force can only be ascertained through the unity of an elementary lawfulness (which is no longer traceable), etc.—which is what entices Helmholtz to the mistaken claim that "force is only the hypothesized law" (see his remark to the text regarding the conservation of force). [Translator: It is not clear from the text which work by Helmholtz Scheler is referring to here.]

55. "Spontaneous"—i.e., originally "directed," and furthermore, not clearly determined through some "thing" from the sphere of the spatial-temporal environment.

56. And psychic and physical dimensions presuppose as kinds of givenness presupposed a more than vital, i.e., spiritual subject to which they are "given."

57. Armin von Tschermak-Sysenegg, *Allgemeine Physiologie* (Berlin: Springer, 1924), 4.

58. A thoroughgoing theory of the drives will be given in my "Anthropology."

59. That feeling-urges is a possibility exclusively for the problem of the souls of plants—but can in no way be considered as "sensation" or consciousness, as Fechner proposes—should be addressed elsewhere. Jennings correctly contends in his famous studies regarding the soul-life of the lowest animals in the research of the movement of the paramecium that there is something introspective comparable to attention, interest, and fear, something that is genetically psychic in its "most elementary form."

60. For this, see William James, *The Principles of Psychology*, vols. 1 and 2

[Newburyport, Mass.: Dover, 2012], who speaks correctly of the "poverty of willful attention."

61. An insightful overview of the "physiology of work" is given by W. R. Hess in his identically titled report, "Die Physiologie der Arbeit," *Die Naturwissenschaften*, 12 (1924), 1031–39.

62. Schilder, *Medizinische Psychologie*, 141.

63. Jaensch, "Der Umbau der Wahrnehmungslehre und die kantischen Weltanschauungen."

64. Rubin, *Visuell wahrgenommene Figuren.*

65. It cannot be our task here to examine the stuff of specific normal and pathological appearances that become intelligible through the proposition of the drive-motor conditionality of perception. For more on this, see H. Bergson, *Matèrie et mémoire: Essai sur la relation du corps a l'esprit* (Paris: Félix Alcan, 1908); translated by N. M. Paul and W. S. Palmer as *Matter and Memory* (New York: Cosimo, 2007). See also the works of Schilder (as well as his instructive book *Über das Wesen der Hypnose* [Berlin: Springer, 1922]), A. Pick, and E. Jaensch.

66. See D. Katz's recent work regarding this question, *Der Aufbau der Tastwelt* (Leipzig: J. A. Barth, 1925); translated by Lester E. Krueger as *The World of Touch* (New York: Taylor and Francis Group, 2016).

67. I have shown this already in my *Formalism in Ethics and Non-Formal Ethics of Values.* The above claim is confirmed so convincingly by Edinger, Uexküll's analysis of the "mark-worlds" [*Merkwelten*] of the animal species, A. Pütter and others, and recently through the beautiful investigations of K. von Frisch regarding color meanings to the bees, that it withstands any critique.

68. See E. Hering's introduction to his *Grundzüge der Lehre vom Lichtsinn* (Berlin: Engelmann, 1925).

69. E. Jaensch has recently demonstrated the same for the primitive conceptual constructs about which we have yet to speak. See also Schilder's concept (in *Medizinische Psychologie*) of "spheres of consciousness which *lag behind* as a vague unity of objects reciprocally justifying themselves in their *affective* meaning for the person in the dismantling of levels of consciousness in the schizophrenic consciousness and determine the particularity of the image symbols that are conscious representations of the affective sphere."

70. See R. Ehrenberg, *Theoretische Biologie* (Berlin: Springer, 1923), 299.

71. See Johannes Müller, *Über die phantastischen Gesichtserscheinungen* (Coblenz: J. Hölscher, 1826).

72. See Carl Stumpf, *Empfindung und Vorstellung* (Berlin: Abhandlung der königlich preussischen Akademie der Wissenschaft, 1918).

73. E. Jaensch has shown that that this is to be expected brain-physiologically and morphologically.

74. See my *The Nature of Sympathy* and also *Formalism in Ethics and Non-Formal Ethics of Values.*

75. Wilhelm Dilthey, *Weltanschauung und Analyse des Menschen seit Renaissance und Reformation*, vol. II of *Gesammelte Schriften* (Leipzig: B. G. Teubner, 1921), 164ff.

76. See Paul Häberlin, *Der Geist und die Triebe: Eine Elementarpsychologie* (Basel: Kober, 1924), 158.

77. See Melchior Palágyi, *Naturphilosophische Vorlesungen: Über die Grundprobleme des Bewusstseins und des Lebens* (Leipzig: Barth, 1924).

78. Erich Jaensch, *Über den Aufbau der Wahrnehmungswelt und ihre Struktur im Jugendalter* (Leipzig: Barth, 1923).

79. See the preface to my book *The Nature of Sympathy.*

80. See Dilthey, *Weltanschauung und Analyse des Menschen,* 175.

Chapter 6

1. For these questions, I must refer to my upcoming work "Metaphysics."

2. We will have to do this in the first volume of our metaphysics.

3. See Wilhelm Dilthey, "Beiträge zur Lösung der Frage vom Ursprung unseres Glaubens an die Realität der Aussenwelt und seinem Recht," in *Die geistige Welt: Einleitung in die Philosophie des Lebens: Abhandlungen zur Grundlegung der Geisteswissenschaft,* vol. V of *Gesammelte Schriften* (Leipzig: Teubner, 1924).

4. Unfortunately, the new and deeply penetrating investigations by David Katz, *Der Aufbau der Tastwelt,* could not be taken into consideration in what follows.

5. See H. Rickert, *Der Gegenstand der Erkenntnis* (Tübingen: Mohr, 1904).

6. See Gyula Pikler, *Schriften zur Anpassungstheorie des Empfindungsvorganges* (Leipzig: Barth, 1919).

7. Pikler, *Schriften zur Anpassungstheorie,* 143.

8. Pikler, *Schriften zur Anpassungstheorie,* 145.

9. See Dilthey, "Beiträge zur Lösung," 100.

10. See Schilder, *Medizinische Psychologie.* 341.

11. See also Julius Pikler, *Sinnesphysiologische Untersuchungen.*

12. See my "Metaphysics," vol. 1, which will be published next. [The work on metaphysics was published posthumously: Max Scheler, *Schriften aus dem Nachlass II: Erkenntnislehre und Metaphysik,* ed. Manfred S. Frings, vol. XI of *Gesammelte Werke* (Bern: Francke Verlag, 1979).]

13. For this point, see the impressive elaborations by M. Geiger: "Fragment über den Begriff des Unbewussten und die psychische Realität," *Jahrbuch für Philosophie und phänomenologische Forschung,* vol. 4 (1921): 1–137.

14. See Kant's *Critique of Pure Reason,* refutation of idealism [note added to the second edition].

15. See W. Dilthey, "Bestätigende Schlüsse aus den Modifikationen des Bewusstseins der Realität," in *Die geistige Welt: Einleitung in die Philosophie des Lebens: Abhandlungen zur Grundlegung der Geisteswissenschaft,* vol. V of *Gesammelte Schriften* (Leipzig: Teubner, 1924), 117.

16. See my forthcoming "Metaphysics."

17. These four laws have up to this point only been partially established by me. The first law was dealt with in detail in my essay "Probleme der Religion," in *Vom Ewigen im Menschen,* ed. Maria Scheler (Bern: Francke Verlag, 1954); trans-

lated by Bernard Noble as "Problems of Religion," in *On the Eternal in Man* (New York: Routledge, 2017). For the second law, see my book *On the Nature of Sympathy*; the third and fourth laws have been treated so far only in my lectures on the "Essence of Death" and in my "Metaphysics," which still awaits publication.

18. See E. Durkheim, *Les Forms élémentaires de la vie religieuse: Le Système totémique en Australia* (Paris: Presses Universitaires de France, 1912) [translated by Joseph W. Swain as *The Elementary Forms of Religious Life* (Mansfield, Conn.: Martino, 2012)]. See also my comments in the preceding essay, "Problems of Religion."

19. See Karl Joël, *Seele und Welt: Versuch einer organischern Auffassung* (Jena: Diedrichs, 1918); see also Karl Bühler, *Die geistige Entwicklung des Kindes* (Jena: Gustav Fischer, 1921); K. Koffka, *Die Grundlagen der der psychischen Entwicklung: Eine Einfuhrung in die Kinderpsychologie* (Osterwieck am Harz: A. W. Zickfeldt, 1921); and Lévy-Bruhl, *La Mentalité primitive*; see also my book *On the Nature of Sympathy*.

20. See W. James, *Der Pragmatismus*, German translation by W. Jerusalem, ibid.

21. See F. C. S. Schiller, *Humanismus: Beiträge zu einer pragmatischen Philosophie*, trans. Rudolf Eisler (Leipzig: Klinkhardt, 1911); originally published in English as *Studies in Humanism* (London: Macmillan, 1907).

22. See Hans Vaihinger, *Philosophie des Als-Ob: System der theoretischen, praktischen und religiösen Fiktionen der Menschheit auf Grund eines idealistischen Positivismus, mit einem Anhang über Kant und Nietzsche* (Berlin: Reuther und Reichard, 1913).

23. See Pierre Duhem, *Ziel und Struktur der physikalischen Theorien* (Berlin: J. A. Barth, 1908).

24. See Johann Carl Friedrich Zöllner, *Über die Natur der Kometen: Beitrage zur Geschichte und Theorie der Erkenntnis* (Leipzig: Engelmann, 1872).

25. See Ludwig Boltzmann, *Populäre Schriften* (Leipzig: J. A. Barth, 1905); see in particular the essay "Über die Entwicklung der Methoden der theoretischen Physik in neuer Zeit."

26. See P. Duhem, *Ziel und Struktur der physikalischen Theorien*.

Index